Philosophy of Mind:
Brains, Consciousness,
and Thinking Machines
Part I

Professor Patrick Grim

THE TEACHING COMPANY ®

PUBLISHED BY:

THE TEACHING COMPANY
4151 Lafayette Center Drive, Suite 100
Chantilly, Virginia 20151-1232
1-800-TEACH-12
Fax—703-378-3819
www.teach12.com

ISBN 1-59803-425-1

Patrick Grim, B.Phil., Ph.D.

Distinguished Teaching Professor of Philosophy
State University of New York at Stony Brook

Patrick Grim is Distinguished Teaching Professor of Philosophy at State University of New York at Stony Brook. Graduating with highest honors in both Anthropology and Philosophy from the University of California at Santa Cruz, Professor Grim was named a Fulbright Fellow to the University of St. Andrews, Scotland, from which he received his B.Phil. He received his Ph.D. from Boston University with a dissertation on Ethical Relativism, spent a year as a Mellon Faculty Fellow at Washington University, and has been teaching at Stony Brook since 1976. In addition to being named SUNY Distinguished Teaching Professor, he has received the President's and Chancellor's Awards for excellence in teaching.

Professor Grim has published extensively on such topics as theoretical biology, linguistics, decision theory, artificial intelligence, and computer science. His work spans ethics, philosophical logic, game theory, philosophy of science, philosophy of law, philosophy of mind, philosophy of language, contemporary metaphysics, and philosophy of religion. Professor Grim is the author of *The Incomplete Universe: Totality, Knowledge, and Truth*; the co-author of *The Philosophical Computer: Exploratory Essays in Philosophical Computer Modeling*; the editor of *Philosophy of Science and the Occult*; and a founding co-editor of more than 20 volumes of *The Philosopher's Annual*, an anthology of the best articles published in philosophy each year. He has taught a course titled *Questions of Value* for The Teaching Company.

Professor Grim is perhaps best known for his critical logical arguments in the philosophy of religion and for his groundbreaking work in philosophical computer modeling. In this course, he draws from his broad interdisciplinary background to concentrate on philosophical issues of minds and machines, brains and subjective experience, the phenomena of perception, and the mysteries of consciousness.

Acknowledgments

First and foremost, thanks to my wife, L. Theresa Watkins, for her work in shepherding lectures and supporting materials through multiple drafts. I have relied throughout on her ability to be scrupulous and critical while also creative and encouraging. I am also grateful to Christine Buffolino, Marcus Dracos, Rob Rosenberger, and Chris Williams for supplementary research and background support and to Marshall Weinberg and Marvin Levine for useful discussion. A special debt of gratitude for helpful feedback and discussion is owed to the students in my graduate and undergraduate courses in Philosophy of Mind.

Table of Contents

Philosophy of Mind:
Brains, Consciousness, and Thinking Machines
Part I

Philosophy of Mind:
Brains, Consciousness, and Thinking Machines

Scope:

What is the relation between the brain and the mind? Is free will an illusion? Could a machine ever be creative? What is consciousness? The discipline known as *philosophy of mind* encompasses a range of questions about subjective experience, perception, intelligence, emotion, and the role of the mental in a physical universe.

Contemporary philosophy of mind is actively interdisciplinary. A broad range of disciplines is involved in the ongoing attempt to understand what minds are and how they work: psychology, neuroscience, cognitive science, artificial intelligence, computer science, and even robotics. This course highlights scientific results, provocative theories, and technological accomplishments in all of these fields in an exploration of what we know about our own mental functioning and what we do not. The overriding goal of the course is to develop a deeper philosophical understanding of our minds and of ourselves.

Each of the lectures focuses on a handful of intriguing questions in philosophy of mind: Is intelligence the same as IQ? Do minds function as parts or wholes? Do you see the same color I see? Do animals have a sense of self? Will our machines become smarter than we are? How can I know what other people think? Topics of investigation include color perception, body image, artificial intelligence, the structure of the adaptive brain, free will, self-identity, and current controversies regarding the nature of consciousness.

Thought experiments are an important conceptual tool. Here, science-fiction zombies, transporters, the inverted spectrum, Wittgenstein's beetles in the boxes, the Molyneux problem, Daniel Dennett's Chase and Sanborn, John Searle's Chinese room, and Ned Block's Chinese gym all play a role in philosophical exploration. The characteristics of injured brains offer a further conceptual resource, both real and tragic: the color-blind painter, the surprising phenomenon of blindsight, split answers from split-brain patients, the isolation of autism, phantom limbs, prosopagnosia (the inability to recognize faces), the facts of psychopathology, and the strange case of Phineas Gage.

The history of ideas is woven throughout the course, from Greek concepts of the soul to the notion of mental substance in Descartes, sense-data in Locke and the Empiricists, Behaviorism in B. F. Skinner and Wittgenstein, and Functionalism in contemporary philosophy and cognitive science. Parallel ideas in philosophy, psychology, and the neurosciences are emphasized in examinations of eyewitness testimony, a mind in the world, the insanity defense, our understanding of other people, the "inner theater," and questions of conscious experience. The history of technology also plays a part, from ancient calculating devices to contemporary computers, from the golden age of automata to robots on Mars. Examples are frequently drawn from literature and the arts, with illustrations from Ovid's myth of Pygmalion through Shakespeare's *Macbeth* to science fiction films, such as *Blade Runner* and *The Matrix*.

Questions of mind are among the most hotly debated in philosophy today. This course outlines major positions in the debate in terms of their prominent contemporary defenders. Reductive Materialism and the new Dualism are considered using the work of Paul Churchland and Patricia Smith Churchland on one side and arguments from David Chalmers, Thomas Nagel, and Frank Jackson on the other. Functionalism and its critics are considered using the positions of Hilary Putnam and Daniel Dennett on one side with counterarguments from John Searle and Ned Block on the other. The philosophical debates spill over into other disciplines as well. The course features theory in computer science and the future of robotics by Rodney Brooks, Hans Moravec, Marvin Minsky, and Ray Kurzweil. It highlights work in psychology and neuroscience by J. J. Gibson, Francis Crick and Christof Koch, Oliver Sacks, Antonio Damasio, and V. J. Ramachandran.

The goal here, as in all philosophy, is conceptual clarification and rational argument. Philosophy has always thrived on controversy, and one goal of the course is to clarify core controversies in philosophy of mind by laying them out in terms of a range of intellectual options. What are the arguments behind Dualism and the considerations that have led most contemporary thinkers to reject it? What is it that we see when we see color? Are there reasons to think that consciousness is *forever* beyond the reach of science? The aim of the lectures is always to open and articulate intellectual options, to capture the excitement of intellectual controversy, but never to lay down a single dogmatic position. Even where it is argued that one position is more plausible than another, the lectures attempt to present each side fairly enough so that the student may arrive at a different conclusion. One point about minds on which everyone agrees is that there is a great deal we do not yet know. It is important for continued progress to avoid closing off options too quickly.

The road map for the course starts with six lectures that lay out basic concepts, classical theories, and current hypotheses in philosophy of mind. Functionalism has emerged as a dominant trend in current research and continues as a theme in the next six lectures. This part of the course concentrates on perception, and our conceptions of ourselves and minds as they function in the world. Real robots play an interesting role in that exploration. In the third section of the course, we will focus on questions of intelligence—yours and mine—but also the idea of artificial intelligence. Strong conceptual connections through the course tie together an interdisciplinary examination of mind: Concepts introduced against a philosophical background may be illuminated in a later lecture with results from the neurosciences, compared with achievements in artificial intelligence, and then examined philosophically once again. The final six lectures of the course focus on subjective experience and the continuing mystery of consciousness.

The study of mind is inevitably double-edged. Here, as in all areas of inquiry, we use our minds to try to understand something. But in this area of inquiry, the object of the study—the thing we want to understand—is the mind itself. The fact that the mind is both subject and object of investigation opens wonderful opportunities for learning. The lectures sometimes rely on simple experiments, and because the subject of these experiments is mind, each listener will have all the equipment needed to participate. Auditory experiments are used at a number of points in the lectures to illustrate surprising aspects of the way in which we process sounds. Visual experiments appear in the lecture outlines, with further links to examples online.

Students can expect to gain from the course a rich understanding of rival theories and continuing philosophical controversies regarding minds and brains. Set in the context of intellectual history, that understanding will also be informed by some of the latest and most exciting work in psychology, the study of the brain, and information sciences. Everything we learn about minds makes them seem more interesting rather than less so. There is nothing more obvious than our own subjective experience, but there is also nothing more mysterious.

Lecture One
The Dream, the Brain, and the Machine

Scope:

Many of our questions about brains, minds, and machines are not only questions for which we do not have answers, but questions for which we do not even have approaches for finding answers. What is consciousness? How could our three-pound brains possibly produce our rich experience of the world? Could a machine have subjective experience? These are the questions of philosophy of mind.

This introductory lecture outlines the kinds of topics to be covered using three examples: a particular dream, a specific brain, and the history of an intriguing machine. The dream is one that the young René Descartes had one night in 1619: a dream of the science of the future that would make clear the different realms of matter and mind. The brain is that of Albert Einstein, extremely similar to other brains—a little smaller than average, as a matter of fact—but with some unique characteristics as well. The machine is the Analytical Engine, designed by Charles Babbage in the mid-1800s. If the Analytical Engine had been built, it would have been a full-fledged computer constructed of steel and brass and driven by steam.

This lecture also offers a road map of the course and illustrates the general approach to be used. The philosopher takes as input the range of different perspectives and the wealth of information available from all the arts and sciences. That input, however, is merely a first step. A genuine understanding of the mind's role in the universe requires distinctly philosophical work as well: the disentangling of complex questions, the careful examination of alternative positions, and the search for rational argument and conceptual clarification.

Outline

I. This course covers both some amazing facts we know about the mind and some perplexing mysteries that remain. This first lecture offers a sample of topics to be covered in terms of three "exhibits":

    A. Exhibit A is a series of dreams that Descartes had in 1619.

    B. Exhibit B is Einstein's brain.

C. Exhibit C is a steam-driven computer designed before the Civil War.

II. Exhibit A: In 1619, the young René Descartes envisaged a new science in a series of dreams.

    A. He dreamed of a philosophical unification of all the sciences, grounded in certainty and the solidity of mathematics.

    B. The core of that science was a radical distinction between minds and bodies. According to Descartes, the world is composed of two fundamentally different kinds of substances.

        1. Mass, energy, and the motion of atoms in the void belong to the physical substance of the universe.

        2. Feelings, ideas, and the taste of pineapple belong to the mental substance of the universe, as does Descartes' dream.

    C. Descartes' Dualism gives us the mind-body problem, an issue we will deal with in various forms throughout these lectures.

III. Exhibit B: What happened to Einstein's brain?

    A. Einstein's brain was "kidnapped" after his death, taken on a wandering journey from New Jersey to Kansas.

    B. Einstein's brain was both similar to, and different from, other people's brains.

        1. It was no bigger than the average brain.

        2. Its anatomy was different: An area associated with mathematical thought had taken over an area associated with language.

    C. Brain function and brain plasticity are themes that will reappear throughout this course.

IV. Exhibit C: In the mid-1800s, Charles Babbage designed a computer.

    A. Babbage's Difference Engine was a special-purpose computer designed to calculate logarithms. It was financed by the British government in the 1830s but abandoned before it was built. A Difference Engine was built in the 1990s from Babbage's plans and is now on display in the London Science Museum.

B. Babbage's Analytical Engine, designed well before Edison invented the light bulb, would have been a full-fledged, all-purpose computer made of steel and brass and driven by steam.

C. Could a machine really be intelligent? Could it be creative? Could it be conscious? One way these lectures will look at minds is in terms of thinking machines.

V. History offers a tantalizing link between Descartes' dream and the concept of mechanical minds: the legend of Descartes' robot daughter. It is a story of minds, machines, dreams, and emotions.

VI. Philosophy began in a general "love of wisdom."

A. As time went on, philosophy progressively gave birth to mathematics, astronomy, physics, anthropology, sociology, linguistics, and psychology as specialized scientific disciplines.

B. Once we think we have the techniques needed to answer specific questions, they become scientific questions rather than philosophical questions.

C. Philosophy continues to tackle the core questions that remain—questions that are not only unanswered but elusive in terms of methods for finding answers.

D. The goal of philosophy of mind is a unified understanding of mind and its place in the world.

    1. The focus is on conceptual clarification, the disentangling of complex questions, and the careful examination of alternative approaches.

    2. Philosophy's major tool is rational argument.

VII. Throughout the course, we will lay out issues in terms of a range of intellectual options and alternatives.

A. The first six lectures introduce basic concepts, classical theories, and current hypotheses.

B. The next six lectures follow the theme of Functionalism through issues of perception, self-conception, and minds in the world.

C. A third section focuses on questions of intelligence, both natural and artificial.

D. The final six lectures focus on subjective experience and the mystery of consciousness.

VIII. A crucial prerequisite for the course is your mind, which will function both as the subject and the object of study.

Further Resources:

Daniel Dennett, "Where Am I?" *Brainstorms*.

William Gibson and Bruce Sterling, *The Difference Engine*, 1st ed., pp. 1–71.

Douglas Hofstadter and Daniel Dennett, *The Mind's I: Fantasies and Reflections on Self and Soul*.

Questions to Consider:

1. Do you think the mind is the same thing as the brain?
2. Do you think a computer could ever be creative?

Lecture One—Transcript
The Dream, the Brain, and the Machine

I'm Patrick Grim and I'll be your guide through Philosophy of Mind. The philosophy of mind represents intriguing questions regarding minds and brains that run from the mysteries of consciousness to prospects for thinking machines. There are little bits we know, a range of things we have intriguing hints about—both conceptual and scientific—and a great deal of which we remain abysmally ignorant. That's what the course is all about, some of the amazing things we do know and the many questions that remain. Let me introduce the kinds of topics we'll be covering by starting with a handful of examples. I'll focus on three "exhibits"—A, B, and C—as if this were a court case. These three exhibits will give something of the flavor of the exploration.

The first exhibit, exhibit A, is a series of dreams, a particular series of dreams of a particular person at a particular time. The second exhibit, exhibit B, is a brain, the very special brain of a very special person. The third exhibit, exhibit C, is a piece of machinery built from plans over 150 years old. It's currently on display in London. First, the dreams: The year is 1619. The Thirty Years' War is continuing between the Catholic forces of the Holy Roman Empire and the Protestant princes of northern Europe. It's the night of November 10th, the eve of the Feast of St. Martin of Tours. We're focusing on a 23-year-old Frenchman. After a solid education for his era, he has decided to see the world. He's fighting in the army of the duke of Bavaria. It's November, and the army's wintering in the German city of Ulm.

In autobiographical notes, he says he has been pondering the "disunity and uncertainty" of all his knowledge. That night, he had a series of dreams, which he interpreted as a sign directly from God. What they offered was a glimpse of an all-encompassing body of knowledge—a philosophical unification of all the sciences, built with the solidity of mathematics. That young soldier was René Descartes. He took his visions as a mandate to build a new kind of knowledge. He was so convinced that his dreams signaled a divine endorsement of that mission that he made an extended religious pilgrimage in thanksgiving for the divine favor of his dreams.

In one of the dreams, Descartes saw two books in front of him. The first was a dictionary that appeared to him to be of little interest and use; it was a mere collection without internal conceptual structure or organization and without certainty. The dictionary represented the broken fragments of the wisdom of the past. The second book was entitled *Corpus Poetarum*, and it contained what he saw to be a philosophical union of all science. It's interesting that he envisaged it as written in poetry. Descartes is considered the foremost of the Rationalists, but in describing his dream, he speaks of the "might of fantasy," a poetic force that strikes sparks of wisdom from men's minds like steel strikes sparks from flint. As Descartes tells it, those dreams changed his life. It was through those dreams that he "discovered the foundations of a marvelous science."

The day of his dreams, Descartes had been pondering the "disunity and uncertainty" of his knowledge. As if in continuation of his thinking through the day, his dreams that night seemed to show him the route to conceptual unification and certainty. The course of Descartes' life from that point on is a circuitous one, but there is one major piece of conceptual unification crucial to our modern knowledge for which Descartes is quite directly responsible. It's analytical geometry, our ability to treat matters of two-dimensional space in terms of algebraic formulae. Most people are familiar with Cartesian coordinates. What those allow you to do is to convert the spatiality of a line into a simple equation. Cartesian coordinates are named after Descartes.

The pursuit of certainty, of a foundation for a unified scientific philosophy as certain as mathematics, is most apparent in Descartes' *Meditations*. Here, the theme of dreams reappears. How do I know I'm not dreaming? Could this all just be a dream? In the next lecture, we'll trace the reasoning that leads him from there to "I think, therefore I am." Descartes' *Meditations* is the source for a major philosophical position that bears his name, *Cartesian Dualism*. Dualism is the idea that there are two basic kinds of things in the universe, two basic kinds of "stuff": the physical stuff—mass, energy, the motion of atoms in the void—and the mental stuff—the taste of pineapple or the feel of a frozen car handle in the morning.

The physical and the mental, Dualism says, are essentially different kinds of stuff. One is supremely objective. One is essentially subjective—the stuff of imaginings and tastings and feelings. On the one side is the physical universe. On the other is the mental universe, the universe of how things taste and feel; the universe of consciousness; also the universe of ideas, of imaginings, and of Descartes' dreams. Are the realms of the physical and the mental two essentially different universes? If so, how could they possibly interact? And if they're not essentially different—if there's some sense in which, say, the mental is ultimately physical—precisely how does *that* work? Descartes' dreams invoke a central group of questions that we'll be dealing with throughout the course, questions of mind and body or mind and brain. How could our three-pound brains possibly produce our rich experience of the world? That's the mind-body problem, which I'll examine further in the next lecture. How could consciousness ultimately be physical? And what does it mean if it isn't?

The first exhibit was a dream. The second exhibit is a brain. On April 17, 1955, Albert Einstein checked into Princeton Hospital complaining of chest pains. He died the next morning of a burst aortic aneurysm. He was 76. The autopsy on Einstein was performed by Thomas Stolz Harvey, a young pathologist. Einstein had left explicit directions that his remains be cremated and scattered in secret. He was used to being idolized. He hated it. He didn't want some idolization of his body to continue after his death. Despite those instructions and despite the fact that Dr. Harvey wasn't any kind of brain specialist, he removed Einstein's brain. He also removed Einstein's eyes. He later pressed Einstein's son for permission but only after the fact. He guaranteed him that the brain would be used solely for purposes of research and that results would be published in primary journals.

Harvey gave the eyes to Einstein's ophthalmologist—they're still in a safe deposit box in New York City—but Harvey took the brain. Upon removal, he weighed it, he photographed it, he dissected it into about 240 distinct blocks encased in a plastic-like material called *celloidin*. Within months, he was fired from his position at the hospital for refusing to surrender the specimen. Harvey kept Einstein's brain in the basement of his house in Princeton, but he'd lost his job—he was soon to lose his marriage—so he took the brain with him to a new job in a biological testing lab in Wichita, Kansas. It was kept in a cider box stashed under a beer cooler. From there, he moved to Weston, Missouri, and practiced medicine until he failed a state competency exam. He started working on an assembly line in Lawrence, Kansas, and again, he took the brain with him. When anyone asked, he would say he was studying the brain in his spare time and that he'd soon publish a report. He kept saying that for 43 years. Harvey would occasionally offer pieces of the brain to researchers; in 1985, he sent a piece to the neuroscientist Marian Diamond at UCLA, for example.

In the early 1990s, Harvey returned to Princeton. He met a magazine writer named Michael Paterniti, and together, they conceived the plan of a cross-country trip to California to meet Einstein's granddaughter. Einstein's brain traveled to California in the trunk of a Buick Skylark. Paterniti eventually published a book about the trip called *Driving Mr. Albert*. Around 1995, Harvey sent a fax to Sandra Witelson, a neuroscientist at McMaster University, asking if she would like a part of the brain. She'd never made such a request. She'd never met Harvey in her life. "Needless to say," she says, "it was unexpected." McMaster University now has about a fifth of Einstein's brain. And in one of the few responsible acts of his life, Thomas Stolz Harvey then returned the remainder of Einstein's brain to the pathology department at the University Medical Center at Princeton.

So what is Einstein's brain like? Did Einstein have a particularly big brain? No. His brain was in the average range, rather on the smallish side. Was there anything special about Einstein's brain? Can you look at it and see wherein his genius lay? There are some tantalizing hints that the answer might be a qualified yes. One part of Einstein's brain, you may remember, had been sent to Marian Diamond at UCLA. Her group published a study indicating that the brain had an unusually large ratio of glial cells to neurons. It's not clear that's correct—controversy remains regarding Diamond's study. But even if it were true, we have to admit that we don't really know what it is that glial cells do.

A later study by Witelson's group at McMaster University is perhaps more interesting. What it shows is that Einstein's brain was different in terms of overall anatomy. If you put your hands above and a little behind your ears, your hands will be over your parietal lobes. Einstein's brain was within normal limits everywhere *except* there. There's a portion of Einstein's brain there—the inferior parietal lobe—that is 15 percent wider in Einstein's brain than in yours. There's a neighboring region in yours—the parietal operculum—that's missing in Einstein's brain. What it looks like is that part of his brain grew larger, taking over the area that would have been occupied by another part of the brain. That is, indeed, Witelson's interpretation: that what we're seeing is an early childhood expansion of part of Einstein's brain at the cost of a neighboring region.

What does that mean in terms of function? The tantalizing fact is that the area of Einstein's brain that is 15 percent wider is an area associated with mathematical thought, visual-spatial cognition, and the imagery of movement. Einstein is known for using visual imagination to arrive at his theories. He asked what would it be like if space-time were curved? What would it be like to ride on a ray of light? The area that's missing may be associated with speech production. We know that Einstein didn't start talking until he was three. We know that he would obsessively repeat sentences up to the age of seven. We know that he failed the Technology Institute language exams when he was 16. Einstein always claimed that he thought visually rather than verbally, and he struggled with language throughout his adult life.

There are two themes here that will reappear through the lectures that follow. One is brain function—that there are particular areas of our brains that are crucial for particular functions. One of the ways we know this is by the strange things that happen to cognitive processing when brains are impacted in particular areas—how damaged brains can result in fractured minds. The other theme we'll be pursuing throughout is brain plasticity—the fact that different brains can grow different capabilities in different areas. The brain, we'll see, is organized in terms of structure, but it can also modify that structure. Here, there are a whole range of questions. We think that we perceive the world a certain way—that light comes to our eyes, sends signals to our brain, and is processed in an inner theater. But do things really happen that way? Could they really happen that way? Or is the brain doing things that we don't know about? Are we interacting with the world, seeing and thinking in ways we don't even realize? Here, there are lots of surprises. Together, we will explore some of the mysteries of consciousness.

So far, I've talked about exhibit A, Descartes' dream, and exhibit B, Einstein's brain. The third exhibit I want to offer is a piece of machinery. This one is on display at the London Science Museum. It's made of brass and steel, with columns of interlocking gears. It's called a *Difference Engine*. Between 1820 and 1830, Charles

Babbage drew up plans for a machine that would calculate and print tables of logarithms. He called it *Difference Engine #1*. According to the plans, it would have had 25,000 parts. It would have been eight feet high, seven feet long, three feet deep, and would have weighed thousands of pounds. It would have been driven by steam. He got financing for it from the British government. Many of the parts were actually machined, but Difference Engine #1 was never built.

One of the reasons it wasn't completed is that it was so difficult at the time to machine the parts that Babbage had designed. Another reason it was never built was problems with financing. Babbage kept having to beg more money from Parliament, and his machinist was holding him over a barrel. When the last bill was paid in 1830, the total came to £17,470. The steam locomotive John Bull built in 1831, about the same time, had cost only £784. Babbage's logarithm machine had already cost more than 20 locomotives, and it still wasn't anywhere near complete. A third reason it was never built was that Babbage came up with a different design, a better design, actually *two* designs. One was *Difference Engine #2*. That wasn't completed in Babbage's lifetime either, but it was built by the London Science Museum in the early 1990s. That's the piece of machinery now on display.

Babbage's other design was the Analytical Engine. It, too, would have been made of steel and brass gears. It, too, would have been driven by steam. But the Analytical Engine wouldn't have been limited to merely computing logarithms. Its range would have been all of mathematics. The Analytical Engine would have been able to compute anything. What Babbage designed in the middle of the 19th century—well before the Civil War, well before Edison invented the light bulb—was a steam-driven, all-purpose computer. What would the world have been like had steam-driven computers been available in 1840? What if the Information Revolution had come simultaneously with the Industrial Revolution? That is, in fact, the theme of a novel by William Gibson and Bruce Sterling. What if Babbage had succeeded? The novel is called *The Difference Engine*.

This brings up a third batch of questions we'll be addressing. Could a machine be more than a calculating device? Could a machine really think, think creatively, for example? Could it be genuinely intelligent in the way that people are? Even further, could a machine really feel in the full sense that we feel? Could a machine be conscious? If that seems outrageous to you, let me offer you a question from Marvin Minsky, one of the pioneers of artificial intelligence. Aren't you a machine, a "meat machine," that thinks creatively, that is genuinely intelligent? Aren't you a machine, a "meat machine," that feels? What's so special about the "meat"? I've offered exhibits A, B, and C—the dream, the brain, and the machine—as a first sketch of the kind of topics we'll be dealing with. When you ponder the relations between these—what's the relation between mind and brain? What is it about machines that would allow them to think or would forever prevent them from real intelligence? Those are the questions in philosophy of mind.

There's a further historical link between the first and the last of our exhibits, a link between Descartes and Babbage, between the dream and the machine. Toward the end of his life, René Descartes was summoned as a tutor by Queen Christina of Sweden. He boarded a ship for Sweden even though he feared a shipwreck might cost him his life. That much is documented. The rest is reported as legend and may be impossible to document. And, of course, it may not be true. The story is that Descartes had told other people on the ship that he was traveling with his daughter, Francine, but no one had seen his daughter. The ship was buffeted by storms, during one of which the sailors sought Francine by creeping into Descartes' quarters.

What they found was a large box, inside of which was an automaton, a life-size clockwork doll that moved, they thought, just like a real girl. Descartes' daughter was a machine. The legend continues that the superstitious sailors thought Francine was an item of black magic and that the captain ordered her thrown overboard. We do know that Descartes had attempted to build automata, figures animated by clockwork, earlier in his life. We also know that Descartes, though he never married, did have a daughter out of wedlock. She had died of scarlet fever years before he left for Sweden. Descartes is said to have spoken of her death as the greatest sorrow of his life, and her name was Francine.

That story is written in terms of minds, machines, dreams, and emotions. We will be talking about those, too. It's clear that our topic areas are wide-ranging: minds, brains, and machines. As such, they are clearly the stuff of psychology, computer science, and the neurosciences. We will, in fact, be drawing heavily on those fields throughout the course. I want to say a bit more, however, about what makes the approach that I'll take a philosophical approach, why this is philosophy of mind. The best way to do that, I think, is with a very quick thumbnail sketch of the history of philosophy, in particular, a thumbnail sketch of the relation between philosophy and the sciences.

In the beginning, there was no such distinction. *Philosophy* was simply the Greek for "love of wisdom," and anyone who devoted themselves to wisdom, to knowledge of any kind, was called a philosopher. That's why Thales is often recorded as the first Greek scientist. He's also recorded as the first Greek philosopher. In the beginning, there was no distinction between philosophy and other disciplines. *Philosopher* just meant "lover of wisdom," any kind of wisdom. As time went on, however, particular areas of thought became elaborated enough, or systemized enough, or established enough in other ways to peel off as distinguishable disciplines in their own right.

One of the first to peel off was mathematics. Pythagoras and the Pythagoreans, who gave us both the Pythagorean theorem and the existence of irrational numbers, undoubtedly considered themselves philosophers, not mathematicians. In fact, the Pythagoreans drew no distinction between number theory, musical theory, and the speculation on the role of number and harmony as basic philosophical principles in the universe. Only later, in Euclid—and, interestingly enough, in the systematic axiomatization of geometry— does mathematics start to be treated as a distinct field in its own right. Now, you've got philosophy here and mathematics over here.

Astronomy is probably the next discipline to peel off, though in the archaic amalgam of astronomy and astrology that appears in Ptolemy. Most importantly, astronomy peels off only with a substantial step in systemization around 100–150 A.D., Ptolemy's *Almagest*, and with an applicable technology of astrological prediction. Until after Isaac Newton, there's no physics. Newton thought of himself as a "natural philosopher." Only with the astounding intellectual achievement of his *Principia* of 1687 was there a field distinct enough—with its own Newtonian systemization, with its own experimental techniques—to be thought of as a separate field of physics. Usually, people refer just to Newton's *Principia*. The full title is *Philosophiae Naturalis Principia Mathematica*: the mathematical principles of natural philosophy.

Other disciplines have peeled off in our own century. There used to be part of philosophy called *philosophy of man*. With the development of ethnographic techniques in the early 20th century and with its own smatterings of theory, philosophy of man became the science of anthropology. The key here is the same throughout. Once an area has some real systematization, agreed theoretical basics, and/or experimental techniques, it becomes a science on its own. But there are also more ambiguous cases. Some of what used to be called *social philosophy*—as in social and political philosophy—part of that's now called *sociology*, but not all of it. It was essentially the agreed parts, pursuable by agreed techniques, that became the science of sociology. The *controversial* parts—especially about social values—those remained as part of philosophy. Much the same happened with "philosophy of language." Some of that became linguistics, a science in its own right, but there are plenty of questions that remain. It was only the easy and systematizable questions that became the science of linguistics.

The story is essentially the same in that part of philosophy called *philosophy of mind*. William James taught philosophy at Harvard from the 1880s to 1907, and he's, of course, known as a proponent of philosophical Pragmatism. But it was through his influence that parts of philosophy of mind started to be seen as developed enough to count as a science—the science of psychology. James once said, "The first lecture in psychology that I ever heard was one I delivered." William James published *The Principles of Psychology* in two volumes in 1890. It still reads as half philosophy, half psychology. William James was a philosopher and psychologist; his brother, Henry James, [was] the novelist. But *The Principles of Psychology* was so well written, with such literary flair, that people quipped that William James was the real novelist of the two brothers, a novelist who wrote about psychology. Henry's novels, on the other hand, are known for their deeply psychological insights; he was a psychologist who wrote novels. A publisher convinced William James to create a shorter book to use as a classroom text, which came out as *Psychology: The Briefer Course*. The original longer book became known as "The James." The briefer course became known as "The Jimmy." That was the birth of psychology.

About the same time, in Europe, the break between the philosophy of mind and what was conceived of as the science of mind took the form of psychoanalysis. Freud's first book, *On Aphasia*, was published in 1891. The term *psychoanalysis* was coined in 1896, and later, with somewhat different histories, neurophysiology and neuropsychology became established as sciences. The story throughout is the same. The easier stuff becomes the science, the stuff that's more readily systematized and that yields to experimental technique. The harder stuff is the questions that are not only unanswered but that we're not even sure how to answer. Those are the fundamentally controversial bits—areas in which we're not even sure what basic theory should look like. Those are the areas in which we don't yet even quite know what we don't know. All of that remains part of philosophy. That's the philosophy of mind.

The goal of philosophy of mind is a unified understanding of mind and its place in the world. The focus is on conceptual clarification, the disentangling of complex questions, and the careful examination of alternative approaches. Its major tool is rational argument. Philosophy has always thrived on controversy. One goal of this course is to clarify the core areas of controversy in philosophy of mind. What are the arguments behind Dualism that have led most contemporary philosophers to reject it? What is it that we see when we see color? Are there reasons to think that consciousness is *forever* beyond the reach of science? I'll sometimes be arguing for a particular approach to questions like these, but I'll never be laying down a single dogmatic answer. In each case, I'll be trying to capture the excitement of intellectual controversy by laying out issues in terms of a range of intellectual options and alternatives.

Here's a rough road map for the course: The first six lectures will lay out basic concepts, classical theories, current hypotheses in philosophy of mind. Functionalism has emerged as a dominant trend in current research, and we'll follow its lead in the next six lectures. Those concentrate on perception, our conceptions of ourselves, and minds as they function in the world. Real robots play an interesting role in that exploration. In a third section of the course, I'll focus on questions of intelligence—yours and mine—but also the idea of artificial intelligence. Just how much alike and just how different are brains and computers? The final six lectures of the course focus on subjective experience and the continuing mystery of consciousness.

At every point, I'll be talking about philosophical theories but also about the structure of brains and the most recent data from the neurosciences. At every point, I'll be raising psychological questions but also bringing in issues from robotics and the history of smart machines. Contemporary philosophy of mind is actively interdisciplinary, and it's from the cross-fertilization of these different fields that some of the most interesting perspectives often arise. I'll be drawing examples from literature, from the arts, and from the movies and the history of film—from Fritz Lang's *Metropolis*, to Bogart and Bacall in *To Have and Have Not*, to Arnold Schwarzenegger in *The Terminator*, and Harrison Ford in *Blade Runner*. We'll be doing it all.

The exhibits I've tried to show you—the dream, the brain, the machine—are emblematic of precisely those kinds of questions: questions about minds, brains, and machines for which we don't have solid theory or experimental techniques. These are the questions about minds, brains, and machines for which we do not even know yet quite how to look for answers. There is, by the way, one piece of equipment you'll need for this course. In order to do philosophy of mind, you'll have to get hold of a … mind. Well, isn't that lucky? You already have a mind. You, therefore, have the necessary prerequisites for the course. That's not a very good joke, but it does highlight something that'll come up again and again in our work. In order to do philosophy of mind, you need a mind in two senses. What we're talking about is the mind, so you'll need a mind to examine in the same way you'd examine language in philosophy of language or politics in political philosophy. The mind is the object of our study. Call that the objective side.

But, of course, you couldn't philosophically examine anything without a mind. It's the necessary tool for any examination at all. So it's you, with your mental equipment, that is subjecting this thing to study. You're the subject as well. In this discipline, unavoidably, your mind is both subject and object. That may be part of what makes some of these questions so interesting. It may also be part of what makes them so hard. In the next lecture, I'll dive right into one of the central issues: the mind-body problem.

Lecture Two
The Mind-Body Problem

Scope:

This lecture is based on five "obvious philosophical facts":

1. You have a mind and a body;
2. These normally work together;
3. Your body is physical and, thus, publicly observable;
4. Your mental life is essentially private; therefore,
5. You have privileged access to the contents of your own mind.

The simplest position that makes sense of these philosophical facts is Dualism, developed in the work of René Descartes. This lecture uses a logical principle from Leibniz and Descartes' assertion "I think, therefore I am" to present a major argument for Dualism. The lecture then reveals a crucial conceptual problem that has convinced many philosophers that Dualism must be incorrect. In the Cartesian picture, physical things exist in physical space. The realm of the mental does not. But if mind and body are as radically distinct as Descartes says they are, how could they possibly interact?

Outline

I.   The mind-body problem will be a central issue throughout these lectures.

    A. The central problem will appear in a philosophical guise, a psychological guise, a neuroscientific guise, and in the guise of computer science.

    B. In this lecture, we will tackle the problem head-on, in terms of a position called *Dualism*.

II. We start with five "obvious philosophical facts"—things believed by just about everybody.

    A. Philosophical fact #1: You have a mind. You also have a body.

    B. Philosophical fact #2: Under normal circumstances, the mind and the body work together.

        1. When you die, mind and body will not work together.

    2. Some people think your mind will continue without your body, as a "disembodied" spirit or soul.

    3. Some think that both your body and mind will simply cease to exist.

C. Philosophical fact #3: Your body is physical.

    1. It is composed of matter and occupies space.

    2. As a result, the realm of bodily behavior is publicly observable.

D. Philosophical fact #4: Your mental life is essentially private.

    1. When you imagine a sunset, you alone can see it.

    2. No one else can literally "feel your pain."

    3. Unlike the physical realm, the mental realm is not publicly observable.

E. Philosophical fact #5: You have *privileged access* to your own mental realm.

    1. Suppose we ask Mary, "Does your knee itch?" Suppose we then ask John, "Does Mary's knee itch?" Mary says yes while John says no. Whose testimony should we trust?

    2. Mary has privileged access to her own mental states.

    3. Some have thought that privileged access extends to infallibility—that we cannot be wrong about our own mental states.

F. Why do we think these obvious philosophical facts are true?

    1. Some have proposed that they are the legacy of philosophical theories of the past.

    2. Philosophers often do their best work by spelling out or making explicit concepts that are already part of common sense.

G. Whether the obvious philosophical facts are, in fact, true is a question that will be open for further examination throughout these lectures.

III. If the obvious philosophical facts are true, what must the universe be like? The simplest theory of the universe that fits these facts is Dualism.

A. According to Dualism, the universe is divided into two radically different halves.

1. The physical realm contains all those things made of matter, which occupy space and are governed by the laws of physics.
2. The mental realm contains those things that are essentially mental: hopes, emotions, imaginings, and consciousness.
3. A can of pineapple is entirely physical. The taste of pineapple is something mental.

B. This position is *Cartesian Dualism*, outlined in Descartes' *Meditations*, first translated into English as *Six Metaphysical Meditations: Wherein it is Proved that there is a God. And that Man's Mind is really Distinct from his Body.*

IV. Descartes offered logical arguments that Dualism must be true. The best is that attributed to Descartes by Antoine Arnauld.

A. The argument has two related conclusions.
1. The first conclusion is that your mind is in no way the same thing as your body or any part of your body.
2. The second conclusion is that what is essential to you is not your body but your mind.

B. Crucial to the argument is a basic principle from Leibniz, the "indiscernibility of identicals":
1. If two things are identical—if two things are the same thing—then anything true of one is true of the other.
2. We should keep this principle in mind as we follow Descartes through the *Meditations*.

C. Recall Descartes' dream from Lecture One.
1. Descartes sought complete certainty.
2. His method was to try to doubt everything. If anything could be genuinely certain, it would be impervious to doubt.
3. Let us follow Descartes in trying to doubt everything. Perhaps everything I've ever been told was a lie and nothing is as it seems. Perhaps even other people don't exist.
4. In the *Matrix* movies, human beings are fed false subjective experiences, deceived into thinking that they are living normal lives. Suppose a race of robots, a master computer, a mad doctor, or an "evil demon" is trying to deceive me in any way it can.

5. The next crucial step in this process of doubting takes two forms.

    a. Is there anything I cannot doubt? Yes, that I am doubting. Were I to doubt that I was doubting, I would still be doubting.

    b. Is there anything I cannot be deceived about? Yes, that I am thinking. Were something to deceive me into merely thinking that I am thinking, I would still be thinking.

D. Two conclusions seem to follow:

    1. If I am doubting, I must exist. If I am thinking, I must exist. *Cogito, ergo sum*: I think, therefore I exist.

    2. If I doubt, I must have a mind. If I think, I must have a mind. Therefore, I cannot doubt that I have a mind.

E. When the pieces of the argument are put together, they entail the conclusion that Dualism must be true.

    1. Leibniz's principle is: If two things are identical, everything true of one must be true of the other.

    2. I can doubt that I have a body or any part of a body. I can even doubt that I have a brain—maybe that is part of the illusion. I cannot doubt that I have a mind.

    3. There is, therefore, something true of my mind that is true of no part of my body: I cannot doubt that I have it.

    4. It follows by Leibniz's principle that my mind cannot be my body or any part of my body. My mind cannot be my brain.

V. Cartesian Dualism tells us that the mental and the physical are essentially different kinds of things.

    A. Physical things, Descartes says, are always extended and occupy space. Mental things do not have physical dimension in the same way.

    B. Dualism is the simplest theory that accords with our obvious philosophical facts, and we have a logical argument for it.

    C. But Dualism also has a central philosophical problem.

        1. According to Cartesian Dualism, the mental and the physical are entirely different realms. One is a realm of things that obey physical laws and occupy space. Another is a realm of ideas, sensations, and feelings that don't even exist in space.

2. If those realms were entirely distinct, it would seem that nothing mental could cause anything physical, and nothing physical could cause anything mental.
3. But we know that the mental does affect the physical: Our desires result in physical behavior. We know that the physical does affect the mental: Physical events in the world affect our beliefs and feelings.
4. The "completely separate realms" view of Dualism must, therefore, be wrong.

D. Gilbert Ryle referred to the Cartesian view of mind as the "myth of the ghost in the machine."

E. Can we find a way out of this dilemma? Here is a suggestive analogy, the spirit of which will reappear in later lectures:
1. Your fist is not identical to your hand. You can make a fist and then open your hand: Your fist has ceased to exist, but your hand has not. By Leibniz's law, they cannot be identical.
2. Yet there is a sense in which your fist isn't something extra. To make a fist is just to put your hand in a particular position.

Further Resources:

René Descartes, *Meditations on First Philosophy*, First and Second Meditations.

Gilbert Ryle, *The Concept of Mind*, chapter 1.

Questions to Consider:

1. Our fifth "obvious philosophical fact" was that you have privileged access to the contents of your own mind. Some people have taken this to mean that you cannot be wrong about the contents of your own mind. What do you think? Can you be wrong about whether you are in pain? Can you be wrong about what you believe?

2. Consider this thought experiment: We haven't proven anything like this, but suppose the following beliefs turned out to be inconsistent. In order to remain consistent, you have to abandon at least one. Which of these beliefs would you keep, which would you reject, and why?

a. The mental and the physical are radically different aspects of reality.
b. The physical and the mental are causally linked.

Lecture Two—Transcript
The Mind-Body Problem

I used our first lecture to give an outline of the kinds of topics we'd be covering in this course. I used three exhibits: a dream, a brain, and a machine. A problem that came up clearly to the fore in that discussion was the mind-body problem. That's a problem that we'll be tracking throughout the course in one way or another—in a philosophical guise, a psychological guise, in the guise of computer science, and in terms of the neurosciences. In this lecture, I'll tackle the mind-body problem head on in terms of a position called *Dualism*. I want to start with five "obvious philosophical facts" or, at least, what seem to be obvious philosophical facts; these are things that just about everybody believes. These are even *pre*-philosophical facts, in a sense. Everybody thinks they're true even before they start doing philosophy. Here they are:

Philosophical fact #1: You have a mind. You also have a body.

Philosophical fact #2: Normally, hopefully, these work together. When you die, they won't. When you die, we'll have a dead body on our hands—*your* dead body. At that point, one of two things might happen, and here people disagree. Some people think your mind will continue without your body. It will then be a "disembodied mind" or a "disembodied spirit." Some people think that when you die, you cease to exist. We will have nothing but a dead body on our hands. Your mind will no longer exist. There'll be no more you. We don't have to settle that dispute here. Philosophical fact #2 is just that normally, hopefully, and while you're alive, your mind and body work together.

Philosophical fact #3: Your body is physical. It's made of matter—physical stuff—and it occupies space. Because of that, what you do with your body is something other people can observe. If you raise your arm, people can see it. If you turn sideways, that's the kind of thing people can see. If you shout, it can be heard. The things that bodies do are like that. Bodies are physical space-filling things, observable in the same way other physical space-filling things are. We can put it this way: The realm of bodily behavior is publicly observable.

Philosophical fact #4: The other side of this coin: What you do with your mind, in contrast, may not be publicly observable. Imagine a sunset. Imagine it in full color and great detail. Now you may see that sunset in your mind, but we don't. What you see—your mental image—is not publicly accessible. Your mental life is essentially private. Here's another example: When you're in pain, even excruciating pain, that's just *your* pain. You might express your pain by some public and physical way—by moaning, for example—so that we become aware that you're in pain. But no matter how sympathetic we are, we don't literally "feel your pain." Unlike the physical realm, the mental realm is not publicly observable. You can mentally picture things that are essentially private or inner. You can also mentally do things that we can't see. You can add two numbers in your head. You can make plans for the future. As long as you don't tell us, we can't get to those.

Philosophical fact #5: The mental realm, then, is somehow private. Something that goes along with that is what's called *privileged access*. Suppose there are three of us in the room. I'm sitting with Jim and Mary. Nobody's hidden. We're just sitting in the open and talking. Suppose I ask both Jim and Mary how many chairs there are in the room. Is there any reason for me to think that one of their responses is going to be more accurate than the other? No. How many chairs there are in the room is an observable physical fact. Both Jim and Mary have access to that fact. I have no reason to believe that one of them is going to give me a more reliable report than the other. Now suppose I ask Mary whether her right knee itches. Independently, somehow simultaneously, I also ask Jim whether Mary's right knee itches. Mary tells me her knee itches; Jim tells me that it doesn't. Whose testimony should I take regarding Mary's itches—Jim's or Mary's?

Or suppose that I ask them both whether, right now, Jim feels a little pain in his lower right molar. Jim says he doesn't; Mary says he does. Whose testimony should I take as to whether Jim has a toothache—Jim's or Mary's? Jim's, obviously. Why? Because he knows whether he has a toothache a lot better than anybody else does. Some people have characterized this in terms of our privileged access to our own mental realm, to the contents of our own minds. It's your mind. Mental stuff is internal, and nobody else can get in there. You're the one who knows. Some people have thought that what this gives you is not only privileged access but infallibility, that you can't be wrong about your knee itches, or your headaches, or your toothaches. The idea is that this can't happen. "Oh, oh, oh, oh,

I'm in terrible pain. Uh, no, I guess not. How silly of me; my mistake." The claim is that you can't make mistakes about that kind of stuff. You can't be wrong about your own mental realm. Whether the infallibility claim is true or not, you get the general idea of privileged access.

We have, then, five obvious philosophical facts. Let's reiterate: You have a mind and a body. Normally, hopefully, they work together. The body is physical and, so, publicly observable. The realm of the mental, in contrast, is private. And, finally, it is you who have privileged access to the contents of your own mind. Those are claims regarding minds and bodies that just about everyone thinks are true. Why do we think they are? Some have proposed that these are the legacy of philosophical theories of the past that have somehow trickled down to become part of common sense. Bertrand Russell speaks of common sense as the "metaphysics of the Stone Age," and perhaps these are common conceptions that are a legacy from the philosophical views of—well, not exactly the Stone Age but maybe the Renaissance.

The road between philosophy and common sense runs in both directions, however. The work of philosophers and other thinkers can trickle down to become common sense. But philosophers often do their best work by making concepts explicit that are already part of common sense, by developing and sharpening ways people already tend to think of minds and bodies, for example. My guess is that these philosophical facts were sharpened and formalized in philosophical work, but that they were part of common ways of thinking long before that. There is also the possibility that some of these obvious philosophical facts aren't true. That's still up for grabs. In the course of these lectures, we'll be looking at some of the conceptual problems that our pre-philosophical views can lead us into, whatever their history. At certain points, I'll introduce you to some reasons to think that we should perhaps abandon or qualify one or more of these conceptions of minds and bodies.

For now, I want to do something different. Let's suppose that these five claims are precisely what they appear to be—obvious philosophical facts. Let's see what follows if they are. If these claims are true, what must the universe be like? What must the universe be like in order for minds and bodies to work this way? Here's the simplest theory of the universe that fits with all of these; it's a theory called *Dualism*. This is a philosopher's theory; in the form I'll outline it, it's Descartes' theory. But it's not just a philosopher's theory; in a broad outline, this is precisely the way most people think about people, minds, and bodies. The simplest story we tend to tell is a Dualist story. Here's the basic Dualist picture:

There are really two radically different halves of the universe: the physical realm and the mental realm. The physical realm contains all the physical things—the things composed of matter. These are the things that have physical dimension: length, height, depth. Descartes speaks of this as "extension." These are the things that exist at particular places, at particular times, that occupy space, that are governed by the laws of physics. Your body is a physical thing, something with extension that occupies space. Your body is part of the physical universe. But there are also things in the universe that are essentially mental: the way things look to you, the way they appear in your imagination, the mental calculations you do when figuring something out, your thoughts, your hopes, your emotions, your imaginings, and your consciousness.

Consider a can of pineapple, the can itself, made of metal, and its physical contents—that stuff inside with a particular acidic pH. All of that is part of the physical universe, but the taste of pineapple is something different. It's something essentially mental. You can imagine how pineapple tastes right now, and in doing so, you are accessing the mental side of the universe. This is *Substance Dualism*. In more highfalutin and traditional terminology, the position is that there are two essentially different substances in the universe: the mental and the physical. Substance Dualism fits our obvious philosophical facts to a T. The physical is the objective stuff of the universe; the mental is the essentially subjective realm. The physical is something that exists independently of us, publicly observable by all, and about which we can be wrong. The mental is a private and internal realm to which only we have access and about which we cannot be wrong in the same way.

Descartes holds precisely that view. Substance Dualism is also called *Cartesian Dualism*. Your body is part of the physical universe. Your mind is something essentially different, part of a very different universe—the universe of mental phenomena. Descartes' meditations were first translated into English with a very appropriate subtitle: *Six Metaphysical Meditations: Wherein it is Proved that there is a God.*

And that Man's Mind is really Distinct from his Body. Descartes didn't just have a position. Like any philosopher worth his salt, he also offered logical arguments for that position, reasons beyond just intuitive philosophical facts or the fact that everyone believes something like this. Descartes offered reasons for thinking that this is what the universe really has to be like.

I'm going to focus on just one argument for Dualism. I think it's Descartes' best argument, if it really is Descartes'. Finding this argument in Descartes' text is actually very difficult. It is attributed to Descartes by one of his contemporary critics—by Antoine Arnauld. In the end, what I'm offering as Descartes' best argument may actually be Arnauld's. What we care about, however, isn't where an argument comes from. What we care about is how good it is and what it shows, and this is a powerful argument for Dualism. If it works, the argument really has two conclusions. One conclusion is that mind and body really are two different things—that your mind is in no way the same thing as your body nor the same thing as any part of your body. Your mind could not possibly be your brain. The second conclusion is that what's essential to you is not your body but your mind. The argument is a complicated one. It demands an experiential journey of a certain sort, so sit back and let the argument flow over you.

Crucial to the argument is a basic philosophical principle that's most clearly expressed not in the work of Descartes but in the work of the philosopher Gottfried Wilhelm Leibniz. The principle is this: If two things are identical—if two things are really the same thing—then anything true of one is true of the other. This is the most obvious half of Leibniz's "indiscernibility of identicals." If two things are identical—if they're really the same thing—then anything true of one is true of the other. They are, after all, the very same thing. It follows immediately that if we find two things where something is true of one of them and isn't true of the other, they can't be identical; they can't be the same thing. Keep that principle in mind as we follow Descartes through his *Meditations.* Here's where the experiential journey comes in.

In the last lecture, I told you about Descartes' dream. During that day in 1619, he said he had been pondering the uncertainty of all of his knowledge. In his dream that night, the dictionary represented the disorganized and unreliable bits and pieces that had been passed down to us as human wisdom. What Descartes wanted was a breathtaking alternative. What he wanted was dead certainty. What he wanted to do was build up a unified worldview from a firm foundation, a foundation that we could be absolutely sure of. Descartes' technique was correspondingly breathtaking. If you want absolute certainty, you have to start by throwing out everything that might in any way be subject to doubt. If you throw out everything that you could possibly be wrong about, what's left—if anything is left—will be something that's absolutely certain. That will be something about which it would impossible to be wrong.

So let's follow the Cartesian methodology of trying to doubt everything. Suppose that everything I believe is a lie; suppose it's all false. Suppose the sky isn't blue; there's no real sky. Suppose all the people I think I know are merely figments of my imagination. How could that happen? In the *Matrix* movies, human beings are fed false subjective experiences. They're deceived into thinking that they're leading normal human lives, moving about in an actual world. In reality, their bodies are being exploited as energy sources, cocooned line upon line in a giant battery, out of any real touch with any real world. So suppose I'm a captive of the *Matrix*. Suppose there's a race of robots, or a master computer, or a mad doctor, or an "evil demon" that's manipulating my subjective world, feeding me false experiences, out to deceive me in any way it can.

I think I'm lecturing about Descartes, but maybe I'm not. The evil demon might be making things appear that way when they're not. I'm not really talking to anybody. I'm mumbling in my sleep or merely dreaming that I'm talking. I guess I can't be certain that I'm really talking. We're using Descartes' method in pursuit of absolute certainty, and I could be wrong about that. Even that goes on the trash heap of possible doubt. I think I've got two legs, but maybe I don't. Maybe the evil demon is deceiving me into thinking I have two when I only have one or none. In fact, I could be wrong about just about anything about my body. I think I see what I look like by looking in a mirror, but maybe I don't look like that at all. Maybe those images are all a fabrication. In good Cartesian style, what I think is true of my own body goes on the trash heap of possible doubt as well. Maybe I'm not the kind of thing that has a body at all. Maybe there's no physical universe at all in the sense I think there is. The evil demon may have fooled me into thinking even that. You see how devastating the acid of Cartesian doubt really is. That is step one in the experiential journey—the Cartesian route of doubting everything.

There are a couple of forms of the next crucial step of the argument. Is there anything I can't doubt? Well, here I am, just like Descartes, doubting everything in sight. Can I doubt even that? Can I doubt that I'm doubting? Interestingly, and for the first time, the answer is no. If I were to doubt that I was doubting, I'd still be doubting, right? So doubt about doubting would still be doubting. As long as I'm doubting, I can't doubt that. Aha, finally something I can't doubt— the fact that I'm doubting. Here's an alternative form of the same step: Is there anything I can't be deceived about? Well, consider the fact that I'm thinking about being deceived. Or just consider the fact that I'm currently thinking. Could the evil demon be deceiving me about that? I'm not really thinking at all, but he's making me think I am ... oops, then I really am thinking, right? So as long as I'm thinking, he couldn't be deceiving me about that. That's the crucial second step in Descartes' meditation: I can't doubt that I'm doubting. I can't be deceived about whether I'm thinking.

Two things seem to follow. The first is that if I'm doubting, I must exist. In order to doubt, you've got to have something that does the doubting. If I am thinking, I must exist. *Cogito, ergo sum*; I think, therefore I exist. This piece of argument is called the *cogito*. It is the *cogito* that Descartes hopes is going to be the cornerstone of certainty. The second thing that follows is that if I'm doubting, I must have a mind. If I'm thinking, I must have a mind. Doubting and thinking are something that minds do. So I think, therefore I exist; I think, therefore I have a mind. It's time to put the pieces of the argument together. We started with Leibniz's principle: If two things are identical—if they're the same thing—anything true of one is true of the other. From there, we followed Descartes' trail of doubt, finding something central that I cannot doubt (that I am doubting), something I can't be deceived about (that I'm thinking). From those, it follows that I must have a mind.

The final step puts these two things together. The evil demon may deceive me into thinking I have a body when I don't, but he can't deceive me into thinking I have a mind when I don't. I can doubt I have a body, but I can't doubt I have a mind. So here is something true of my body: I can doubt it exists. Here's something that's not true of my mind: I can doubt it exists. So different things are true of my body and my mind; I can doubt one of them exists, but I can't doubt the other exists. By Leibniz's principle, it follows that they can't be the same thing. My mind cannot be the same thing as my body or any part of my body. Let me repeat just that crucial transition in the argument. If two things are the same, everything true of one must be true of the other. So if my body and my mind were the same, everything true of one must be true of the other. But I can doubt that my body exists; I can't doubt that my mind exists, so they cannot be the same thing.

If you think your mind is any part of your body—if you think your mind is your brain, for example—the argument works just as well. If they were the same, everything true of one would have to be true of the other. But you can doubt even that you have a brain; maybe that's all part of the illusion. You can't doubt that you have a mind, so your brain and your mind cannot be the same. So here's where we stand. The simplest theory that makes sense of our obvious philosophical facts is Dualism, the theory that there are these two essentially different parts of the universe—the realm of the mental and the realm of the physical.

What that theory tells us is that these are *essentially* different kinds of things. According to Descartes, physical things are always extended and occupy space. Physical things, like billiard balls and sandwiches and automobiles, always have a particular size and shape and are located in some particular physical place. Mental things, Descartes says, do not have physical dimension in the same way. There seems something right about that. Consider the taste of pineapple, that very particular taste. How tall is it? How wide? Mental things don't have physical dimensions like that. Consider subtraction. Where is that located—Chicago or New York? Mental things don't have physical locations like that. The physical and the mental are essentially different kinds of things, one of which exists in space and one of which doesn't.

We have Dualism as a position—a position suggested by our obvious philosophical facts. We also have the Cartesian argument that Dualism has to be true, at least with regard to minds and bodies. But we're doing philosophy, and there's a major philosophical problem right here. The problem is that despite its intuitive appeal and despite Descartes' argument, we also have good reasons to think that Dualism couldn't possibly be true. The core problem is this: If the mental and the physical realms are essentially different—if they represent such radically different kinds of things—how could they possibly interact? Here's the problem in the form pressed against Descartes by critics in his own time: Consider what happens when one thing causes another—for example, when a billiard ball hits another one, knocking it into the corner pocket. We have a physical billiard ball, which rolls on a physical table toward another physical billiard ball, makes physical contact with it, and transfers its physical force to the other ball—a physical cause producing a physical effect.

But the mental realm is supposed to be something entirely different from the physical. Mental things aren't even located in space, remember? So how could something mental produce a physical effect? You can stand there all day and dream that the ball is going to go into the corner pocket, wish that the ball would go into the corner pocket, *imagine* the ball going into the corner pocket. Parapsychology aside, it won't. It needs a physical push. What Dualism tells us is that the mental realm is something completely different and apart. How could something that's purely mental possibly give anything a physical push? Mental things on the Dualist picture look like the wrong kinds of things to have physical effects. Because it so radically separates the realms of the mental and the physical, Dualism makes causal interaction between the two realms look impossible. And yet we know perfectly well that there are causal links between the physical and the mental, so Dualism has to be wrong.

We know that mental things cause physical things all the time. You're thirsty; that sensation is part of the mental realm. Because of that sensation and because of your mental desire, you make a mental decision. As a direct result, your physical legs take you down the physical hall; you drop a physical piece of metal into a physical machine. The mental *causes* the physical. If you want to see a physical cause that causes something mental, buy yourself a full physical bottle of scotch. There it is, real physical liquid with a real physical alcohol content, physically resting in its physical bottle. Raise it to your physical lips and pour it down your physical throat. I guarantee you things will change in the mental realm as a direct result.

So where do we stand? We have a set of obvious philosophical facts that seem to lead us to Dualism. We have, for good measure, a solid

Cartesian argument for Dualism. But if full Substance Dualism were true, it looks like there would be no causal interplay between the mental and the physical. We know perfectly well that there is. It follows that Dualism cannot be true. Indeed, the strong majority of philosophers working today think that Dualism has to be wrong for precisely that kind of reason. In the 1950s, the British philosopher Gilbert Ryle called the idea that I have this thing called the mind—somehow separate from, but contained in, my body—he called it the "myth of the ghost in the machine."

I'll return to the issue in the lecture after next. At that point, I'll talk about possible ways out of the dilemma, about some subtle defenses of weaker forms of Dualism and important philosophical alternatives. For now, let me give you just the merest hint. Let me show you how the conclusion of the Cartesian argument could be right—the conclusion that mind and body are two different things—and yet how full Substance Dualism might still be wrong. I'll do this by showing you two different things that are somehow also the same. Here is a suggestive analogy, a suggestive analogy the spirit of which will reappear in later lectures. Hold out your right hand and make a fist. Now consider two things: your hand and your fist. There are very different things true of those. If you open your hand, your hand is still there. What happened to your fist? You no longer have a fist. Different things are true of your hand and your fist. There is certainly a sense in which your hand is not identical to your fist, but we don't think it follows that your fist is something extra, above and beyond your hand. We don't think there are, therefore, two kinds of basic substances in the universe: hand substance and fist substance.

We started with five obvious philosophical facts. Let me add a sixth. It's obvious that there is some close relation between my fist and my hand. There's some sense in which my fist *is* my hand. My fist is my hand in a particular posture, perhaps, or doing a particular thing, and maybe something like that is also true of minds and brains.

Lecture Three
Brains and Minds, Parts and Wholes

Scope:

The brain and the mind seem to work in parallel: The brain is the physical understructure of the mind. That fact suggests a strategy for investigation. We should be able to find out things about the brain by seeing how the mind works. We should be able to find out things about the mind by seeing how the brain works. This lecture offers a historical view of a number of things we have learned about minds and brains using precisely this strategy.

In 1848, a railroad foreman named Phineas Gage suffered a horrible accident: An iron rod was blasted through his head. Amazingly, Gage survived the accident, but he underwent a radical personality change. Together with the story of phrenology, the strange case of Phineas Gage is used to explore the history of a basic question about mental faculties and the brain: Does the brain function as a thing of distinct parts or as a unified whole?

Outline

I. This lecture emphasizes an investigative strategy suggested by the interaction between the mind and the brain.

    A. If mind and brain are correlated, we will be able to learn things about the brain by studying the mind, and we will be able to learn things about the mind by studying the brain.

    B. This lecture also considers moral implications from some of the facts of interaction.

II. The accident suffered by Phineas Gage presents a classic case used to explore the question of mind-brain interaction.

    A. In September 1848, Gage was working on the railroad when a blasting charge sent an iron rod through his head.

    B. Gage showed no evidence of speech or memory problems, but he experienced a radical change in personality.

        1. Previously, he had been "the most efficient and capable" man in the railroad's employ.

    2. After the accident, Gage was described as fitful, irreverent, profane, impatient, and obstinate yet capricious and vacillating.

  C. In reconstructions using Gage's skull, Hanna Damasio and her students concluded that the rod passed through the ventromedial region of the frontal lobe.

  D. Such cases raise questions on both sides of the issue of mind-brain interaction.

    1. One set of questions relates to how brains function.

    2. Another set involves the character of our mental lives and moral experience.

III. Is the mind one thing or many?

  A. In one picture, the mind is a thing of distinct parts or mental "faculties" located in different parts of the brain.

  B. Another picture is an image of mind as a homogenous whole.

    1. William James noted the unity or "stream of consciousness."

    2. In that picture, we should perhaps expect to find a holistic brain of undifferentiated "mind stuff" that does everything everywhere.

  C. Which view is right? The case of Phineas Gage played an important role in the historical debate.

    1. Francis Gall's phrenology of the early 1800s was based on the concept of localizing mental faculties and personality characteristics in distinct places in the head.

    2. Phrenology was a pseudoscience, unscientific even by the standards of the time.

    3. Because Gage's memory and linguistic abilities were intact, his case was used at the time as an empirical argument for a *holistic* view of the mind.

    4. Today, Gage's case is used as one piece of evidence among many on the other side. Gage's personality changes fit a *localization theory*, reconfirmed daily in CAT scans, PET scans, and functional MRIs.

IV. What mental functions did Gage lose?

  A. Gage no longer behaved in socially appropriate ways, and his decision-making abilities were seriously impaired.

B. Antonio Damasio's patient "Elliot," who suffered brain damage in the same area, shows similar personality changes.

    1. Elliot does well on all standard intelligence testing, with no evident impact on memory or linguistic abilities. Tests also indicate a normal level of moral development.

    2. With regard to practical decisions in his own life, however, he has everything necessary for responsible action except the ability to put it into play.

    3. Elliot's is a case of *volitional dysfunction*. He knows right from wrong but behaves as if he does not.

V. These concepts are central to the history of the insanity defense.

    A. By the criterion adopted into American law in 1882, a defendant is "not guilty by virtue of insanity" if he or she did not know the nature and quality of the act or did not know that the act was wrong as a result of laboring under a defect of reason from disease of the mind.

    B. A more modern criterion has both a "knowledge" and a "volitional" prong. Defendants are "not guilty by virtue of insanity" if they lacked substantial capacity to appreciate the criminality of their acts or lacked substantial capacity to conform their conduct to the requirements of the law as a result of mental disease or defect.

    C. Phineas Gage and Damasio's Elliot might have a defense of insanity under the second criterion but not the first.

    D. Because of the volitional prong, the jury found John W. Hinckley, Jr., "not guilty by virtue of insanity" for the attempted assassination of Ronald Reagan in 1981. As a reaction to that decision, the second criterion has largely been abandoned; insanity is once again treated as a matter of what one knows.

VI. Cases like those of Elliot and Phineas Gage also raise moral questions.

    A. We will examine the issue of free will in a later lecture. Many philosophers agree that we do act freely.

    B. But do people with brain damage like that of Elliot and Phineas Gage have free will? Antonio Damasio says no.

C. Imaging studies show a high incidence of similar frontal lobe abnormalities in our prison population, with clear links to violent crime.

D. Do these facts about minds and brains have implications for our system of criminal justice?

Further Resources:

Rita Carter, *Mapping the Mind*, chapter 1.

Antonio Damasio, *Descartes' Error: Emotion, Reason, and the Human Brain*, chapters 1–3.

Malcolm Macmillan, *The Phineas Gage Information Page*, http://www.deakin.edu.au/hmnbs/psychology/gagepage/.

Questions to Consider:

1. Mind and brain seem to work together, yet we seem to have a single, unified stream of consciousness, despite the fact that different aspects of perception, judgment, and emotion are processed in different parts of the brain. How can that be?

2. Consider this thought experiment: You are on a jury in a murder case. The defense argues that the defendant suffered brain trauma from an automobile accident a year earlier; as a result, he no longer acts from his own free will.

   Describe a piece of evidence that would convince you that the defense is right and the defendant does not have free will.

   Describe a piece of evidence that would convince you that the defense is wrong and the defendant does act of his own free will.

Lecture Three—Transcript
Brains and Minds, Parts and Wholes

In the last lecture, we saw that the reality of mental-physical interaction posed a basic problem for Substance Dualism. If these really were two radically distinct, essentially different kinds of things, how could they possibly interact? We know, of course, that they do interact. Our mental decisions do have clear physical effects. The physical world does influence our mental life, or else perception itself—seeing, hearing, and tasting—would be impossible. But it's not merely that the two interact. We take it to be a fact that the mental and the physical are very closely connected. To put it simply, the mind has a physical understructure. The physical understructure of the mind is the brain.

However, merely stating that the mind has a physical understructure in the brain doesn't answer the major questions about the relation between mind and brain. It doesn't tell us what the physical understructure is. It doesn't tell us in precisely what ways aspects of our mental lives are linked to aspects of our brains. It also doesn't answer the philosophical question of how that's possible. We still stand in the shadow of Dualism. If the mental and the physical are so radically different, how could they interact? More on that question next time. For this lecture, I want to concentrate on what we do take to be a fact: the fact that mind and brain are correlated—that they run in parallel—whatever our ultimate philosophical understanding of that fact is going to be.

Here is the theme of this lecture: If mind and brain are correlated—if they function together—things we discover about the mind may tell us important things about how our brains work. If mind and brain are correlated in this way, things we discover about the brain may also reveal important things about how our minds work. I will be talking about a classic case from which conclusions regarding both the brain and the mind can be drawn in precisely this way. This particular case points up something more; it has implications for our understanding of our physical brains and implications for our understanding of the character of our mental lives. But it also has implications regarding important questions of morality.

This is the strange case of Phineas Gage. It was September 1848. Phineas Gage was 25 years old and a construction foreman for the Rutland & Burlington Railroad. His job was to supervise the laying of new tracks across Vermont. One of the things Gage was in charge of was blasting. The way they did this in the mid-1800s was to drill holes in the rock, pour in gunpowder, insert a fuse, cover the gunpowder with sand, tamp it down, and set it off. Gage worked with an assistant. He poured in the gunpowder. The assistant put in the sand. Gage tamped it with an iron rod. On September 13th, 1848, he was distracted for a minute. The assistant didn't put in the sand. Gage went to the next step, dropping in the rod to tamp it. The rod was 1¼ inches in diameter; it was about 3½ feet long. It was pointed on one end. He dropped it directly into the gunpowder, and the gunpowder exploded. The rod shot up through his head, through his face, brain, out the top of his skull, and off into the sky.

The amazing thing was that Phineas Gage wasn't dead. Even more amazing was the fact that he was conscious and able to talk. A doctor who examined Gage about an hour after the accident describes the broken fragments of skull and of being able to see the "pulsations of the brain." Gage was entirely lucid throughout the examination, answering questions and describing what had happened to him. He had survived having a 3½-foot iron rod rammed through his head. But Phineas Gage was nonetheless a changed man. Before the accident, he had been considered polite and reliable, "the most efficient and capable" man in the railroad's employ. He was still an able-bodied and intelligent adult; he had no impairment of movement or speech. He had no memory problems regarding either his life before the incident or after. But he now acted in inappropriate and irresponsible ways. Dr. John Harlow describes the new Gage as:

> … fitful, irreverent, indulging at times in the grossest profanity … manifesting but little deference for his fellows, impatient of restraint or advice when it conflicts with his desires, at times pertinaciously obstinate, yet capricious and vacillating, devising many [future] plans … which are no sooner arranged than they are abandoned. …

The new Gage [flouted] authority and couldn't be trusted. The railroad wouldn't rehire him. At one point, he became an exhibit in P. T. Barnum's museum in New York. He wandered from job to job as far as South America, eventually ending up in San Francisco. There are indications that he suffered from seizures toward the end of his life. It may have been one of those seizures that finally killed him, 13 years after the accident, at the age of 38. There was no autopsy on Gage's brain when he died, but his skull still exists, as does the rod that went through it. On the basis of those, several attempts have been made to reconstruct the trajectory of the rod through his head, how he could have survived, and what explained the radical change in his personality.

One of those reconstructions was done by neuroscientist Hanna Damasio and her students. The conclusion was that the rod had passed through the ventromedial region of the frontal lobe. If you grasp your forehead with your hand, the area under your hand is the frontal lobe. *Ventro* is the underbelly of that lobe. It curls under in there just above your nasal cavities and your eyes. *Medial* means that we're talking about the midline of the brain, drawn lengthwise. The area impacted by the rod, on this reconstruction, was the middle underside of the front part of the brain, the ventromedial region of the frontal lobe. Working on the hypothesis that the mind and brain are linked, cases like that of Phineas Gage raise a range of important questions. [Specifically,] they raise questions of two kinds.

One set of questions concerns the physical side of the mind-brain linkage—questions as to how brains function. Another set of questions concerns the mental side of the mind-brain linkage—questions regarding the character of our mental lives. As I'm going to develop it, these questions include questions regarding the true character of our own moral experience. Let's start with the physical questions, exploring these with some help from the mental side as well. We're working with the assumption that the brain is the physical understructure of the mind. But is that physical understructure a matter of distinct bits and pieces of differently functioning parts, or is it a matter of some unified whole? Is the mind one thing or many? Is the physical brain beneath it a matter of differently functioning bits or a homogenous whole?

We have two options here. On the one side is the image of the mind as a thing of different parts, with the physical understructure of the brain as a thing of distinct parts as well. The idea that the soul is a matter of different parts goes back to Plato. Plato envisages a tripartite soul composed of reason, appetite, and *thumos*, a force of courage shown in battle. Plato thought of these as different functions and associated them with a physical understructure. For example, he speaks of *thumos* as being located in one's chest. Faculty psychology—the idea that the mind functions in terms of distinct mental "faculties"—is evident in medieval writings but becomes most fully developed in the 1800s. On such a view, your mental life is a thing of many parts, operating in terms of the faculties of sense, memory, imagination, sympathy, intellect, and the like. We still speak of someone "losing their faculties." If the mind has different faculties and the brain is the physical understructure of the mind, you might well expect to find those faculties in different parts of the brain.

The other option is an image of mind as a homogeneous whole. If the mind is one thing and the brain is the physical understructure of the mind, we might expect the brain to be working as a homogeneous whole as well. Our mental lives don't usually feel like a thing of bits and pieces. William James speaks of a "stream of consciousness." Even as my attention shifts from one thing to another—even as I start working on a problem in logic rather than listening to music—it clearly feels as if it's one thing, one uniform stream of consciousness, that's moving from one activity to another. When the transitions are less than smooth, we express discomfort. "I don't know what's wrong with me today ... I feel so scattered." But no matter how scattered or distracted I am, it clearly feels like one me that is scattered or distracted. If the mind has this kind of unity, perhaps we shouldn't expect a differentiated physical understructure. Perhaps we should expect to find a brain that does everything everywhere—a locus of uniform, all-purpose "mind stuff."

Which picture of the mind and the brain is right: the faculty psychology view of mind and brain as composed of bits and pieces or the *holistic* view of the mind and brain as a unified whole? The strange case of Phineas Gage played an interesting historical role in that debate. Here's some of that history: A few decades before Phineas's accident, the idea that the brain is a thing of parts—that distinct functions are localized in distinct places in the head—had been made into a so-called science (today, we consider it pseudoscience) of phrenology. In the early 1800s, Francis Gall attempted to identify precisely what faculties were located where. He did this on an experimental base, although it was an extremely limited and crude experimental base, even by the standards of the day.

Gall's science of phrenology also came with a technology. It could be used as a diagnostic tool to analyze parts of your character. He thought there should be characteristic differences in the skull, detectable from the outside, which correspond to developed areas in the brain. If a particular faculty was particularly well developed, we should be able to tell by detecting a bump in that area of the skull. If a particular faculty or character trait was underdeveloped, we might see a dip or a valley. So phrenologists would feel your skull and find a bump in the "acquisitiveness" area or a dip in the "memory" area. That would show that you liked money or you had a bad memory. From bumps on your head, they claimed they could tell how good a friend you were, how good a husband, how spiritual or conscientious or self-destructive you were.

Put a finger on the nape of your neck and slowly trace a path up from there toward the top of your skull, mostly on the left side. You'll feel a bump. How big is that bump? Do you have a big bump there or just a small bump? Phrenologists interpreted that as an "amativeness" bump—your "romantic" bump, your "sexual love" bump. Go up from there another inch or two toward the top of your left ear. Do you have another bump there or not? Are you climbing a hill in that area, or are you passing over a plain? If you have a bump, it is a "combativeness" bump—an indication of combativeness or even potential violence. If you don't have a bump, you must be a peace-loving type. Sex and violence laid out right there on the back of your skull, bumps on the back of your skull.

I said that Gall's phrenological map had a very limited experimental base. Here's just how limited: Gall based the amativeness bump on studying two recently widowed young women. Boy, they probably had a lot of amativeness, and they had big bumps. The mapping of the combativeness organ was based on the fact that Gall thought it was smaller in certain Asian populations, and he thought those Asian populations were passive and noncombative. That's a pretty poor sample and a pretty bad methodology. So much for reading your potential for sex and violence off your skull. Phrenology was a pseudoscience, unscientific even by the standards of the 1800s. It was a popular fad for a while, in the same way that reading Ouija boards and stage hypnotism were fads. Phrenology eventually took its proper place alongside crystal balls and palm reading.

Because Gall's phrenology was so clearly pseudoscientific, the idea on which it was based got a bad press. "What? The brain does different things in different areas? Baloney; that's the stuff of Gall's character bumps on the skull. That's the stuff of pseudoscience." Bad press for a localization theory was good press for a unified-whole theory. Phrenology has to be wrong, so it must be that the brain functions as a unified whole. At the time, the case of Phineas Gage was also used as an argument for the homogenous whole theory. When that rod went through Phineas's head, it clearly damaged a massive amount of brain tissue. But did he die? No. Did he lose the power of speech? No. He continued to function with all major faculties intact.

Holists pointed to Phineas Gage as evidence that it must not matter if you knock out major parts of the brain. That must mean the brain is just filled with undifferentiated mind stuff, and Gage had enough left to fill in any functional gaps. If you attend to the details of the Phineas Gage story more carefully, as we have, you know that it did matter that parts of Gage's brain were knocked out. There was much of Gage that remained, but he was a changed man nonetheless and changed in very definite ways. Why? Because the brain is differentiated in terms of localized function. It was a very particular functional area that was obliterated in Gage's brain.

Today, Phineas Gage is used as a primary exhibit not for the homogeneous whole theory of the brain but for the *localization theory*. The localization theory now guides all brain research. It's reconfirmed daily with CAT scans, PET scans, and functional MRIs, scans of activity in living brains that were impossible in the days of Francis Gall or Phineas Gage. Phrenology was a pseudoscience, but Gall's fundamental guess was right. It's not true, of course, that those areas are detectable from bumps and valleys on the skull, and Gall was almost always wrong about what function was in what area. We know that language abilities are located in Broca's and Wernicke's areas on the side of your head, a little above your ears. Gall thought the language faculty was just beneath the eye.

There is one strange coincidence. If you put your hand on the very top of your head, you go a little forward and then a little down to the left toward the top of your forehead, you'll be in Gall's region of "mirthfulness." That's where he thought your organ of humor was located. Researchers at the UCLA Medical Center have described the results of applying a tiny electric current close to that point in the left brain of a 16-year-old girl. With stimulation at that spot, she began to laugh. "You guys are so funny, standing around." A short time later, they stimulated the same spot again. There was a picture of a horse in the room, and she suddenly thought that was a terribly funny horse. On that particular area, perhaps by chance, Gall seems to have gotten it right.

What we've explored so far are some of the questions that cases like this raise on the physical side of the mind-brain linkage—questions as to how brains function. Cases like this also raise questions concerning the mental side of the mind-brain linkage—questions regarding the character of our mental lives. We know there were particular parts of Gage's physical brain that were lost. What precisely were the parts of his mental functioning that were lost? There are two points about the changed Gage that are clear from the historical record. First, it's clear that he no longer behaved in socially appropriate ways. He manifested "but little deference for his fellows," the reports say, and his profanity was so bad that women were warned to stay away. The second point is that his decision-making was clearly shot. Here's the description again. He:

> ... was impatient of restraint or advice when it conflicts with his desires, at times pertinaciously obstinate, yet capricious and vacillating, devising many [future] plans ... which are no sooner arranged than they are abandoned. ...

Hanna Damasio's reconstruction indicated the ventromedial area of the frontal lobe as the site of the brain damage. Hanna's husband, Antonio Damasio, has studied a contemporary patient with damage in much the same area. He refers to him as "Elliot." Damasio and his colleagues were able to give Elliot the full gamut of contemporary psychological testing. Elliot does quite well on all standard intelligence tests; we'll talk about intelligence testing in a later lecture. Standard memory tests indicate no memory problems. Tests on motor abilities, on language comprehension and generation, and perceptual abilities all come out normal. What about judgments regarding behavior, including moral and ethical judgments? Abstract tests of judgment indicate nothing out of the ordinary. Elliot's moral principles are no different from yours or mine. He can envisage alternatives. He's conscious of consequences, including social consequences, just as we are.

But when Elliot has to make day-to-day decisions in his own life, he is a mess. He can't organize his time to task in a normal job. He will fail to do the important things because he is distracted by the small things. People advise him against taking certain courses of action. He pays attention; he even agrees that he shouldn't do those things, and he turns around and does them anyway. In Elliot's case, his unbelievably bad decision-making resulted in a chain of life disasters: repeated job loss, divorce, and bankruptcy. It is not his intellectual or moral judgment about decisions in the abstract that is impacted. It's his practical decision-making as it relates to his own life. He's a lot like Phineas Gage—capricious yet vacillating, making future plans only to abandon them. It's as if Elliot has everything that's necessary for responsible and ethical action, except the ability to put it into play.

I think this tells us something about the structure—the mental components—of our own personal and moral decision-making and of our own moral lives. We've said that our mental lives appear to have a unity; certainly that seems true of our personal and moral decisions. We face a difficult situation. We consider the alternatives. We consider consequences for the people involved. We deliberate in terms of moral principles. We decide what we should do, and we do it. This is what Aristotle called *practical reasoning*. Reasoning often gives us a statement as a conclusion, a concluding statement, which on the basis of our reasoning, we take to be true. But practical reasoning does something more. It doesn't just result in a statement; practical reasoning results in an action.

For most of us, most of the time, this kind of practical reasoning operates smoothly. We reason about an issue, decide, and therefore, act. We act from judgment. The entire process seems seamless. Cases like that of Elliot and Phineas Gage show us that the process is not as smooth as it may appear to be. Moral action is more complicated than we think. Underneath lies an elaborate machinery that links a number of distinct mental capabilities. The component parts of that machinery become obvious only when something goes wrong, like it does in the case of Elliot or of Phineas Gage. These are cases of *volitional* or *willing dysfunction*.

The amazing thing is that abstract judgment can be so entirely intact, as it appears to be in the case of Elliot, yet the application of that reasoning to something as immediate as individual decisions in your own life can be so radically disturbed. It's as if the whole chain of practical reasoning is there, except the very last step—the thing that it's all for: the willed action that it's meant to produce. We often talk of people not knowing right from wrong, but cases like that of Elliot show us that there are people who *know* right from wrong and yet behave as if they don't. Their abstract moral and social judgments are perfectly normal, but what they do has come unhooked from what they know. The flawless flow from knowledge to action that we take for granted has been broken.

There's an interesting aside here on the history of the insanity defense. The criterion of insanity adopted in American law in 1882 says that someone has a legitimate defense of "not guilty by virtue of insanity" if they did not know the nature and quality of the act or did not know that it was wrong because [of] laboring under a defect of reason from disease of the mind. On that definition, in order to get off on grounds of insanity, there had to be something you didn't know. A more modern criterion added a second prong, recognizing that insanity could impact either what you know or your ability to control your actions. The more modern criterion allows someone a legitimate defense of "not guilty by virtue of insanity" if they lacked substantial capacity to appreciate the criminality of their act—that's like the "knowledge" prong—or they lacked substantial capacity to conform their conduct to the requirements of the law, either of those as a result of mental disease or defect.

People with frontal lobe damage, like Elliot and Phineas Gage, would not qualify as insane in terms of the first prong because they do know right from wrong. But they might qualify as insane in terms of the second prong because they may nonetheless be unable to conform their conduct to the requirements of the law. I said that this second criterion was a more modern one, but it's not the legal definition of insanity most widely in use today. The second definition was the one that was used in trying John W. Hinckley, [Jr.,] who tried to assassinate Ronald Reagan in 1981. Hinckley was found not guilty by a Washington jury. People thought the verdict was wrong, and they put the blame on that definition of insanity. They thought the problem was the second prong, the "volitional" prong. As a result, American law took a giant step backwards. Under federal law and in most states, insanity is once again treated exactly as it was in 1882, purely as a matter of what you know.

The physical lesson I have drawn from these cases is a lesson of functional localization—the parts of the brain. The lesson regarding our mental life is that it, too, is a thing of parts—much more so than may be evident from how it normally seems to us. There are also a range of moral questions that are raised by cases like this. I'll devote a later lecture to the perplexing problem of free will and determinism. If the physical universe operates in terms of deterministic laws and if we're part of that physical universe, how can our actions ever really be free? I won't take on the whole of that question here. I, like many philosophers, want to say that we do act freely, although we have a lot to learn about what that really means.

But even if it's true that you and I act freely, with our intact physical brains and our unified moral lives, it remains an open question whether that holds for people whose brains have been impacted in the way that Elliot's and Phineas Gage's have. People like this are missing some of the neural understructure crucial for personal decision-making. Should they be held responsible for their actions? Antonio Damasio, for one, thinks the answer is no. These are people, he says, who lack the major control systems that most people have. Their decisions are *not* free in the sense that ours are. In a sense, decision isn't an option for them. They are incapable of guiding their action in the way we are. Damasio proposes that they do not have free will and so should not be held responsible for their actions.

Were this just a matter of a few individuals, it might be shrugged off as a merely academic issue. But there are indications it might not be so limited. Imaging studies show an unusually high incidence of frontal lobe abnormalities among the populations of our prisons, with particularly clear links to violent crime. Those kinds of data have to be handled with care; frontal lobe abnormalities are also associated with substance abuse, and there may be lots of reasons why people end up in prison. But suppose for a minute that the physical substrate of the brain is so connected to the mental structure of our lives that damage to the frontal lobes does reduce free will and, therefore, does reduce moral responsibility. If that's true, what are the implications for how we currently handle our prison populations?

Our explorations of the mind-body problem in the last lecture ended with the *interaction problem* for Dualism. If they are separate kinds of things, how could the mental and the physical interact? In this lecture, we've explored some of the things to be learned from the fact that they do interact. We've explored what brains may have to tell us about minds, and minds about brains. In the next lecture, I want to return to Dualism and the obvious philosophical facts we began with last time. I'll be examining the way many people think about their own mental processing. Next time, we'll be taking a critical look at the "inner theater of consciousness."

Lecture Four
The Inner Theater

Scope:

What happens when you see? A naïve characterization is as follows: Something in the world reflects or refracts light, which enters your eyes and impinges on your retinas. From there, an image is sent to your brain and is projected onto something like an inner screen. Images in this "inner theater of consciousness" also seem to explain the phenomena of memory, imagination, illusion, hallucination, and dreaming. This characterization fits well with Dualism and accords with many of the "obvious philosophical facts" outlined in Lecture Two.

This lecture challenges the "inner-theater view" directly. A range of experiments in touch, hearing, and conscious willing seem to show that something much more complicated is happening in perception and volition. Logical arguments against the inner theater are even stronger, demonstrating that this naïve conception of our mental processing could not possibly explain what it is supposed to.

Outline

I.   The purpose of this lecture is to outline and challenge an "inner-theater picture" of consciousness.

    A. We use the terms *conscious* and *consciousness* in a number of ways.

        1. In a limited sense, someone is *conscious* if he or she is not asleep or in a coma.

        2. We speak of someone as *conscious of* something when he or she responds to it.

    B. The sense that will be at issue in this lecture is *phenomenal consciousness*: the realm of subjective experience.

II. According to the inner-theater theory of vision, light enters your eyes and impinges on your retina, and an image is sent to your brain. What happens when you see is that the image from the external world is projected on something like an inner screen.

A. The same pictures-in-my-head theory could explain a range of other mental phenomena, including memory, imagination, and dreaming.

B. The inner theater is also conceived as the place in which we make decisions and initiate movement.

C. The picture of an inner theater is so culturally ingrained that we have come to think of it as "common sense." But there are reasons to think that major parts of the theory are simply not true.

III. Empirical evidence counters the inner-theater theory of perception.

A. In the inner-theater theory, images should show up on the inner screen in the order they come in from exterior sources.

B. The *cutaneous rabbit* is evidence of a much more complicated phenomenon.

   1. If you are given a series of 12 taps spaced 50 milliseconds apart at three distinct points—your wrist, halfway up the forearm, and your elbow—you will perceive them as a continuous series of evenly spaced taps. It will feel as if a small rabbit is hopping all the way up your arm, including hops at places that were not tapped at all.

   2. The *auditory rabbit* is a similar effect with sound. Although equally balanced clicks are sounded in two widely spaced speakers, you hear an even series of clicks moving across the space in between.

   3. These experiments create a problem for the inner-theater theory because the taps perceived in the middle appear in consciousness before the taps at the end. But the effect appears only when there are taps at the end.

   4. How does your brain know to perceive taps in the middle before they have occurred at the end? The only explanation seems to be that the illusion of taps in the middle is created after the entire series of real taps has taken place. That account, however, violates the A-B-C aspect of the inner-theater theory.

C. Related phenomena occur in visual perception.

    1. Movies and animations depend on the *phi phenomenon*, in which a series of still pictures is perceived as showing genuine motion.

    2. When dots of one color are flashed one after another at distinct points on a screen, the appearance is of a single dot that moves.

    3. If the color of the dots changes, the dot is seen to change color as it moves.

    4. How does your brain know to perceive dots in the middle moving in the right direction? How does it know to perceive a dot changing in color toward the correct shade? A story of continuity must be constructed after the data of the endpoint are already in.

IV. Empirical evidence also counters the "control-center" aspect of the inner-theater theory.

    A. In the 1980s, Benjamin Libet and his team timed both subjective and objective events in simple voluntary movement.

        1. On the subjective side, the researchers timed the points at which people reported they (a) were conscious of willing their arms to move and (b) were conscious of their arms moving.

        2. On the objective side, the researchers timed (a) a readiness potential in the brain that results in an arm movement and (b) the point at which the muscles in the arm actually contract.

    B. The results showed that the consciousness of willing came almost half a second after the readiness potential. The brain is already going full speed to produce a movement before you are aware of willing that movement.

V. Conceptual arguments against the inner theater are even stronger.

    A. Consider this thought experiment:

        1. Imagine a pirate standing with his arms crossed beside an open treasure chest.

        2. Can you honestly say whether he is missing any fingers, or how many buttons are on his coat, or what color the jewel is in the upper left-hand corner of the treasure chest?

3. Perhaps imagining is not like looking at a picture in an inner theater.

B. We seem to think we know where the inner theater is—right behind our eyes. But historical evidence indicates that that notion is merely a matter of cultural indoctrination.

1. The Egyptians carefully preserved many of the body parts for the afterlife but threw the brain away.

2. Aristotle thought that the heart was the seat of reason. The function of the brain was merely to cool the blood.

3. No aspect of your subjective experience tells you the location of the inner theater. It could be anywhere or nowhere in space at all.

C. If correct, the inner theater should work equally well for all senses.

1. Visual images come in and are projected on an inner screen.

2. Tastes come in and are projected as … what?

3. Smells come in and are projected as … what?

4. When you think about it, the theory really works only for sight.

D. The theory doesn't explain what is happening in perception and systematically cannot explain what is happening.

1. In order for images on the screen to amount to seeing, something would have to be watching the inner screen—the *homunculus*, or "little man."

2. How does this inner being feel things? Taste things? See things?

3. If we need an inner being to explain seeing, we will need another inner being to explain the first's ability to see, and another being inside the second, and so on.

4. In the end, the theory appears ridiculous, impossible, and pointless.

VI. The inner-theater demolition crew has done its work, but questions remain.

A. Given that both experimental and conceptual evidence indicates that the theory is wrong, why is the inner-theater view so tempting?

1. We import analogies from the outside. We know that we see something when we look at a picture; perhaps, then, seeing everything is like looking at pictures in our heads. We know that we can be fooled by pictures; maybe hallucination is being fooled by pictures in our heads.

2. The analogy breaks down, however, under empirical and conceptual arguments.

B. If this inner-theater theory is not how experience works, how does it work? We do not yet have a better theory to replace the inner theater.

Further Resources:

Daniel Dennett, "The Nature of Images and the Introspective Trap," *Content and Consciousness.*

Daniel C. Dennett and Marcel Kinsbourne, "Time and the Observer: The Where and When of Consciousness in the Brain," *Behavioral and Brain Sciences* 15.

David I. Shore, *Measuring Auditory Saltation,* http://www.mohsho.com/dshore/sound_top.html (a version of the auditory rabbit).

University of North Carolina at Charlotte, http://www.philosophy.uncc.edu/faculty/phi/Phi_Color2.html (an interactive exploration of the color phenomenon).

Questions to Consider:

This lecture explored attempts to demolish the concept of the inner theater. But the truth may be that parts of the concept work and others do not. In that light:

1. In what ways is imagining a pirate like seeing a picture of a pirate and in what ways is it different?

2. In what ways is memory like retrieving a picture from the files and in what ways is it different?

Lecture Four—Transcript
The Inner Theater

In the lecture before last, I started with five obvious philosophical facts—let me remind you of those: (1) You have a mind, and you have a body. (2) Normally, hopefully, these work together. (3) Your body is physical. Because of that, what your body does is, in principle, publicly observable. (4) Your mind, on the other hand, is essentially private. (5) Your access to your own mind is, therefore, privileged; you have privileged access. In that lecture, I used these philosophical facts to introduce Substance Dualism, the theory that there are two essentially different sides of the universe: the physical side and the mental side. We tracked that position through Descartes' argument and saw some of the problems it leads to, in particular, the problem of explaining how two such radically different realms could possibly interact.

In this lecture, I'll turn to an everyday notion of how our minds work that's suggested by those philosophical facts. My topic isn't really a formal philosophical theory, but it is a common concept of mental processing—the concept of the "inner theater of consciousness." It's the idea of an inner theater that I want to talk about and want to challenge in this lecture. We use the terms *conscious* and *consciousness* in a number of ways. In a limited sense, someone's *conscious* if they're awake rather than asleep or in a coma. We speak of people as being *conscious of* something when they respond to it. But we also speak of consciousness as a personal realm of subjective experience. Philosophers sometimes call this *phenomenal consciousness*. If you attend to the range of your sensory and subjective experience right now, how things look to you now—the colors and shapes you see, the sounds you hear, and the feelings you feel—that's the sense of consciousness that's at issue.

We'll start with the idea of the inner theater as it applies to visual processing. What happens when you see? There's something in the world that reflects or refracts light. That light enters your eyes, impinges on your retina, and an image is sent to your brain. According to this view, what happens when you see is that the image from the world is then projected on something like an inner screen. As the data stream comes in, it's projected, image by image, onto the screen. The inner theater is sensory central. You can see why it's called the "inner-theater view." But it isn't just a concept of seeing;

the inner theater seems to explain all kinds of things. What happens when you remember something, when you remember a scene from your childhood, for example? That, too, appears as an image on your inner screen. It's just the causal mechanism that's different. The image is retrieved from the film files rather than delivered direct from the outside.

What happens when you imagine something? You *create* an image on your inner screen—that's what imagining is. Thinking? We say you "see it in your mind's eye." What about dreaming? It's something like memory, something like imagining, perhaps something like a projector that's projecting random images. Deep asleep, you watch images on your inner screen. Illusion? Hallucination? What's being projected on your inner screen has come unhooked from the image source, from what's really out there in the world. There's also another aspect of the inner theater. It's also the place where we initiate movement, where we make decisions. Sensory data come together on our inner screen, and on the basis of[those data], we decide to act in certain ways. Our decisions are carried out by way of messages sent to our muscles. So the inner theater explains a whole range of mental functions. It offers a theory of what happens when you see, when you remember, when you imagine things, [and] when you dream and what conscious decision is about.

It also fits well with our obvious philosophical facts. Why is it that the mental is somehow private? Why is it that you have privileged access? It's private because it's an inner theater, and you have privileged access because it's yours. This isn't exactly the same as Substance Dualism, but it sure does fit. The inner theater is so culturally ingrained that we've come to think of it as "common sense." It's so entrenched that we think it's obviously true. We think we can see that it's true just by looking at the character of our mental experience. A picture that's so deeply ingrained in how we think is going to be difficult to dislodge, but that's what I'll try to do in this lecture. I'll release a demolition crew of arguments intended to demolish the concept of the inner theater. A number of these arguments, I owe to the philosopher Daniel Dennett. There are reasons for thinking that at least major parts of the "inner-theater picture" just aren't true. It's a story we tell ourselves about our mental functioning, but it turns out that things aren't really like that at all.

What I'll give you first are some empirical reasons for thinking the theory isn't true, pieces of scientific data that seem to indicate the picture has to be wrong in major ways. An even stronger set of arguments are conceptual. These are arguments that [say,] not only isn't the theory, in fact, true, but it *couldn't* be true. And yet the picture is so tempting and so ubiquitous that even when you see reasons to think it isn't true, that it can't be true, you can't help but slip back into it in unguarded moments. I'm not sure that the demolition crew will succeed, by the way, but I hope they convince you that the inner-theater theory shouldn't just be assumed to be true—that it is at least open to question whether major parts of it are right or wrong.

Let me start, then, with some empirical reasons for thinking the inner-theater theory can't be right. All of these have to do with time. If there's an inner theater of consciousness at which we receive sensory messages from the outlying senses, the images should show up on the screen in the order they come in from the exterior sources. The messages come in A, B, C and show up on the screen A, B, C. The fact is that something much more complicated than that is happening. There's an experiment in the literature reporting an experience we can produce in the lab. It's called the *cutaneous rabbit*. Although originally discovered by accident, the cutaneous rabbit is a clear and repeatable effect.

Here's what happens in this experiment. I give you an evenly timed series of taps on your wrist, very fast, at 50-millisecond intervals, 50/1000 of a second. Those are followed immediately by a series of taps halfway up your forearm and a final series on your elbow. I'll have given you a series of rapid, evenly spaced taps at three different spots on your arm, but it won't feel like three sets of taps in three separate places. It'll feel instead something like a small animal hopping its way in small, evenly spaced steps all the way up your forearm. It'll feel like a little rabbit hopping from the spot I started tapping (on your wrist) to the place I stopped (at your elbow) with lots of evenly spaced hops in all those areas in between that were not tapped at all.

There's also an auditory version of the illusion, the *auditory rabbit*. Here it is, as developed by David Shore, a psychologist at McMaster University. This is a little tricky and much more subtle. It may not work, but we'll give it a try. The illusion requires that you be centrally spaced between two well-balanced speakers—one on the left and the other on the right. If it doesn't happen to work for you now, the outlines guide you to a website where you can experiment further. Here [is] a quick series of clicks in the left speaker. Those should have sounded like they just came from one side. Here [is] a quick series of clicks on the right. But now, if the conditions are right, you may hear a fast series of clicks that move quickly but evenly all the way from one speaker to the other, not just on the left and then on the right but moving from left to right. Here it is again: left …, right …, and all the way in between.

What you actually hear in the third case is just the clicks on the left followed immediately by the clicks on the right. But when it works, people say it sounds like someone dragging a thumb across the teeth of a comb, with the sound transitioning through the space in between, from one speaker to the other. Here's why the cutaneous and auditory rabbit experiments offer a problem for the inner theater of consciousness. According to that theory, messages should come in A, B, C and show up on the screen A, B, C. But suppose you feel 12 rabbit hops coming up your arm; 1, 2, 3, 4, 5, 6, 7, 8, 9, 10, 11, 12. Hop 1 corresponds to the initial place we tapped on your wrist. Hop 6 corresponds to the place we tapped halfway up your forearm. Hop 12 corresponds to our final tap on your elbow. But think about those taps 2, 3, and 4 that you felt moving up from your wrist to your mid-forearm. If those came into your inner theater in order, they would have to come in before we tapped your mid-forearm. But the effect only happens if we tap the second place, the one you feel later. So how did hops 2, 3, and 4 "know" that we were going to tap your mid-forearm a second later?

The auditory rabbit presents the same problem. With just the clicks in the left speaker, there's no illusion of movement. It's only when we immediately follow clicks on the left with clicks on the right that the sound moves through the spaces in between. So think about the clicks happening between the left speaker and the right. If order in the inner theater matched order in the world, there would have only been clicks on the left at the point people hear clicks in the middle. The illusion happens only if those are followed by clicks on the right. How would our perceptual system know that there were going to be clicks there, too? The only way to explain these kinds of results is to say that it's only after the later taps and only after the later clicks that the illusion of motion is created.

It's as if some part of the brain processes both the clicks on the left and the clicks on the right and then, later, produces the illusion in the inner theater of movement from left to right. But that means that the inner theater isn't the stimulus reception area it's cracked up to be—receiving input bit by bit and throwing it up on the screen bit by bit. The theater, if there is one, is much further down the line. Reception happens somewhere else, reception of clicks on the left and on the right. Something else then cooks up a story—an illusory story about moving sensations—that only then is sent to conscious awareness in the inner theater.

The cutaneous rabbit works in terms of taps that you feel. The auditory rabbit works in terms of clicks that you hear. The same thing happens with what you see, and you are already quite familiar with it. In the visual case, it's called the *phi phenomenon*. All movies and animations depend on it. As the film goes through the projector, what's actually flashed on the screen [is] a series of still pictures, but that's not what it looks like, at least not since the time of silent films. With the right timing, Lauren Bacall moves oh-so-smoothly toward Humphrey Bogart. Belle and the Beast are nothing more than a series of static drawings, but they look like they glide smoothly across the dance floor. The only difference in television or video is that the series of images is created by a pixilated scanning procedure across the screen, left to right and top to bottom.

In the very simplest experimental case, phi can be produced by dots that appear one after the other on a screen. With the right time interval, the right distance, and the right intensity of light, successive dots at different spots on the screen are perceived not as individual dots but as a single dot that moves from one spot to another. The philosopher Nelson Goodman asked researchers on phi: What would happen if you changed the color of the dots? Would that destroy the illusion? Would it look like a green dot and, later, a red dot somewhere else, rather than one dot moving from one place to the other? What people often report is that it doesn't destroy the illusion at all. The dot still moves, but it changes color as it moves from one spot to the other.

Phi offers the same problem for the inner theater as the cutaneous and auditory rabbits do. We see the dot as moving from one place to the other—moving across the screen in a particular direction—but the effect doesn't happen without the second dot. How do we know to see the dot moving in that direction? It has to be because the information of the second dot is already in, shaping our perception of the moving first dot. In the Goodman case, we see the dot is changing color through intermediate shades. But in order for that to happen, we must already know what color it's going to be. In all of these cases, it looks like the only explanation for the illusion is that there is already a prepackaged story of movement before it goes to the inner theater. The inner theater doesn't show first-run movies.

Here's another aspect of phi, by the way. When you see automobiles driving along in films or on television, how come it sometimes looks like the hubcaps are revolving backwards? The answer is that phi works by writing in motion in the direction of the smallest distance between images, frame by frame. Because hubcaps have radial symmetry—every fifth lug nut looks the same—it sometimes happens that the smallest movement that would convert a hubcap position that looks like the one in frame 32 to a hubcap position that looks like the one in frame 33 is motion backwards rather than forwards. Therefore, we see it that way, with the hubcap merrily spinning in reverse even though we know that couldn't be true.

So far, we've talked about sensation. But it's also part of everyday thinking that your inner theater is your "control center." That's where you make your decisions, conveyed as messages to your muscles. Here again, the empirical data [don't] seem to fit. There are now many studies that confirm a core result first reported in the 1980s by Benjamin Libet and his team at the University of California, San Francisco. Libet was interested in voluntary action— the sequence of mental and physical events that happen when you decide to move your arm, for example. What these researchers did was to time two subjective events and two objective events. They had people indicate the point at which they were conscious of willing their arm to move. They had them indicate the point at which they were conscious of their arm moving. The idea was to pinpoint the timing of those subjective events. The researchers also used probes to time two objective events: (1) the timing of a readiness potential in the brain and (2) the point at which the muscles in the arm actually contracted.

Their timed results showed that the readiness potential comes before the muscular contraction. That was no surprise. People's consciousness of willing a movement comes before their consciousness of the movement itself. That was no surprise either. What was surprising was this: The consciousness of willing comes almost a half-second after the readiness potential. Here's one way of putting the result: The brain is already going full speed to move your arm before you are aware of willing that movement. Interpreting empirical results can be tricky, but if Libet's conclusions are right, the picture of the inner theater as a control center has to be wrong. What we perceive as the point at which we make a decision is coming too late; the real decision has already been made elsewhere.

What I've given you so far are some empirical reasons to be suspicious of the inner-theater story; things don't seem to work the way the story says they do. Let me give you another experiment halfway between an empirical result and a conceptual argument. Our research subject is going to be you. One thing that will be required is that you be absolutely honest in your reporting. Okay, I want you right now to imagine a pirate. There he is in your imagination, standing with legs apart and arms crossed beside his open treasure chest. The treasure chest has no gold in it, though; it's filled to the brim with jewels. Okay, have you imagined the pirate? This is where you have to be scrupulously honest. If the inner-theater story were right, imagining should be like looking at a picture on your inner screen.

Without changing anything—without adding anything to your mental picture—does the pirate have a hat on? What color is his hair? Without changing anything, is he missing any fingers? How many buttons are there on his coat? Look at that jewel in the upper left-hand corner of the treasure chest. What color is it? If you're like me, and if you don't quickly fill in the blanks with things that weren't there before, you don't have answers for a lot of those questions. But if you were looking at a picture of a pirate, you'd be able to answer those questions. You'd just have to look at it more closely.

Maybe imagining isn't very much like looking at a picture. In fact, it has been suggested that what you have when you imagine something is less like a picture and more like a description, not because it's in words, but because it is usually incomplete, just as a description is usually incomplete. If you have a picture of a pirate, there's either a hat in that picture or there isn't. But if you have a description of a pirate, it may be incomplete. It may not specify either that he has a hat or that he doesn't. When I imagined my pirate just now, I don't think there was anything at all about how many buttons he had on his coat or what color that jewel was. Maybe imagination isn't much like a picture in your inner theater after all. I think the most powerful arguments against the inner theater are conceptual arguments. It's these that convinced me that the story is wrong not only in its details but in its essentials.

Here's a historical consideration: We not only tend to think there is an inner theater, [but] we think we know where it is. It's here in our heads, somehow behind our eyes. We can feel it there. But we have historical evidence that the location of our inner theater is purely a matter of cultural indoctrination. The Egyptians carefully prepared their mummies, making sure they had everything they needed for the afterlife. They carefully preserved the liver, the heart, the kidneys, but they fished the brain out of the skull and threw it away. Nobody needs a brain in the afterlife. They certainly wouldn't have done that if they thought it was the location of the inner theater of consciousness.

Aristotle thought the seat of reason was in the heart. The function of the brain was merely to cool the blood, a sort of radiator at the top of your body. If you pay attention to your own processing, I think you'll find that there is no aspect of your subjective experience that tells you that your inner theater is there. Your eyes are in your head, of course. Your ears are on your head. But that's just where the messages come from. As seen from the inside, the processing center itself could be anywhere or, like Descartes thought, nowhere in space at all. Neurophysiologically, by the way, there's no evidence of any single place in the brain that it all comes together. We can localize a range of different mental functions. There are clearly separated language areas, auditory areas, and visual processing areas, but all current evidence indicates that any inner theater where it all comes together is something the whole brain does, not something itself located at any place in the brain.

Here's another conceptual argument against the inner theater: It works a lot better for some senses than others. When I first outlined the standard inner-theater view, I did so in terms of vision. You see because of what's projected on your inner screen. Memory, imagination, dreaming, and illusion are all a matter of projections on the inner screen as well. But the inner theater is supposed to be where all sensation comes together—not just sight but sound, touch, smell, and taste. So how exactly is the story supposed to go with respect to the other senses?

In the sight case, the images come in and are projected on the inner screen. In the case of taste, what happens? The images come in—well, no, the taste *messages* come in, and then … and then … what? They're not projected on a big screen because we don't taste things by seeing them on a screen. Are they projected onto some kind of taste screen? Are they projected onto a big tongue? Smells come in as what? And are projected as what? How do sounds come in? When you think about it, the inner theater really works only for sight. If it were a decent theory of perception, it should work equally well for the other senses. There, it just seems to break down, which makes you think it may not be that good a story for any of it.

I've left the strongest conceptual refutation of the inner theater, and the easiest, for last. Indeed, you may have seen it coming long ago. The whole purpose of the theory is to explain what happens when we perceive things, but it's a terrible failure. It doesn't explain what happens, and it systematically can't. The story is that the eyes send images into the brain, where they're projected on the inner screen. But in order for that to amount to seeing, there would have to be something that's watching the inner screen, some inner me that's watching the show as it comes in. That inner me is often called a *homunculus*, or a "little man." I see things because he sees them on the inner screen. I hear things, I guess, because he's hearing them from the speakers in the inner theater. How is he smelling things? The theater must have smell-o-vision with little perfumes wafting in. How is he feeling things? Do we have a vibrachair underneath him and little touchers on his skin? How is he tasting things? Are there little inner chemicals hitting his little inner tongue?

When you fill in the all the blanks that a real inner theater would demand, it's clearly ridiculous. It's also impossible. We would need not just one little man in your brain but an infinite number. If we need an inner man to explain seeing, how are we to explain what happens when that inner man looks at the screen? How are we to explain the fact that he can see the inner screen? Inside the little man's head is another little screen, and I guess we'll need another little man inside him. And how does he see? Oh, there must be still another little man. We have an infinite regression of homunculi inside homunculi. It's ridiculous, it's impossible, and in the end, it's clearly pointless. The inner theater is supposed to explain how we see things, but it only works if we have the inner man inside and he sees the screen. How does he see things? That part doesn't get explained, so seeing doesn't really get explained at all. The theory just pushes the problem of seeing inside to the little man. We should have just admitted that we don't have an explanation. All the inner theater does is allow us to pretend we know things that we don't.

However attractive the picture of the inner theater is, there are strong reasons to think it's wrong. There are empirical reasons to think that neither perception nor decision-making work the way the inner-theater picture would tell us that they work. When we really consider what happens when we imagine things, imagination doesn't seem all that much like looking at a picture. For me, the strongest arguments are the conceptual ones. The picture just doesn't do its job. It breaks down fairly badly when it comes to senses other than sight, for example, and the infinite regression of homunculi shows that it ultimately couldn't explain what it's supposed to explain. Okay, the inner-theater demolition crew has done their best. I hope they've convinced you that the inner-theater view at least can't be taken for granted—that we shouldn't just assume that it's true. Even if they've succeeded at that, there are still some major problems that remain for the demolition crew. There's some major cleanup to do.

Here's one question they haven't answered: If the story is so wrong, why is it so tempting? I think the inner theater may be tempting because there are things that really do work the way images on the inner screen are supposed to work. The things that really do work that way are real images—pictures, and paintings, and photographs. We don't really have a good explanation for how we see things, or remember things, or imagine things, but we do know about paintings and pictures. We know that we see something when we look at a painting. So maybe seeing everything is like looking at a painting inside our heads. We know that we can create pictures of our own of unicorns and mermaids, of people with trees for arms. So maybe imagining things is like drawing a picture inside our heads.

We can even be fooled by pictures that look like a door into another room, but then we find it was just a clever painting. We're fooled when we're hallucinating, so maybe we're fooled by a picture then, too, a picture in our heads. On this suggestion, it's the fact that we have visual images of visual things, paintings and photographs, that makes the picture theory tempting in the first place. What about the other senses? Do we have smell-o-graphs that we can flip through like old photographs, smelling again the smell of Grandma's chocolate chip cookies? No. Do we have taste-o-graphs that allow us to taste those cookies again? No. Do we have touch-o-graphs? No. That may be why the inner theater doesn't even get off the ground in terms of the other senses.

There's another problem that remains for the demolition crew, and it's much harder. If this is not how things work, how *do* they work? It would certainly help in trying to leave a bad picture of our mental processing behind to have a better picture to replace it with. If my suggestion is right, it's because we didn't have a better picture that we went for inner images in the first place. I'm afraid that better picture of how things work—the one that we need to replace the inadequate inner theater—that's a picture we don't yet have. It's the picture of minds and bodies that Dualism paints that gives us the interaction problem. How could the mental and the physical possibly interact? It's something like Dualism that gives us the problems of the inner theater as well. Maybe Dualism is the problem. Are there other ways of looking at minds and bodies? Are there alternatives to Dualism? That'll be the focus of the next lecture.

Lecture Five
Living in the Material World

Scope:

Despite its initial plausibility, Dualism has been shown to have basic conceptual problems. A crucial difficulty is the *interaction problem*. If the mental and the physical realms are as radically distinct as Dualism says they are, how could they possibly interact in the ways we know they do? Historically, philosophers made some valiant efforts in the attempt to save Dualism, but to the contemporary eye, those attempts look futile. What are our intellectual options if we give up Dualism? Do we have more plausible options?

This lecture presents a range of intellectual options, from the idea that the universe is purely mental (Idealism) to the view that the universe is purely physical (Materialism). According to Reductive Materialism, mental phenomena—emotions, beliefs, feelings, and sensations—ultimately reduce to physical phenomena. By contrast, Paul Churchland and Patricia Smith Churchland's Eliminative Materialism proposes that mental phenomena don't exist. Concepts of belief and sensations are like concepts of witches and will be left behind as science progresses. Materialism has seemed particularly attractive to many scientists and philosophers; we will consider it both in terms of its promise and the conceptual problems it raises.

Outline

I. Despite its initial plausibility, Dualism has been shown to face some basic conceptual problems. The purpose of this lecture is to consider alternatives. If Dualism is not true, what might be true instead?

II. Historically, a number of attempts were made to answer the interaction problem within Dualism.

   A. Descartes thought mind meets body in the pineal gland.
      1. Most parts of the brain form symmetrical pairs, but the pineal gland does not. Descartes thought mistakenly that animals do not have a pineal gland.
      2. The central question, however, is not where the mental and the physical interact, but how they possibly could.

B. The idea that Dualism is true clashes directly with the idea that the mental and the physical interact.

    1. To address this conflict, we could give up the idea that Dualism is true.

    2. Alternatively, we could give up the idea that a connection exists between the mental and the physical.

    3. At the time of Descartes and for a significant period afterward, the second route was seriously explored.

C. *Epiphenomenalism* holds that physical events do not cause mental events. Mental events nonetheless "float above" the physical events. Thomas Huxley argued for Epiphenomenalism.

D. *Occasionalism* holds that physical events do not cause mental events or vice versa. On every occasion, God makes both happen, producing an illusion of interaction. Nicolas de Malebranche was the classic proponent of Occasionalism.

E. *Parallelism* holds that God sets up the universe from the beginning with a "pre-established harmony" between the physical and the mental. From that point, the two operate side by side, like two clocks wound up in parallel. Leibniz is the classic proponent of Parallelism.

F. These attempts to shore up Dualism look increasingly desperate.

III. If Dualism is not true, what is? A number of philosophical viewpoints are major contenders for answering this question.

A. The *interaction problem* boils down to how two distinct substances could possibly interact. One answer might be that perhaps there is only one kind of "stuff." This position is called *Monism*, and it comes in several different forms.

B. One version of Monism, *Idealism*, asserts that there is just one kind of stuff, and it is the mental stuff.

    1. What evidence do we have of the existence of anything physical? Only our sense impressions—and those are mental.

    2. Idealism leads directly to *Solipsism*: the view that there is no universe (and no people) beyond my mental realm.

    3. Idealism and Solipsism look like dead ends.

C. Another form of Monism is *Materialism*. There is only one kind of stuff, and it is the physical. But if everything is physical, then everything in the mental realm must ultimately be physical: sensations, pains, pleasures, belief, and love. The problem for the Materialist is to fill out that "ultimately."

IV. Most Materialists have characterized themselves as *Reductive Materialists*, asserting that all mental phenomena ultimately reduce to physical phenomena.

   A. Reductive Materialists often claim that mental states reduce to brain states: chemical or neurological patterns in the brain.

   B. How plausible is Reductive Materialism? A central form of the position, known as *type identity theory*, argues that all types of mental states are identical to types of brain states.

   1. If that argument is true, then two people who hold the same belief would be in the same brain state.

   2. But brains differ from person to person. We have no reason to think that the way your brain encodes a particular belief is identical to the way mine does.

   C. The theory also faces a more general problem: If pain is a brain state, what brain state is it?

   1. The closest people have gotten to answering this question is to say that to be in pain is to have C fibers firing.

   2. But because C fibers are carbon-based, it would follow that no silicon-based creature on some other planet could possibly feel pain.

   3. That result seems both intuitively wrong and ethically dangerous.

   D. It appears that pain, fear, love, and hope could be multiply instantiated. If so, Reductive Materialism's identification of these mental states with any particular physical state must be wrong.

V. *Eliminative Materialism* is another form of Materialism, championed by the philosophers Paul Churchland and Patricia Smith Churchland.

   A. According to Eliminative Materialism, mental phenomena do not really exist; there aren't really any fears, hopes, or beliefs.

B. We will eventually develop a science of human beings that will cover everything about them. When we do, we'll find that concepts of fears, hopes, and beliefs will not be part of this science.

VI. If Dualism is not a satisfactory theory, what might be? Are we out of options?

Further Resources:

Patricia Smith Churchland, "Reduction and Antireductionism in Functionalist Theories of Mind," *Neurophilosophy*.

Paul Churchland, "Eliminative Materialism and the Propositional Attitudes," *Journal of Philosophy* 78.

U. T. Place, "Is Consciousness a Brain Process?" *British Journal of Psychology* 47.

Questions to Consider:

Below is a list of positions mentioned in the lecture. On a scale of 1 to 10, from "not plausible" (1) to "very plausible" (10), rate each in terms of how plausible you think it is right now. You can change your mind later, of course.

Cartesian Dualism: The universe consists of two radically different substances.

1   2   3   4   5   6   7   8   9   10

Epiphenomenalism: The mind "floats" above the brain but has no causal effect on it.

1   2   3   4   5   6   7   8   9   10

Occasionalism: There is no causal link between the mental and the physical, but God intervenes on every occasion to make it appear that there is.

1   2   3   4   5   6   7   8   9   10

Parallelism: There is no causal link between the mental and the physical. It appears that a link exists because God set the two realms working in parallel at the beginning of the universe.

1   2   3   4   5   6   7   8   9   10

Idealism: Everything that exists is ultimately mental.

1   2   3   4   5   6   7   8   9   10

Solipsism: Everything and everyone that exists, exists only in my mind.

1   2   3   4   5   6   7   8   9   10

Materialism: Everything that exists is ultimately physical.

1   2   3   4   5   6   7   8   9   10

Reductive Materialism: The mental reduces to the physical. Mental states are a kind of brain state.

1   2   3   4   5   6   7   8   9   10

Eliminative Materialism: Our concepts for mental states—fears, hopes, beliefs—will be eliminated in an eventual science of human functioning, rejected as concepts of witches and humors are now.

1   2   3   4   5   6   7   8   9   10

Lecture Five—Transcript
Living in the Material World

I first introduced Dualism as the simplest theory that makes sense of a range of obvious philosophical facts. It's a theory with a logical argument behind it in the work of Descartes. But Dualism has taken a number of serious knocks in previous lectures. I argued last time that a picture of our mental functioning that goes along with Dualism—the picture of the inner theater—doesn't hold up very well under more careful examination. To the extent that the inner theater is part of our obvious philosophical facts, it may no longer be so obvious that these are genuine facts rather than just common assumptions. Dualism also faces the *interaction problem*. If Substance Dualism is true—if there are two radically different kinds of "stuff" in the universe—how could they possibly interact?

In this lecture, I want to talk about some philosophical alternatives. If Dualism *isn't* true, what might be true instead? But let me first talk about some alternatives within Dualism. Descartes was a Dualist; it's Cartesian Dualism, after all. He was perfectly aware of the interaction problem; even in his time, his critics made sure of that. You say the mind and body are essentially different kinds of things? Then how could they possibly interact? Descartes did, in fact, have an answer. It doesn't appear in the *Meditations*, but it does appear in his book on the *Passions of the Soul*. There, Descartes admits that the two essentially different substances *must* interact. There is, he says, a place where mind and body are causally linked. Where? Descartes' answer was the pineal gland. If you dissect a brain all the way down—as Descartes actually did—you would find, just about in the center of your head, sitting on top of the spinal column, a small reddish-gray organ about the size of a pea. That's the pineal gland. That's where Descartes proposed that the mental universe meets the physical universe. That's where mind meets body.

Descartes had several reasons for settling on the pineal gland as the magic organ of interaction. First, most visible parts of the brain come in symmetrical pairs. You have two hemispheres, two clear sides of the hippocampus, a left and a right thalamus, but you have only one pineal gland. It's also true that the pineal gland sits above the spinal column like some precious thing on a pedestal. It just *looks* like some spot of central importance. Finally, Descartes thought that people were essentially different from animals—that people alone had souls—and he mistakenly thought that animals didn't have a pineal gland. But, of course, when you think about it, none of this really answers the interaction question. The question is not where mind and body interact. The question is how they possibly could. Pointing to the pineal gland or any other physical structure doesn't solve that basic problem.

It looks like we have to face facts: Causal interaction between the mental and the physical is real and obvious, but it poses a crucial problem for Dualism. There are two things you could do in the face of that. One would be to give up Dualism precisely because it makes causal interaction a mystery. Or one could keep one's Dualism and give up the idea that there really is causal interaction between the mental and the physical. The first route is the modern one. That's the one I'll explore through most of this lecture; because causal interaction is so obvious, Dualism has to be wrong. But at the time of Descartes and for a significant period afterwards, people seriously explored the second route, so let's start here. It sure does seem as if there are two radically different dimensions of the universe, so maybe the idea of causal interaction is an illusion.

One theory that was proposed is called *Epiphenomenalism*. It works like this: Maybe we're wrong about interaction; maybe physical events *don't* cause mental events or vice versa. But maybe mental events nonetheless ride piggyback on physical events—they just come along for the ride. It's hard to get analogies that really work, but here's a try: As a horse runs, its shadow glides beside it. Maybe the brain is like the horse, doing all the work, and the mental realm is just its shadow. The rush of a locomotive makes a whistling sound as it goes by. Maybe the brain is like the locomotive, doing all the work; the mind is just the whistling sound as it rushes by. *Epi* means "above," and what Epiphenomenalism maintains is that mental events "float above" physical events.

There were proponents of Epiphenomenalism even into the 1800s. Thomas Huxley was one of them, though he was better known as "Darwin's bulldog" for defending the theory of evolution. In the Epiphenomenalist view, alcohol consumption doesn't cause mental confusion. What alcohol consumption causes is a particular brain state, which may, in turn, cause stumbling or slurred speech. It's just that the brain state casts a mental shadow. Mental confusion is an epiphenomenon of that particular brain state. Okay, does that solve anything? For me, it just points up another question: What do we mean by *cause*? That's a big question; it's one I can't pursue here in full detail. What the Epiphenomenalist admits is that every time I'm in a certain brain state, I find myself in a certain mental state. And if I weren't in that brain state, I wouldn't have that mental state. That certainly sounds like a causal connection. The analogies don't help much either. The movement of the train does cause that whistling sound, and the movement of the horse does cause the movement of its shadow. Why would we see this parallel between the mental and the physical if there weren't a causal connection?

Another view explored at the time tried to answer that very question; it's called *Occasionalism*. The classical proponent of Occasionalism was Nicolas de Malebranche. In this view, physical events do not cause mental events. Admittedly, it looks like the two go together, but that's because on every occasion, God is there making both happen. It's as if God had a puppet in each hand—the physical puppet on one hand, the mental on the other. God is there, minute to minute, making them dance together, hence the illusion of interaction.

Just one step away from Occasionalism is *Parallelism*, a view championed by Leibniz. Leibniz thought that the Occasionalist view didn't offer a very dignified picture of God, with these two puppets. The God of the Occasionalist is constantly meddling in the affairs of the world in order to keep the mental and the physical in sync. Hasn't he got more important things to do? Instead, Leibniz asks us to consider two clocks running side by side in perfect synchrony. It may look like what one does causes the other to do the same thing, but that's not what's happening; it's just that they were wound up at the same time, and they're set running in parallel. That's what God does. He predetermines the physical universe, and he predetermines the mental universe. Leibniz calls it "pre-established harmony." The two are not connected, but they run in parallel since the beginning, hence the illusion of interaction.

Epiphenomenalism, Occasionalism, Parallelism—if all of those seem pretty desperate to you, you are in good company. That's the general verdict in the philosophical community today. If one has to go as far as these theories in order to save Dualism, maybe Dualism isn't worth saving. Maybe it's time to seriously rethink the whole question. What are the modern alternatives to Dualism? I want to lay out some major contenders for you to think about. As we go through them, you should be asking yourself whether we've hit on a theory that sounds plausible to you, that sounds right. But you should also give yourself plenty of room to consider new arguments and to change your mind. So where do we go if we leave Dualism behind?

A major problem with Dualism is that it gives no plausible story about interaction between the universe's two substances. But if interaction is the problem, it won't help to postulate more substances. If instead of two basic substances, we postulated three or four—if we went from Dualism to Triplism or Quadruplism—we'd just have more interaction problems to answer for. No, if we're going to give up Dualism, it'll be in favor of some form of *Monism*. Monism includes all those views in which there's just one kind of basic "stuff." The universe, whatever its complexities, is ultimately a single, unified universe composed of a single, unified kind of stuff. Let's move, then, from Dualism to Monism. Dualism says there are two basic kinds of things, the mental and the physical. A Monistic view says there's only going to be one kind. Which kind? Clearly, there are two options here.

One way to go from Dualism to Monism is to say, that's right; there aren't two kinds of stuff. There's ultimately only one kind of stuff—let me see, physical or mental—and the one kind of stuff is the mental. Okay, on this view, everything is ultimately mental. Despite appearances, there are no physical things. It is quite literally all in your mind. This position is called *Idealism* or, sometimes, *Subjective Idealism*. What evidence do we have of the existence of anything physical, the Idealist asks. Only our sense impressions—sights and sounds and the feel of things. But those sense impressions are purely mental. We have no reason to think there's anything beyond or behind them. We have no reason to think there's anything but those sense impressions, no reason to think the universe is anything but mental. Plausible? Well, maybe.

Unfortunately, Subjective Idealism leads quite directly to *Solipsism*. I have access to my sense impressions, but I don't have access to yours. Why should I think those exist? In fact, why should I think there's any "you" with a mental life at all? That's Solipsism, the view not only that there's no universe beyond the mental realm, but that there's no universe beyond *my* mental realm. Bertrand Russell points out that Solipsism would be psychologically impossible to believe. Anyone who really tried to hold such a position would end up denying it in nearly everything they did. Russell tells the following story:

> I once received a letter from an eminent logician, Mrs. Christine Ladd Franklin, saying that she was a solipsist, and [that she] was surprised that there were no others. Coming from a logician and a solipsist, [her] surprise surprised me.

Subjective Idealism looks like a dead end. How did we get here? We went from Dualism to Monism, from [saying that] there are two basic substances to there's only one. But when it came to choosing which one, we took the mental option. So let's try the other option. You could call it *Physicalism*, the position that the universe is made of just one kind of stuff, and that stuff is the physical stuff. Everything in the universe is ultimately physical. More standardly, the position is called *Materialism*, with precisely the same meaning. If Dualism has a persistent problem, however, so does Materialism. The essential problem for Dualism is the interaction problem. If there are two radically different kinds of things, how could they interact? Materialism doesn't have that problem. If there's only one kind of thing, interaction is entirely to be expected. The problem for Materialism is different. If there's only one kind of thing, how come it seems like there are two?

Remember the obvious philosophical facts with which we began. Certainly, there does seem to be an important difference between the taste of pineapple, on the one hand, and its chemical composition, on the other. Certainly, there does seem to be an important difference between things like hope, on the one side, and things like dirt, on the other. If everything's physical, as the Materialist maintains, then even the mental things must ultimately be physical. Sensations, pains, pleasures, love, and belief must ultimately be physical. The problem facing any Materialist is to fill out that "ultimately." In precisely what ways are these physical things?

Most Materialists have characterized themselves as *Reductive Materialists*. What's the relation between the mental and the physical? What the Reductive Materialist says is that mental phenomena—*all* mental phenomena—ultimately reduce to physical phenomena. Here are two immediate questions for any Reductive Materialist: What kind of physical phenomena do you think they reduce to, and what precisely do you mean by *reduce*? Reductive

Materialists have given different answers to those questions, offering subtly different shades of the position, but here's a common answer to the first question. What do mental phenomena reduce to? They reduce to brain states. Unfortunately, Materialists have never been much more specific than that, and some of them have admitted that they can't be.

But the idea is that when you're in a certain mood—when you're depressed, say—there's something true of your brain; your dopamine levels are low, for example. That's a kind of brain state. When you're afraid, there's something true of your brain. Maybe it's not a matter of chemistry but of neural wiring; a particular part of your limbic system is activated. That's a kind of brain state. The general theory is supposed to hold for everything you do mentally and for all mental states. When you're concentrating, or trying to remember a name, or you suddenly do remember that name, or you start to suspect that your neighbor's having an affair—in all those cases, there's something happening in your brain. It may be something chemical, or activation of a particular area of the brain, or a complex pattern of neural firing, and all of those are meant to be included as brain states. It's those brain states that the Reductive Materialist thinks mental phenomena reduce to.

And what precisely does the Reductive Materialist mean by *reduce*? It's here especially that different theorists give different answers, but the core idea is a familiar one. You can make a good case that chemistry reduces to physics. Atoms of particular elements are combinations of specific particles in specific bonds. An atom of hydrogen, for example, is composed of a bonded proton and electron pair. The bonds and the particles are the stuff of physics. Molecules of particular kinds are just bonded combinations of specific atoms; that's what they are. Ammonia is formed from an atom of nitrogen bound with hydrogen in a particular way. Those molecules are the stuff of chemistry. The stuff of chemistry, then, can be defined in terms of the stuff of physics. Chemistry reduces to physics. If you did everything right, in fact, it looks like you'd be able to deduce the laws of chemistry from the laws of physics alone. You can make the case that molecular biology reduces to chemistry, just like chemistry reduces to physics, so molecular biology ultimately reduces to physics, too.

Note that there are really two relationships at issue in reduction. One is a relation between the things we are studying. DNA is a family of particularly interesting, complicated molecules, which are composed of simpler molecules, which are composed of atoms in quantum mechanical bonds. That's a reduction of things to the smaller things they are composed of. The other relationship at issue is between the sciences of these different levels. If we do things right, the idea goes, our theories of one level—our theories of one level—will reduce to theories of a lower level. If we do things right, our theories of the higher-level phenomena will directly follow from our theories of the lower-level phenomena. These two reductive relationships are precisely what the Reductive Materialist has in mind. Mental states, he says, reduce to brain states. All types of mental phenomena—our loves, our fears, our hopes, our beliefs—even very specific beliefs— are nothing more than types of brain states. Just as molecules are nothing more than bonded atoms, mental phenomena are nothing more than brain states. From the science side, the claim is that psychology reduces to neurobiology.

In 1953, Francis Crick and James D. Watson discovered the molecular structure of DNA. They were awarded the Nobel Prize in 1962. Watson went on to play a major administrative role in the mapping of the human genome. Francis Crick did something different; he turned his sights on understanding the human mind. He went from trying to understand the mysteries of life to trying to understand the mysteries of consciousness. Crick was a Reductive Materialist of the first order. He calls [the theory] the "astonishing hypothesis." Here's what he says:

> … your joys and your sorrows, your memories and your ambitions, your sense of personal identity and free will, are in fact no more than the behavior of a vast assembly of nerve cells and their associated molecules. As Lewis Carroll's Alice might have phrased it, "You're nothing but a pack of neurons."

How plausible is Reductive Materialism? Let's look at a central form with all the details filled in. This form of Reductive Materialism is sometimes called *type identity theory*. What the theory says is that all mental states—all types of mental states—are identical to particular types of brain states. Depression is a particular kind of brain state; fear is a kind of brain state; love and hope are particular kinds of brain states. Since the position is that *all* types of mental states are identical to particular types of brain states, it'll apply to more specific mental states as well. Specific hopes and specific beliefs will be identical to specific brain states. Fear of elephants will be identical to a specific kind of brain state.

The position starts to look less plausible when you fill in all those details. If this were true, it would mean that everyone in love would have the same brain state. If it were true, then if Bill is afraid of elephants and George is afraid of elephants, there will be some specific brain state they both have. What kind of brain state could that possibly be? If the theory held for all mental states, it would hold even for very specific mental states. If I believe that Lincoln was our greatest president and you believe the same thing, the theory says there is a brain state we both have; there is some physical Lincoln-belief–specific property that our brains have in common. What physical property could that possibly be?

Everything we know about brains indicates that although they follow a common structural plan, they differ from person to person, particularly in detail. There seems no reason to think that how your brain codes a specific belief is exactly how my brain codes that belief and lots of reason to think that our brains could code the same belief very differently. If so, at the very least, it can't be true that specific types of mental states are specific types of brain states. The position also faces a fundamental problem on a much more general level. Consider being in pain. If Reductive Materialism is right, to be in pain is to have a certain brain state. What brain state could that be? The closest people have gotten to answering this question is to say that to be in pain is to have a certain kind of nerve fiber firing. The specific types of nerves involved are unmyelinated, unsheathed C fibers. What's pain? The Reductive Materialist would say that pain just *is* the firing of C fibers.

Here's the problem: If we say this is what pain is—pain is the firing of C fibers—it follows immediately that if you don't have C fibers firing, you cannot possibly be in pain. After all, that's what pain is. C fibers are essentially a carbon-based thing, like all our neurons are. But let's do a thought experiment: Suppose there are creatures on another planet that aren't carbon-based; perhaps they're silicon-based. If pain just *is* the firing of C fibers, it follows that those creatures cannot possibly feel pain. So when we go to another planet on which life is silicon-based; and we shoot one of the aliens there; and it writhes screaming in the dust, shouting, "Ow, ow, ow, ow," we can rest assured it's not really in pain. It can't be pain; pain is the firing of C fibers, and the alien doesn't have any. That seems wrong. It also seems ethically dangerous. If that's what the theory entails, it looks like the theory can't be right.

This thought experiment establishes a quite general point about *multiple instantiation*. The problem with identifying pain with the firing of C fibers, or any other specific state of the brain or nervous system, is that pain might be differently instantiated in different kinds of organisms. In us, it might be C fibers. In aliens, it might be S fibers or something very different. Particular kinds of nerve fibers and particular kinds of nervous systems might be different in different organisms, and yet they might all still feel pain. Multiple instantiation indicates that pain itself must be something more general, something that shouldn't be thought of as identical to any specific aspect of just one operating system. It shouldn't be identified with carbon-based C fibers, for example.

What goes for pain goes for fear, and love, and hope, and particular beliefs. These things, too, are going to be multiply instantiated. The way I code up a particular belief about Lincoln may be different than the way you do, even though we hold the same belief. The neural mechanisms for fear in a squid and a mammal or us and a Venutian might be radically different but might still be real fear. An analogy is sometimes made to software and hardware. Microsoft Word is a program that can be run on very different hardware platforms. The way Macs and PCs and UNIX systems instantiate the program can be very different. The way Intel and rival chips implement it might be very different. The program itself, then, isn't identical with any one physical instantiation. It can't be reduced to any one kind of physical instantiation. But reducing mental states to particular physical instantiations is the whole strategy of Reductive Materialism. Maybe the whole strategy is wrong.

I've concentrated on Reductive Materialism, emphasizing some pervasive problems with the approach. There's another form of Materialism as well. This one is championed by the philosophers Paul Churchland and Patricia Smith Churchland. It's called *Eliminative Materialism*. Like all Materialists, the Churchlands think that everything in the universe is ultimately physical. So what about these mental things? What the Reductive Materialist says is that the mental things ultimately reduce to physical things. What the Eliminative Materialist says is that the mental things don't exist; that's the eliminative part. Taken literally, Eliminative Materialism is at the other extreme end from Idealism. Idealism says that only the mental exists; there are no physical things. Eliminative Materialism says that only the physical exists; there are no mental things.

That looks equally unacceptable. There are no mental things? There's no such thing as belief, as fear, as hope? You've got to be crazy. But here's the full story: The idea is that we will eventually have a science of human beings which will cover everything about them, all those things we refer to now by using concepts of love and fear and pain. The Churchlands say that when we write the ultimate science—the one that tells us the full physical story about people—these concepts won't be there. Here is an analogy: Consider witches. That concept was part of a theory of why certain things happened, for example, why people got sick or why certain people acted certain ways. We've now developed better theories, theories of social ostracization, theories of certain kinds of contagious diseases, theories of mental illness. Those occupy, and they occupy better, the theoretical space that we used to deal with by using the concept of witches. It's not that we now have better theories of witches. We've built better theories that do without that concept entirely. We now know that witches don't exist, and they never did.

Here is another analogy: Consider "humors." Medieval medicine was written in terms of draining good and bad humors. We have better medicine now, but it's not that we have a better theory of humors. It's a theory that does without that concept entirely. When the Churchlands say there aren't really any mental events, they mean when the whole theory is in, we'll find out that our ordinary terms—beliefs, desires, sensations—don't really apply. We will eventually find out that our contemporary "folk" psychology is just a bad theory and that all the things it talks about—beliefs and hopes and desires—just don't exist. There aren't any witches, and there never were. We'll eventually find out that there aren't any beliefs, and there never were. It's interesting that the motivation for the theory seems so appealing—the promise of a better theory. Yet what it literally says seems so wrong—that there aren't any mental events at all. That seems as intuitively wrong on one end of the spectrum as Subjective Idealism does on the other.

The purpose of this lecture was to explore intellectual alternatives. If Dualism is not a satisfactory theory, what might be? Subjective Idealism—a denial that physical things exist at all—looks like a dead end. That leaves us with Materialism. But Reductive Materialism, at least in the form of type identity theory, turns out to be less plausible than it might at first appear. That leaves Eliminative Materialism—a denial that familiar mental things exist—and that seems as extreme as Idealism. Are we out of options? Interestingly, the answer is no. Here, as elsewhere in philosophy, it may be that the whole problem has been set up wrong. We may be getting such disappointing answers because we're asking the question the wrong way. That's a line of thought that I want to follow next time.

Lecture Six
A Functional Approach to the Mind

Scope:

This lecture introduces two radically different approaches to mind using two important arguments. First, we'll explore Analytical Behaviorism using Wittgenstein's private language argument, together with his parable of the beetles in the boxes. This philosophical position parallels but is distinct from the psychological Behaviorism of B. F. Skinner. The Analytical Behaviorist claims that mental states—decision, love, or belief, for example—are not part of some inner mental realm but merely complex patterns of behavior.

Hilary Putnam's *multiple instantiation* argument is used to introduce a more contemporary successor to Behaviorism. Functionalism, which is currently the dominant position in philosophy of mind and the cognitive sciences, is the view that mental states are functional states of an organism: complex patterns that link inputs both to behavioral outputs and to other constellations of mental states.

Outline

I. How are we to understand the relation between body and mind, between the mental and the physical? It may seem that we have exhausted all conceptual possibilities, but two further positions take a radically different approach.

   A. Behaviorism was prominent at the mid-20th century, in both a philosophical and a psychological guise.

   B. Functionalism is currently the dominant position in philosophy of mind. The purpose of this lecture is to explain why.

II. Behaviorism and Functionalism offer another route out of both Dualism and Monism.

   A. From the beginning, the debate has been framed in terms of a question about the basic "stuff" of the universe.

   B. Why should we think that the important differences are a matter of stuff?

III. Wittgenstein's *private language argument* was crucial in changing the character of the entire debate.

   A. The *private language argument* is as follows:

      1. If Dualism were right, then my believing, seeing, imagining, and loving would be essentially inner and private, inaccessible to anyone else.

      2. But that very claim was expressed using words we all know: *believing, seeing, imagining, loving.*

      3. Words are learned by correcting incorrect uses and praising correct uses. We must have learned these words in that manner.

      4. But if Dualism were right, these things would be inner and private, inaccessible to anyone else. If so, we could never have learned these words.

      5. We did learn those words; therefore, Dualism must be wrong.

   B. Wittgenstein also expresses the argument in terms of the parable of the beetles in the boxes.

      1. Suppose we each had a beetle in a box into which no one else could look.

      2. One day, I say, "My beetle is so … 'glorp.'" You say, "Mine is, too. No, it's more 'nikiniki' than 'glorp.'"

      3. Those words, Wittgenstein says, could never acquire meaning. If Dualism were right, the same would be true of all mental terms.

      4. Because mental terms do have meaning, Dualism must be wrong.

IV. If our language of mental states is not about some private inner experience, what is it about? One proposal is that talk of mental states is really a way of talking about behavior.

   A. The philosophical form of this position is *Analytical Behaviorism*: the view that mental concepts are definable in behavioral terms.

   B. In psychology, *Behaviorism* is used to refer to the theory of B. F. Skinner, famous for stimulus-response theory and particularly for schedules of reinforcement. But Skinner was far from consistent in talking about Behaviorism.

      1. Sometimes, he talked as if mental states did not exist. Only behavior exists.

  2. Sometimes, he took a methodological stance: The subjective "inside" is scientifically inaccessible.

  3. Sometimes, he seems to be an Analytical Behaviorist: Talk about mental states is a roundabout way of talking about behavior.

 C. When you think about what people do when they are in love, you end up focusing on behavior. Perhaps that is all that love is.

 D. Analytical Behaviorism faces a number of conceptual problems.

  1. If mental terms have publicly observable criteria, we should be able to list them, but no Analytical Behaviorist has ever been able to give an exhaustive list for any mental term. When people have attempted an analysis, they have ended up using other mental terms.

  2. No matter what behavioral equivalent is offered, it appears that someone will be able to add further context that makes it clear that the mental concept does not apply.

V. Although philosophers have abandoned the letter of Behaviorism, its spirit lives on in Functionalism.

 A. Here again, philosophy and psychology have worked in parallel. Functionalism is at the core of contemporary cognitive science.

 B. One of the prime motivations for Functionalism is the *multiple instantiation* argument.

  1. It appears that pain could have any of multiple instantiations: different physical structures in different kinds of organisms. The same will hold for other mental states.

  2. Why? The Functionalist answer is that mental states are functional states of the entire organism.

 C. What does something have to be to qualify as a mousetrap? It just has to catch mice: The concept of "mousetrap" is functionally defined. On the Functionalist view, our concepts of mental states are functionally defined, too.

 D. As a functional state, a mental state is triggered by a particular input that (a) results in particular behaviors, but (b) also triggers further mental states down the line.

VI. Functionalism and multiple instantiation are often expressed using a metaphor of software and hardware, but the historical connection between Functionalism and computers is even closer.

    A. In the 1930s, Alan M. Turing developed a general conception of computation: the Turing machine, thought of as operating step by step on individual symbols. How it functions at any step depends on its inner states, but the symbols also change its inner states.

    B. In introducing Functionalism, Hilary Putnam proposed that mental states are like the states of a Turing machine.

    C. If mental states are functional states, they might be instantiable not only in living organisms but in machines.

        1. If so, the theory entails that an appropriately functioning robot would have beliefs, memories, and hopes, just as we do.

        2. If so, we could do psychology by doing robotics.

VII. Because of the change in perspective, Functionalism is ultimately noncommittal as to stuff. Although Functionalists tend to be Materialists, the position is, in fact, consistent with various views of what the universe is made of—including Dualism.

Further Resources:

Lawrence Durrell, *The Alexandria Quartet, Justine*, and *Balthazar*.

Hilary Putnam, "The Nature of Mental States," *Art, Mind, and Religion.*

Ludwig Wittgenstein, "The Blue Book," *The Brown and Blue Books,* pp. 46–56.

Questions to Consider:

Reflect on these two thought experiments:

1. You arrive as an explorer on another planet and encounter a new kind of organism that looks and moves roughly like a land-going squid. What would convince you that this creature is intelligent? What would convince you that this creature can feel pain?

2. An inventor has announced the first genuinely mechanical organisms. They look and move roughly like metal-jointed squids. What would convince you that they are intelligent? What would convince you that they can feel pain?

Lecture Six—Transcript
A Functional Approach to the Mind

In the last lecture, I promised a new and different approach to some of the central questions we've been tracking, a different approach to questions of the nature of mind, a different approach to the relation between the mental and the physical. We've looked at a range of classical approaches, from Dualism to Idealism and varieties of Materialism. Sometimes they seem crazy from the outset. Sometimes they have strong initial appeal but an appeal that fades with further thought and when we see the conceptual difficulties they bring with them. It may seem like we've exhausted the possibilities, but in fact, we haven't. There are two positions developed in the 20th century that take a radically different approach to questions of the mental and the physical, the mind and the brain. One is a theory most prominent at mid-century, in both a psychological and a philosophical guise; that's *Behaviorism*. One is an approach that has risen to prominence in only the last 25 years or so, in many ways as a development out of Behaviorism, a *Functionalist* approach to mind.

Philosophical research is always a matter of argument and counterargument. It thrives on conceptual controversy. Within continuing controversy, however, Functionalism is currently the dominant theory in philosophy of mind. In this lecture, I want to try to explain why. I want to show you the appeal of a Functional approach to mind. What these approaches offer is another route out of Dualism and out of Monism, too, for that matter. From the beginning, the debate has been defined as a debate about the basic "stuff" of the universe. Descartes divided the universe into two types of substance. Monists, whether Idealists or Materialists, seem to concede that the central questions at issue are questions about basic substance or "stuff." The debate between Materialists and Idealists is just over which kind of stuff is *the* stuff. The question is what kind of stuff mental states are made of, for example.

Maybe that's wrong; maybe that's dead wrong. The world contains beautiful things, and inspiring things, and graceful, and solid, and loving things. Why think the differences between them are, in any important way, a matter of stuff? Consider an example that I used at the end of Lecture Two. Hold up your right hand and make a fist. Now, there are clearly two different things here. We know they are different because different things are true of them. Open your hand

and you still have a hand, but you no longer have a fist. But the stuff of your hand and the stuff of your fist are exactly the same. The difference between those isn't a matter of constituent stuff. To understand what a fist is, you have to understand something radically different than the stuff it's made of. Maybe the same is true of minds.

In previous lectures, I've outlined a number of arguments against Dualism and against the inner theater. There's another argument against both of these that we haven't yet broached. It's an argument that was historically crucial in changing the character of the entire debate. I'm referring to Wittgenstein's *private language argument*. Ludwig Wittgenstein was an amazing philosopher with an astounding personal history. He was born in 1889, the last child of eight, in one of the richest families in Austria. It was an extremely rich family and very much involved in the arts. Brahms was a frequent evening guest, for example. Ludwig's brother Paul became a prominent pianist, despite the fact that he lost an arm in World War I. It was for Paul Wittgenstein that Ravel wrote the *Piano Concerto for the Left Hand*. The Wittgensteins were patrons of the visual arts as well as music. One of the most often reproduced paintings by Gustav Klimt is a portrait of Wittgenstein's sister Margaret.

So Wittgenstein's background is one of wealth, the arts, and depression. Three of his brothers eventually committed suicide. Wittgenstein's brooding intensity was legendary but may also have reflected a deliberate cultivation of the cult of his own genius. Wittgenstein writes in aphorisms, metaphors, and philosophical suggestions. He argues with himself in different voices. That's a style that charms his devotees and annoys his detractors no end. All indications are that Wittgenstein's charisma was irresistible—and, perhaps, dangerous. That charisma infected several generations of British philosophers. Throughout their later careers, his students carried Wittgenstein's mannerisms; they even carried his accent.

Wittgenstein's philosophical work is remarkable because it consists of two radically different periods. The first was the period of the *Tractatus Logico-Philosophicus*, stimulated by work of Bertrand Russell and published in the 1920s. Wittgenstein's second period was that of the *Philosophical Investigations*, published after his death in the 1950s. The *Philosophical Investigations* are an attempt to free us from pervasive philosophical mistakes with roots deep in our own language. Wittgenstein says that one of his primary targets—one of the philosophers he argues most emphatically against—is "the author of the *Tractatus Logico-Philosophicus*," namely, himself.

The *private language argument* is perhaps the most important legacy of the *Philosophical Investigations*. It goes like this: If Dualism were right, then mental phenomena—believing, seeing, imagining, loving, guessing, dreading, fearing—all of those would be essentially inner and private. My believing, seeing, imagining, loving would be inherently inaccessible to you or to anybody. All of these would be private in the most complete sense possible. These would be aspects of my inner experience, impossible to communicate to anyone else. But wait a minute. In saying what I just said, I used a number of words that we all know: *believing, seeing, imagining, loving*. We all know what those words mean. We all know what these words mean: *hating, guessing, dreading, fearing*. Somehow, all of us have learned the meanings of those words.

This is how children learn a word: "Look, Johnny, a truck." "Doggie." "No, Johnny, that's a truck. Can you say *truck?*" "Truck." "That's right, what a nice big truck." Children apply words. They get corrected if they apply them wrong, and they're praised if they apply them correctly. If that's the way we learn words, that's the way we had to learn words for *believing, imagining, guessing*, words for mental phenomena. If Dualism were right, these things would all be essentially private. If that were true, we could never have learned those words at all. We could never have learned the language of the mental, the language of belief, and fear, and pain, and hope. That's the *private language argument*. If Dualism were right about what these mean, we could never have learned them. But we did learn them, and therefore, Dualism must be wrong.

Historically, Wittgenstein's argument was part of an important shift in philosophical thinking in the 20th century. It's sometimes called the *linguistic turn*. Here's the general idea: If you're talking about belief, or knowledge, or perception, you're talking about what we *call* belief, or knowledge, or perception. What we're interested in are concepts that are embedded and expressed in language. If so, philosophical progress may demand careful attention to our language. If you want to know about belief, you shouldn't just sit there trying to peer inside at your beliefs. You should pay attention instead to how the concept of belief really functions in the language. That's what Wittgenstein is trying to do for mental terms in the private language argument. That's why he tries to approach questions of what mental phenomena are by what may seem to be a fairly indirect route—by talking about how we *talk* about mental phenomena. If what we're out to understand is the concept, attention to the language of mental states may not be so indirect after all.

Wittgenstein also expresses the private language argument in terms of a parable: the parable of the beetles in the boxes. Suppose that we each have a little box into which no one else can peek. Everyone has a beautiful beetle in their box, but they can share it with no one; it's somehow impossible to see anyone's beetle but your own. No one has any way of talking about their beetles because the colors of the beetles, the shapes, the strange motions of the beetles are unique in all the world. But we try to talk about them. One day, I turn to you, and I say, "My beetle is so … 'glorp.'" You hesitate a minute and then say, "Yeah, mine, too; glorp, glorp, glorp." Some people say their beetles are glorp, but others say, "No, mine is more 'nikiniki.'" Wittgenstein says that those words could never get a meaning. No one would have any way of knowing whether the words *glorp* or *nikiniki* were being applied in the same way or not. It would be a meaningless language.

The punch line of the parable, like the punch line of the private language argument, is this: If Dualism were right, terms for things inside our private mental realms could never get a meaning. But these terms clearly do have a meaning: *believes*, *doubts*, *loves*, *hates*, *is angry*, *gets the point*. So Dualism has to be wrong. It has to be wrong at least about how these terms work, wrong about what they really mean. If these are terms in agreed public use, as they clearly are, then either the mental realm has to be more public than Dualism says or these words have to be about something other than an essentially private mental realm.

If our language of belief and doubt and love isn't about a hidden inner realm, what is it about? Wittgenstein's positive proposals are much harder to interpret, but a number of his students, including Norman Malcolm and Gilbert Ryle, took him to mean this: What we are really talking about when we talk about mental states is not some private experience in some private inner theater but behavior. That's what these words have to be about if they're ever to be learned.

When we're talking about love or hate or having a new idea, we're really talking about behavior. This is called *Philosophical Behaviorism*, also called *Analytical Behaviorism*. The term *Behaviorism* has a number of uses in both philosophy and psychology. Analytical Behaviorism is a philosophical theory as to what mental terms mean.

In psychology, it may be used differently. The towering representative of Behaviorism in American psychology was B. F. Skinner, famous for stimulus-response theory and particularly for schedules of reinforcement. If you want to train an animal to do something—or a person, for that matter—you should positively reinforce or reward certain behaviors and negatively reinforce or punish other behaviors. But the effectiveness of training doesn't just depend on how much positive and negative reinforcement you do. It depends, in interesting and systematic ways, on how and when you apply reinforcement. Skinner's work on schedules of reinforcement was a milestone.

When he talked about Behaviorism, however, Skinner was far from consistent. Sometimes, he talked as if there were no mental states. There's no inside; it's a myth. There's only behavior. Sometimes, he merely took a methodological stance. The subjective "inside" is scientifically inaccessible. If we're going to do science, we have to use objective indicators—stimulus inputs and behavioral outputs. And sometimes, he talked like an Analytical Behaviorist in the sense at issue here. Talk about mental states—about belief or hope or love—is not a report on some hidden inner realm. It can't be. Talk about mental states is really just a roundabout way of talking about behavior.

The Behaviorist approach is radically different from the approaches to the mind-body problem we've considered before. Those approaches were obsessed with stuff, obsessed with the idea that you were going to understand the mental by understanding the stuff it's made of. The Behaviorist approach is radically different. If you want to talk stuff, maybe there is only one kind of stuff. Perhaps our universe is a physical universe, and there aren't any particles that aren't physical particles. But even if that's true, not everything is particles. There are movements of particles and patterns of movement. There are gentle breezes and hurricanes, and waterfalls and tidal waves. There are complex organisms. And then there are the ways they move, the ways they adapt, the ways they behave. What defines the mental may not be stuff but behavior.

Let me try to get across some of the underlying plausibility of Analytical Behaviorism. Take something like "Joe is in love with Mary." That looks mental, right, like we're talking about something in Joe's inner mental life? But think about what people do when they're in love. Joe moons about saying, "Mary, Mary." He gazes longingly at the object of his affection. He writes down little plans. He turns red in the face and stomps about when other people take Mary out on a date. He smiles when Mary smiles at him. He sulks when Mary doesn't talk to him. He calls up the florist and orders flowers. Hey, that's not mental; that's a complicated pattern of behavior. Maybe the term *love* doesn't refer to some private mental event in your skull. Maybe what the term *love* means is a complex set of behaviors.

Here's another example: Take something like "Joe finally decides to go to the party." That decision is a mental event. But the behavior we're talking about is something like this: At 2:30, you ask, "Joe, are you going to the party?" He says, "Oh, I don't know," and shuffles his feet. You ask him at 3:30 and at 4:30, and he says exactly the same thing. You ask him at 4:35, and he suddenly says, "Sure, let's go; I'll drive." That's a behavioral change, and maybe that's just exactly what the term *decision* means.

Behaviorism was a movement of enormous importance in both its philosophical and its psychological incarnations. In philosophy, it changed the whole character of the debate by changing the kinds of questions philosophers asked. Instead of asking about emotions, philosophers began to ask about our criteria for emotions. There were, however, a number of problems that plagued Analytical Behaviorism. Here's a main problem: According to Behaviorism, mental terms have to come with public criteria. So claims like "Joe loves Mary," "Joe decided to go to the party," and "Mike has a horrible toothache" must have publicly observable criteria for when they're true and when they aren't. These *must* have behavioral equivalents; otherwise, we wouldn't have been able to learn the language of love and decision. That's precisely what the private language argument was meant to show.

But if "Joe loves Mary" comes with some set of publicly observable criteria, we should be able to list those criteria. We should be able to say, "Joe loves Mary" just in case: (a) he sends her flowers, and (b) he sits and stares at her, and (c) he repeats her name in a moody tone of voice, and so on. Despite valiant attempts, no Analytical Behaviorist has ever been able to give any such list of criteria for any mental term. No one has ever been able to give a plausible set of behavioral equivalents for *loves*, or *believes*, or even something as apparently simple as *voluntarily raises his arm*. The attempts seem to fail for two very basic reasons. First of all, when people attempted serious behavior analyses, they ended up using other mental terms. You try to offer a behavioral equivalent for *voluntarily raises his arm*, and you end up with a definition that uses the term *intentionally*, for example. If the theory is right, there should be some pure behavioral equivalent for *decides*. But the only plausible equivalents anyone ever came up with turned out not to be pure. They smuggled other mental concepts in the back door.

The second reason why these analyses failed is central and seems impossible to avoid. It looks like no matter what behavioral equivalent is offered for a mental concept, some clever person will always be able to add context, which makes it clear that the mental concept doesn't apply to that behavior after all. If we say "Joe loves Mary just in case: (a) he sends her flowers, and (b) he sits and stares at her for hours on end, and (c) he repeats her name in a moody tone of voice," I can tell a story in which he does all those things precisely because he *hates* Mary. Joe sends her flowers because someone told him she was deathly allergic to them, and he wants Mary to die. He sits and stares at her for hours, trying to figure out ways to do away with her. He repeats her name in a moody tone of voice, imagining how wonderful the world would be without Mary. The problem is that no matter how complete your behavioral description of what happened, it's always possible to shift interpretation by adding something else. So no behavioral account alone could ever be complete. No behavioral account could be the whole story.

There are novels that turn on precisely that kind of point. No matter how complete your behavioral description of what happened, its interpretation is forever open to reinterpretation. One such example is *The Alexandria Quartet*, a series of novels by Lawrence Durrell. In *Justine*, the first novel of the series, the narrator, Darley, recounts a series of amorous intrigues in Alexandria. In *Balthazar*, one of the characters in the first novel returns to set Darley straight. Nothing he had recounted is false, he tells Darley, but it all meant something radically different than he thought it did. Even the motivations of his mistress were different than he thought they were. Justine's affair with Darley was merely a cover for an affair with someone else.

For these reasons and others, philosophers have largely abandoned strict Analytical Behaviorism, but much of its spirit lives on in a position called *Functionalism*. Here again, philosophy and psychology are working in parallel. It's no longer true that psychology is predominantly Behaviorist. Much of contemporary psychology is *cognitive psychology*, itself forming part of a wider field known as *cognitive science*. If there is currently a dominant theory of mind within both philosophy and cognitive science, that theory is Functionalism. One of the prime motivations for Functionalism is the *multiple instantiation* argument, which I outlined in the last lecture as a problem for Reductive Materialism. There, the setting was this: Suppose, as Reductive Materialism would have it, that mental states are identical to brain states. Suppose that pain is the firing of C fibers. Now consider some organism that doesn't have C fibers, some silicon-based alien on another planet, for example. If pain is the firing of C fibers—if that's what it *is*—that alien could not possibly feel pain. That seems wrong.

What that seems to be telling us is that pain cannot be taken as identical to the firing of C fibers or any other specific physical state. It seems plausible that pain could have multiple instantiations. In one kind of organism with one kind of physical or neurological substructure, pain might be instantiated in one way. In another organism with a very different neurological or physical substructure, it might be instantiated in another way—different instantiations in different structures—but it would still be pain. What goes for pain would go for other mental states as well. Anger might be instantiated in different ways in different organisms. Fear might be differently instantiated. Even if you share my belief that Lincoln was a great president, I'm quite certain that belief is instantiated in a different way in your brain than it is in mine.

If mental states are not the physical states of the brain that instantiate them, what are they? The Functionalist answer is that they are functional states, functional states of the entire organism. What does something have to be to be a mousetrap? Does it have to have that rectangular piece of wood? Does it have to have a little tin trigger with cheese? No. In order to qualify as a mousetrap, all it has to do is trap mice, no matter how it traps mice. Everything that traps mice, by whatever means, counts as a mousetrap. The concept of "mousetrap" is functionally defined. What the Functionalist says is that our mental states are functionally defined, too. A functional state is defined in terms of what it does. Our mental states are functional states that are triggered by particular inputs. They result in particular behaviors, but they also trigger other functional states down the line.

My anger, for example, is a mental state that may have been caused by a series of annoying bureaucratic incidents. Its effects include a range of behaviors—my fist-clenching and shouting back—but its effects also include a range of other mental states, a lingering unease on my part, a painful memory, a tendency to bristle at the thought of facing those people again. The idea is that mental states in general are functional states of that sort. Unlike Analytical Behaviorists, Functionalists are not particularly interested in giving definitions for specific mental states. When viewed as a functional state, both inputs and outputs of a mental state may be other mental states. A fully reductive definition "out of" the language of mental states may be simply impossible.

The multiple instantiation argument is often presented with the analogy of software and hardware. Computer programs are functional states. They give a particular range of outputs for a particular range of inputs. Mental states are like programs in that sense. An anger program gives a certain range of outputs on a certain range of inputs. A remorse program gives different outputs. A belief program gives still others. The same program can be run on very different computers, the same software on very different hardware. Mental states are like programs in that sense, too; the same mental state might be differently instantiated in very different organisms. The software-hardware metaphor is a useful analogy in explaining Functionalism, but it's also more than that. Functionalism is quite closely tied to computers and computing, both in its historical inception and in some of its most interesting implications. Hilary Putnam was one of the prime movers in the development of contemporary Functionalism. His prime example of what a Functional state was like—and, thus, what a mental state might be like—was an example taken from the foundations of computer science.

In talking about the history of artificial intelligence in a later lecture, I'll talk about Alan M. Turing and Turing machines. Turing was a British mathematician with a life fully as fascinating as Wittgenstein's. In fact, Turing and Wittgenstein were friends at Cambridge. Here is Turing's place in the story of Functionalism: In the 1930s, Turing developed a general conception of what computation was all about. Long before we had any real computing machines, he developed an abstract conception of step-by-step calculations that came to be called the *Turing machine*. The crucial point for our purposes is that Turing machines are envisaged as operating step by step, symbol by symbol. At any one step, a Turing machine inputs a symbol, which puts it into some specific inner state, in terms of which it moves a single step and outputs a single symbol.

Because Turing's conception is a totally abstract one, it doesn't matter how you might instantiate a Turing machine. It's the same machine, in abstract terms, whether it works in terms of gears, or electricity, or something else. The amazing thing is how general that conception is. Turing was able to logically prove that anything computable step by step by any machine could be computed by something as simple as a Turing machine. Turing machines are multiply instantiable, and they can be seen as working in terms of functional states. Given certain inputs, they give certain outputs and trigger further functional states. That, said Putnam, is what mental states are like.

Some of Functionalism's most interesting implications can also be phrased in terms of machines. According to the Functionalist account, mental states are functional states. Belief, memory, and hope are all functional states. It follows that anything that has the right functional states will have beliefs, memories, and hopes as well. That's what beliefs, memories, and hopes are. Because functional states are multiply instantiable, they might be instantiable in very different kinds of organisms, from ocelots to octopi. The same functional states might be realized in even radically different organisms on another planet. By the same token, because functional states are multiply instantiable, they might be instantiable in machines.

Theoretically, if it were built with the right functional states, a robot would have mental states as well. An appropriately functioning robot would have beliefs, memories, and hopes, just as we do. Putnam is quite straightforward about the point. If psychology is the study of mental states and if mental states are functional states, then we could study them in anything that could have those functional states. Reductive Materialism seemed to say that we could do psychology by doing neurobiology. A clear implication of Functionalism is that we could do psychology by doing robotics. How plausible is that? That's a question you should keep in mind in the next lecture, in which I'll trace the history of robotics.

In closing, here is one final point of interest: Functionalism, like Behaviorism, radically changes the kind of question we're trying to answer. We have left a presupposition of Dualism, Idealism, and Materialism behind. The question of mind is no longer a question of "stuff." Precisely because of that shift, the Functionalist approach turns out to be entirely noncommittal as to "stuff." Most Functionalists are probably Materialists, but that commitment is not really entailed by the position. The claim that mental states are functional states doesn't imply anything, one way or the other, as to what they are functional states of. As long as they work right, they could be functional states of the Materialist's physical stuff, or of the stuff of Subjective Idealism, or even of the double stuffs of Dualism.

Lecture Seven
What Is It about Robots?

Scope:

What is so fascinating about robots? The concept of machines that are like people has an extensive history in myth and art, stretching from Homer's *Iliad* and the myth of Pygmalion in Ovid's *Metamorphoses* to such movies as *Blade Runner* and the *Terminator* series. Real robots also have an extensive history, from Descartes' influence on the golden age of automata in the 1600s and 1700s to their impressive use in various fields today. One purpose of this lecture is to explore our enduring fascination with robots by tracing their history in both art and reality.

Robotic development has increased dramatically since the late 20th century. This lecture focuses in particular on contemporary robots, emphasizing both the promise they may offer and the threat they may pose. The inventor and theorist Ray Kurzweil foresees a "coming singularity," in which our machines become more intelligent than we are; roboticist Hans Moravec welcomes this possibility as the next step in evolution. The prospect of human-like robots also raises ethical issues of how we should treat our machines.

Outline

I.   People have long been fascinated with the idea of machines that behave like people—what we think of as robots. This lecture traces the history of robots and ends by examining some of the ethical questions that contemporary robots pose.

II. *Robot* is a recent term, but robot-like beings have a long history in myth, literature, and film.

   A. The term *robot* was introduced in Karel Capek's play *R.U.R. (Rossum's Universal Robots)*, first performed in 1921.

   B. Homer's *Iliad* has several references to robot-like beings.

   C. Romance and robots mix in the myth of Pygmalion from Ovid's *Metamorphoses*.

      1. Pygmalion creates a sculpture in the form of a woman and falls in love with it, and Venus brings the sculpture to life.

2. In the 1890s, Jean-Léon Gérôme painted the theme of Pygmalion twice.

3. Ovid's myth inspired George Bernard Shaw's 1916 play, *Pygmalion*, which was the basis for the musical *My Fair Lady*.

4. The Pygmalion theme appears again in the movie *Blade Runner*.

D. Myths of robot-like beings appear in other times and cultural contexts, including the medieval Jewish myths of the golem.

E. To recurrent themes of creation, power, protection, and love, the film robots of Hollywood add the theme of technology gone wrong.

1. By the time the golem appears in film in 1915, he runs amok.

2. In Fritz Lang's 1927 *Metropolis*, a female robot tries to destroy both people and machines.

3. Technology gone wrong is a continuing theme in such movies as *Westworld*, *2001: A Space Odyssey*, and the first movies of the *Terminator* series.

4. A more recent theme is sympathetic robot consciousness, evident in the later *Terminator* movies, *Blade Runner*, *Artificial Intelligence*, and of course R2-D2 and C-3PO of *Star Wars*.

III. The history of real robots is equally fascinating.

A. What was the first "real robot"? That question reveals as much about our concept of robots as it reveals about the history of machines.

1. Archytas of Tarentum, a friend of Plato, is reputed to have built a mechanical bird.

2. Sometime between 100 B.C. and A.D. 100, Hero of Alexandria constructed a series of steam-driven religious altars, some of which incorporated moving statues.

3. The 1354 Strasbourg clock incorporated several automata.

4. In 1495, Leonardo da Vinci may have built a moving knight in armor.

B. Descartes' work inspired the golden age of automata.

1. Lecture One mentioned the legend of Descartes' daughter, Francine. Whether that story is true or not,

evidence exists that Descartes developed plans for automata.

2. By 1633, Descartes had completed his work *De Mundo*. Because Galileo had been convicted by the Catholic Church for similar arguments, Descartes decided to suppress the book. The view of animals and machines in *De Mundo* was developed in his later work.

3. According to Descartes, animals are merely automata. They are purely mechanical and cannot feel.

4. Descartes' philosophical position inspired a burst of automata-building over several centuries. The centerpiece of that work was Jacques de Vaucanson's mechanical duck, mentioned in the work of de La Mettrie, Voltaire, and Goethe.

5. The history of automata continues with increasingly sophisticated machines through the 18th and 19th centuries and all the way up to Walt Disney's theme-park attractions Mr. Lincoln and Pirates of the Caribbean.

6. Some touted automata, including von Kempelen's chess-playing Turk, were fakes. All of these automata lacked genuine *autonomy*.

IV. Contemporary robots come in a variety of forms and have a variety of purposes.

    A. The first to be developed were industrial robots. More than a million are now in use, half of them in Japan.

    B. Robotic development is a major part of the space program. Spirit and Opportunity, robots designed to last 90 days on Mars, have continued to work for years.

    C. Surgery is increasingly being done by robots, with microbots in development that could swim through the human bloodstream.

    D. Humanoid robots are being developed in Japan to serve as nurses.

    E. Pet robots seem to offer therapeutic benefits.

    F. Some experimentation has been conducted with "emotional" robots.

G. Semi-autonomous robots are being developed for military purposes of surveillance, delivery, and aid, but the idea of attack by a robot army is chilling.

V. The future of robotics will bring a range of ethical dilemmas.

    A. What is the possibility of robots taking over?

        1. If we have something to fear, it will be at the point that we hand robot construction over to beings more intelligent than we are—our own robots. This situation is what inventor and theorist Ray Kurzweil means by the "coming singularity."

        2. Could we voluntarily limit the development of more intelligent robots? Would we? Should we?

        3. Roboticist Hans Moravec sees a glorious future in this prospect. Our true descendants will be our "mind children"—robots that will replace us as the next stage in evolution.

    B. Another set of ethical dilemmas concerns the robot as victim.

        1. If Functionalism is right, a machine could have real perception, emotion, pleasure, and pain. Wouldn't it also have ethical rights?

        2. We could design machines that want to do our dirty work, but what right do we have to design another being for our own ends?

Further Resources:

Terrell Miedaner, "The Soul of Martha, a Beast" and "The Soul of the Mark III Beast," *The Soul of Anna Klane.*

Gaby Wood, *Edison's Eve: A Magical History of the Quest for Mechanical Life*, chapter 1.

Fritz Lang, *Metropolis*, 1927, video.

Ridley Scott, *Blade Runner*, 1982, video.

T.I.L. Productions, *Vaucanson and His Remarkable Automatons*, http://www.automates-anciens.com/english_version/ automatons-music-boxes/vaucanson-automatons-androids.php (shows what may be photos of the remains of Vaucanson's duck).

Questions to Consider:

1. Explore this thought experiment: You are offered the opportunity to be one of the first users of the Universal Household Robot, a human-sized robot that will be installed in your house and will follow general English commands to mow the yard, do the housework, balance the checkbook, and tend the kids. According to the company selling the robot, it may still have a few bugs that need to be worked out. The company also insists that you sign a waiver for any negative consequences that may result from use of the robot. Do you accept the offer? What would be the advantages? What could be possible dangers?

2. Ray Kurzweil has predicted that our machines will pass us in intelligence by the year 2040. How plausible do you think that prediction is? What do you think the consequences will be? Should we worry about this possibility? What might help protect us against negative consequences?

Lecture Seven—Transcript
What Is It about Robots?

We ended the last lecture with the following implication of the Functionalist approach: If mental states are functional states, we should be able to study them in anything that can instantiate those mental states. If Functionalism is right, we should be able to do psychology by doing robotics. People have long been fascinated with machines that act like people. One of the things I want to do in this lecture is to trace the history of that fascination. What is it that we see in robots? What makes them so fascinating? Toward the end of the lecture, I'll outline current directions in robotics today, and I'll broach some of the ethical questions we may eventually face. For the moment, those are still questions of science fiction, but they may not remain mere science fiction for long.

The term *robot* is actually a recent invention. It first appeared in a play that opened in Prague in 1921, *Rossum's Universal Robots* by the playwright Karel Capek. *Robot* was Capek's adaptation of the Czech word for tedious labor—actually, a particular kind of feudal labor—unwillingly given. Although *robot* is a recent term, the idea of creating artificial humans is an extremely old one. Homer's *Iliad*, written about 800 B.C., has several references to robot-like beings. Hephaestus, the crippled blacksmith god who forges Achilles's armor for him, has robot-like assistants.

> Golden maidservants hasten to help their master. They looked like real girls and could not only speak and use their limbs but were endowed with intelligence and trained in handiwork by the immortal gods.

I prefer the robots that Hephaestus made for himself.

> … Hephaestus was hard at work and sweating as he bustled about at the bellows in his forge. He was making a set of 20 three-legged tables to stand round the walls of his well-built hall. He had fitted golden wheels to all their legs so that they could run by themselves to a meeting of the gods and amaze the company by running home again.

Humanoid robots are those made to look like people, like the golden maidservants endowed with intelligence by the gods. By contrast, Hephaestus's self-propelled tables were autonomous, non-humanoid robots. These are not the only robots in ancient myth. In Minoan

Crete, there was said to be a bronze giant named Telos who patrolled the edges of the island to repel any enemies. The theme of creation appears in Homer's tales of Hephaestus. Themes of protection and power appear in the myth of Telos.

Sometimes the creatures that appear in the myths are less obviously mechanical, though still like robots in being artificial people created from inanimate matter. There is, for example, the myth of Pygmalion, which appears in Ovid's *Metamorphoses*, completed in Rome in the year 8 A.D. In the same year, the emperor Augustus banished him from Rome for what Ovid refers to mysteriously as "a poem and a mistake." Pygmalion is a sculptor. He hates women. "Even if he closed his eyes, his instincts told him he'd better sleep alone." But he creates a sculpture in the form of a woman and falls in love with that sculpture. Here, Venus, the Greek goddess of love, conveniently steps in and makes the statue real. Pygmalion and the living sculpture he loves run off together and bear a child.

It's the kind of myth that never dies. In the 1890s, the French painter Jean-Léon Gérôme painted Pygmalion embracing his statue as she comes alive. Gérôme painted the scene not once but twice, from two different angles. The myth inspired George Bernard Shaw to write a play called *Pygmalion* in 1916. It was later made into a musical called *My Fair Lady*. There were no robots in Shaw's play. It was about a man who tries to train a woman to be as he wants her to be. The problems that Ovid's Pygmalion had with women are carried over directly to the musical. Rex Harrison sings, "Why can't a woman be more like a man?"

The Pygmalion theme appears again in the move *Blade Runner*, an adaptation of Philip K. Dick's *Do Androids Dream of Electric Sheep?* In *Blade Runner*, Harrison Ford's character runs away with a woman he has proved to be artificial, complete with artificial childhood memories of a spider beneath her bedroom window. As the movie ends, they disappear into the wilderness to live happily ever after—at least, that is, in the upbeat theater version. Pygmalion represents a romantic side of our ancient fascination with robots. What's at issue is a fairly perverse combination of creation and the power of control but also sexual attraction and love.

There are also myths from other cultural contexts of artificial humans created robot-like from inanimate matter. Among these are the Jewish myths of the golem. The myths arose in medieval Prague in a period during which Jews were repeatedly accused of killing their own children. In the golem stories, outsiders attempt to frame the Jewish community by taking dead children and throwing them into the Jewish quarter of Prague. "See, they kill their own children!" In a typical form of the myth, Rabbi Judah Loew uses a Kabbalistic ritual to produce a golem from clay. The golem is a strong and powerful servant, charged with protecting the Jewish people from the unjust charge of infanticide. He captures the perpetrators, ties them up with the dead children, and deposits the bundle at town hall. Here again, the theme is protection, much like the bronze giant Telos on the island of Crete.

Our recurrent themes, then, are creation, power, protection, and love. To these, especially as the myths come into the 20th century, we have to add a sinister fifth theme. The fifth theme is the dark side of technology. Robots increasingly appear with the theme of "things gone wrong." By the time the golem myth appears in film—the first was a German Expressionist film of 1915—the things-gone-wrong theme has come to the fore. In that movie, the golem runs murderously amok. The first mechanical robot in film may have been the iconic female robot in Fritz Lang's 1927 film *Metropolis*. A major theme of that film is industrial oppression in the futuristic year 2026. The robot is produced by hooking up a machine to a living woman. It becomes a force of evil that ultimately tries to destroy both the people and the machines in *Metropolis*.

Murderous robots have clearly established themselves as a Hollywood theme. In *Westworld* (1973), Yul Brynner plays a sophisticated amusement park robot in the form of a gunslinger who tracks down and kills the tourists for real. Arnold Schwarzenegger's *Terminator I* is a cold and unstoppable robot messenger sent from a future robot war. Though not quite a robot, the computer Hal in *2001: A Space Odyssey* attempts to kill his astronaut crew.

Alongside the killer robot, another theme has been growing in recent robot fantasy, the theme of nascent and sympathetic robot consciousness. It happens with Robby the Robot in the 1956 version of *Forbidden Planet*. The Terminator shifts his sympathies to our side in the later sequels. The robot-like replicants of *Blade Runner* commit murder with impunity, but they do so because they've been shortchanged in robot life. R2-D2 and C-3PO are sympathetically comic throughout the *Star Wars* series. Data in *Star Trek*, Johnny

Five in *Short Circuit*, and the robots of Steven Spielberg's *Artificial Intelligence* all play with this same theme. Themes of creation, power, protection, love, things gone wrong, and sympathetic consciousness—it's as if metaphors of mechanical people allow us to examine these ideas in simpler forms, ideas of power, love, and consciousness. Why the fascination with robots? Maybe what we see in them are aspects of ourselves.

So far, I have been talking about robots in myth, fiction, and the daydreams and nightmares of Hollywood. What about the history of real robots? What was the first "real robot"? That's a much more complicated question than it may appear at first. Answering it has as much to do with what we count as a real robot as with the history of animate machines. Here is some of that history; you can decide for yourself what counts as the first real robot. Archytas of Tarentum was a friend of Plato. Around 400 B.C., he's reputed to have built a mechanical bird propelled for 200 yards by steam.

Sometime between 100 B.C. and 100 A.D., Hero of Alexandria constructed a series of animated religious altars that looked like the precursors of robots. The power source in all of these was steam. Hero used fire to produce pressure in a vessel containing water, and that pressure activated levers, ropes, and pulleys to produce some awe-inspiring effects. Here's one example: After lighting a fire to the god on the altar, the doors to the inner sanctuary mysteriously open by themselves. We know from Hero's writings how the device worked. Steam pressure activated by the altar fire opened the doors by pulling ropes under the floor. In a more elaborate example, fire on the altar makes snakes hiss and two statues bend to pour out wine and milk.

Descartes may have known about Hero's altars. He certainly would have known about the famous Strasbourg clock, built in 1354. That clock incorporated several automata, including a metal rooster that opened its beak, put out its tongue, crowed, spread its feathers, and flapped its wings. In 1495, Leonardo da Vinci may have built a robotic knight in armor. You remember the legend of Descartes' daughter, Francine, from Lecture One. If that legend is true—if the crew really did break in Descartes' quarters, really did find Francine in a box, and really did throw her overboard out of shock and superstition—then Francine was an automaton. Descartes was a major figure in the history of automata, whether the Francine legend is true or not. It's fully possible that accounts of earlier automata inspired his philosophical claims regarding people and animals. It's absolutely certain that Descartes' philosophical claims inspired a flurry of invention in the 1600s and 1700s, known as the *golden age of automata.*

Let me take a moment to fill out Descartes' history. In Lecture One, I mentioned Descartes' dream—the dream of a complete and unified philosophical science. In trying to fulfill that dream, Descartes wrote a major work called *De Mundo.* It means "On the Earth." *De Mundo* incorporated anatomy, physics, mathematics, and astronomy. It took him five years to complete. It was ready for publication in November of 1633. But 1633 was also the year that Descartes heard that Galileo had been tried and convicted of heresy by the Catholic Church. Galileo's crime was a book—a book called *Two World Systems*—in which he lays out powerful arguments for Copernicus's theory that the Earth revolves around the Sun. For that crime, and despite his public recantation, Galileo spends the rest of his life under house arrest. He goes slowly blind. He wrote of himself:

> The noblest eye is darkened which nature ever made; an eye so privileged and so gifted with rare qualities that it may with truth be said to have seen more than the eyes of all those who are gone, and to have opened the eyes of all those who are to come.

Galileo was never exactly modest. So in 1633, on the verge of publishing *De Mundo,* Descartes learns of Galileo's trial and punishment. That posed a problem for Descartes because his own work championed the Copernican theory, precisely the theory that had doomed Galileo. Descartes wasn't stupid; he simply decided not to publish *De Mundo.* All that he published of *De Mundo* in his lifetime were bits that he included in later work. One of those bits is a view of men and machines that he developed in his later *Discourse on Method.*

What Descartes says is that animals really are machines. They work like clocks, like automata, clever machines and nothing more. Our bodies are much like animals' bodies, and they are mechanical as well. But Descartes thinks there is one thing that raises us above the animals, one thing that makes us more than machines; it's our reason—our thinking being. You can tell that we have a rational soul from our creative use of language. In Descartes' view, animals don't use language, and they don't have souls. Animals are merely machines. So can animals feel? Machines can't, automata can't, and Descartes thinks animals can't. Some thinkers revolted against that conclusion. On the topic of animals, Pascal writes, "I cannot forgive Descartes."

Descartes' views inspired an astounding burst of automata building over the course of several centuries. We can build machines. If animals *are* machines, we should be able to build *them*. Of all the automata built, the most famous of all was Vaucanson's duck. Jacques de Vaucanson first built a flute player. His flautist stood about 5½ feet tall on a pedestal 4½ feet high and 3½ feet wide. It played the flute just as a human would, moving its mechanical fingers on the keys. But that's not the hardest part of playing the flute. The hardest part of playing the flute is wind control. For that, Vaucanson's mechanism included nine bellows connected to three pipes leading to the figure's chest. His automaton played the flute with fully animated, fully articulated lips and tongue.

But the big show was Vaucanson's duck. It was made of gold-plated copper, about the size of a real duck. Each wing had over 400 articulated parts. The duck could drink, splash in the water with its beak, rise, and settle back on its legs. If fed grain, it would gulp it down like a real duck and even poop. Vaucanson's duck has the distinction of being written about by several great men of letters: de La Mettrie, Voltaire, and Goethe. De La Mettrie called Vaucanson a "new Prometheus." Voltaire writes, "The audacious Vaucanson, rival of Prometheus, imitating nature's action, seemed to use heavenly fire to kindle life in inanimate matter." Voltaire is also quoted as saying, "Without the shitting duck, we would have nothing to remind us of the glory of France."

Vaucanson's duck was exhibited again and again, apparently destroyed and later resurrected. In 1805, Goethe went to visit a Professor Beireis at Helmstadt, who had bought the remains of Vaucanson's automata, but he reports that they were utterly paralyzed. Goethe said:

> In an old garden-house sat the Flute Player in very unimposing clothes, but his playing days were past. A duck without feathers stood like a skeleton, still devouring the oats briskly enough, but had lost its powers of digestion.

Napoleon evidently tried to buy the automata, but Beireis refused to sell. After Beireis died, his heirs approached Napoleon again, but he was no longer interested. It's at that point that the marvelous mechanical duck seems to disappear from history. However, in the 1930s, there were some mysterious photos found in a drawer in the French National Conservatory of Arts and Crafts. It happens to be on the Rue Vaucanson in Paris. The photos date from the 1890s and show what some people think may be the last images of the remains of Vaucanson's duck.

Sophisticated automata continued to be developed throughout the 18th and 19th centuries. There were keyboard players and writers, one of which would use a quill pen to carefully write, "I think, therefore I am." Some of these used an inner mechanism of revolving cogs very similar to the first techniques used by Walt Disney in [the theme-park attractions] Mr. Lincoln and the Pirates of the Caribbean. There are repeated references to chess-playing automata. The most famous of these was Wolfgang von Kempelen's 1769 chess-playing wooden Turk, said to be "for the mind what the flute player of M. de Vaucanson is for the ear." But the chess player was a fake, a cross between a conjuring trick and a fraud. The game play was actually controlled by a small person nestled inside the works. The chess player was exhibited by a range of impresarios for over 50 years. In an article for the *Southern Literary Messenger* in 1836, Edgar Allan Poe offers a chain of inductive reasoning to prove that it has to be a hoax.

These real automata clearly fall short of the robots of myth and fiction. They celebrate the act of creation and control, the cleverness of their makers in imitating life. But none exhibits the power or offers the protection of a Telos or a golem. None seems appropriate as a love object, and none comes anywhere close to a sympathetic consciousness. A quite simple thing that all of these automata lack is *autonomy*. They are mechanical in all the implied limitations of that term. They follow a rigid routine, repeating the same set of actions again and again. The automaton writes, "I think, therefore I am" again and again—"I think, therefore I am; I think, therefore I am"— but it doesn't think, and it doesn't write anything different until a person loads in a new program.

Since the late 20th century and with the resources of contemporary computing, the dream of robots has risen again. Often, the goal is one of genuine autonomy, robots that do act on their own. Let me briefly give some of the high points of current work. The first robots to be developed commercially were for industrial purposes. These are not humanoid in form; they're not autonomous. They can't even move from place to place. Industrial robots are often powerful programmed arms, like those used for spot welding in the automobile industry. They can repeat the same routine 24 hours a day without tiring. More than a million industrial robots are now in use, half of them in Japan. Robotic development is critical to the space program. The robots Spirit and Opportunity were designed to last just 90 days on Mars. They've continued to work for years.

Surgery is increasingly being done with the use of robots. Because surgical robots can be small, they are less invasive than a human surgeon would be with big, clumsy hands. At present, surgical robots are not much more than remote-controlled surgical tools, lacking even a rigid program to call their own. However, there are also microbots being developed that'll be able to swim through the human bloodstream. A vision is emerging of more humanoid robots for use in healthcare. Japan, like many advanced nations, has an aging population and is facing a crisis in elder care. The Japanese have been the first to try to address that problem by developing robots to assume some duties of nursing and support staff, like delivering pills and reminding patients to take their medicine at particular times of the day.

Here's another example of robotics being used in healthcare: A range of studies shows that cats and dogs can be therapeutic for those recovering from treatment or dealing with chronic illness. Pets stimulate companionship, and their need for care helps the patient feel loved and valued. But the places where pet therapy might be useful are also places thought to be inappropriate for real pets, like hospitals and nursing homes. Could pet robots serve a similar role? Experiments have been done with both shiny robotic AIBO dogs and with furry robotic seals. They're not humanoid, but they are "animoid," and as degrees of autonomy increase, so does the illusion of life.

There has also been some experimentation with "emotional" robots or at least robots that can be interpreted by humans as expressing emotion. An early example was Kismet from the MIT lab. Kismet was an animated head that could move lips, eyebrows, and eyes to express surprise, interest, affection, or distress. A second generation of emotional robots is represented by Cynthia Breazeal's Leonardo; a fuzzy gremlin intended not only to exhibit emotion but also to read emotions from *your* facial expressions. The goal was never to make a robot that actually felt emotion. It was merely to build a robot that could interact with people using the emotional language of gesture as well as speech.

There's another area of robotic development that may be more troubling—using robots for military purposes. Remote-controlled and bomb-sniffing and bomb-disabling robots are now a standard of contemporary warfare. Given the dangers, one would certainly rather have a piece of machinery blown up than a human being. Drones are a kind of flying robot that serve a surveillance function, but they're easily outfitted to deliver firepower as well. Here, as elsewhere, the question arises whether it's desirable to develop robots with autonomous judgment. Often, a quick response is the only effective response, but autonomous-attack robots present clear dangers. If things go wrong, they could subject soldiers to another form of friendly fire. Self-guiding military land vehicles are now a reality, autonomous in the sense of being able to find the best route on the ground. Such vehicles can be used for delivery and support services without endangering additional personnel. They can also serve as self-guided tanks.

Companies under government contract are currently developing semi-autonomous robots designed to rescue wounded soldiers in complicated battlefield situations. That sounds like a worthy act of mercy, but the developers themselves have also realized how easy it would be to put a machine gun on each arm of the rescue robot. The U.S. military has developed soldier stand-ins, controlled from a distance using an interface that looks like a video game. Do we want war to look like a video game? As war technologies have progressed over the centuries, there has been increasing emotional distance in the killing. Fighting hand to hand is emotionally intimate. Cannonballs and bullets are less so. In dropping bombs from overhead, you don't even have to see the victims. With physical distance comes emotional distance and emotionless killing. The idea of a robot army would be a further step in the progression, chilling in many ways.

Of all the aspects of contemporary robotics that I've mentioned, it's undoubtedly robots in war that raise the most concern, but I want to mention two other kinds of problems that robots may pose. Here, we return to the realm of myth and science fiction. Neither of these poses an immediate problem, but that doesn't mean we shouldn't start thinking about them. The first is the threat of a robotic rebellion. Should we be concerned about robots taking over and eliminating mankind as they do in the dystopian future of the Terminator? Isaac Asimov outlined the prioritized Laws of Robotics to prevent this kind of disaster. The first law is: "A robot will not injure a human nor, through inaction, allow a human to come to harm." The development of military robots already violates this law. What's to keep a sufficiently intelligent and imaginative race of robots in check?

We have little to fear from the robots now on hand. You shouldn't stand in front of an industrial robot, but don't worry about your laptop or Roomba taking control. If we do have something to fear, it'll be at the point at which we relinquish human control over robot design and construction. Ray Kurzweil is an inventor responsible for major strides in optical character and speech recognition and in synthesized music and speech production. He's also a theorist who talks of the "coming singularity," a predicted historical point at which our machines become more intelligent than we are. When we have succeeded in building machines more intelligent than we are, we can predict that *they* will be able to build machines more intelligent than themselves. The vision is of a chain of generation after generation of increasingly intelligent machines.

Could we voluntarily limit that chain of events? Could we deliberately limit the intelligence of succeeding machines? Would we? Should we? If there's a crucial turning point in the story, this is it: the point at which we take the first step toward machines that design their own descendants, which in turn, design their descendants—descendants that might eventually consider us stupid, obstructionist, and disposable. There are thinkers who don't consider this scenario threatening but, rather, the beautiful beginning of a glorious future. The roboticist Hans Moravec is one of them. He proposes that the next step in evolution will be a step of a radically different kind. Our descendants won't look much like us. They'll be silicon-based rather than carbon-based. Design will replace DNA. Our descendants will be machines. Moravec predicts that robots will emerge as their own species by the year 2040. He welcomes them, calling them our "mind children."

The second set of problems that robots will pose are ethical issues as to how we should treat them. Ethical concerns of this type also appear as themes in fantasy and film, for example, in the questions of humanity raised in the movie *Artificial Intelligence* or in terms of the replicants of *Blade Runner*. If Functionalism is right, all mental states might be instantiated in a machine. If so, we could build machines with conscious perception, emotion, pleasure, and pain, just like ours. But if a machine has those capabilities, won't it also have ethical rights like ours? We have no right to enslave another person. What right would we have to enslave something that was so much like a person?

Perhaps we could avoid the problem by designing happy robots, built to take pleasure in the things we want them to do. We design them to really want to do the laundry, to take real pleasure in washing the dishes—one step beyond the *Stepford Wives*. Would that really be any better? The more you think about it, the more ethically suspect it seems—a deliberate breeding of happy slaves. The robots we are envisaging at this point are robots comparable to people. What right do we have to design another person for our own ends? Here again, questions posed by robotics have immediate relevance to questions about ourselves.

In the next lecture, I'll return to issues of human minds and bodies, though robots have something to teach us there as well. The issue I'll raise next time is different from the mind-body problem as we treated it before. The emphasis will be on minds and brains but on particular conceptions in our minds and brains: our conceptions of our own bodies. The topic next time is body image.

Lecture Eight
Body Image

Scope:

This lecture offers a philosophical examination of a range of psychological phenomena involving our perception of our own bodies. An image of our own body is laid out across the sensorimotor cortex, but the importance and plasticity of that body image are only now becoming clear.

People who have lost legs or arms often continue to feel them as *phantom limbs*, sometimes with intense pain. This phenomenon was long thought to be merely an effect of nerve stimulation in the remaining stump, but V. S. Ramachandran's work shows that phantom limbs are better understood and treated in terms of body image in the brain. The brain's body image also turns out to be amazingly "plastic," or adaptable. A violinist's development of technique is evident not only in performance but literally in his or her brain; areas of the brain are recruited and developed for particular motor skills and sensitivities.

How do we learn our bodies? In some ways, the body is a mental construct. Human infants take a significant amount of time to learn how their own bodies move. In some ways, the body is also a social construct. We have all incorporated cultural stereotypes of "normal bodies" and "perfect bodies," the dark side of which are eating disorders, such as anorexia and bulimia.

Outline

I.   Our emphasis in previous lectures has been on the mind side of the mind-body problem: How could a body produce a mind?

   A. This lecture approaches the problem from the other side: how a mind produces a body.

   B. This lecture also emphasizes a perspective different from that in much of the history of philosophy of mind: the perspective of the embodied mind.

      1. A standard philosophical thought experiment is the brain in the vat. How do you know you are not a brain in a vat?

2. That approach to minds assumes that they could be removed from "normal bodies" in normal interaction with the world. Antonio Damasio labels it "Descartes' error."

3. The Functionalist mind, in contrast, is an "embodied" mind.

II. The somatosensory cortex registers sensation from different areas in the body and reveals much about the mind's body.

    A. The areas of your body that are more sensitive to touch occupy a greater proportion of the somatosensory cortex.

        1. With time and a few toothpicks, you and a friend can map the sensitivity of different body areas.

        2. A model of a person in which more sensitive areas are portrayed as larger is called a *sensory homunculus*. This sense of *homunculus* is different from that used in discussing the inner theater in Lecture Four.

    B. Just as the area of brain tissue corresponds to the sensitivity of body area, the organization of brain tissue corresponds roughly to the organization of the body.

        1. The head, mouth, and pharynx occupy about half of the somatosensory cortex, right-side up in the lower portion. The rest of the body occupies the upper area, upside down, with the feet at the top of the head.

        2. Some areas that are not next to each other on the body, such as the feet and genitals, are next to each other on the brain's map. Neurologist V. S. Ramachandran asks whether this proximity explains foot fetishes.

III. The mind's body is not permanent: The plasticity of the brain allows for a takeover of one area for another function.

    A. Finger-sensitivity areas in the brains of people who use their fingers for fine coordination are larger than those in the brains of people who don't. This enlargement has been shown for both violinists and those who read Braille.

    B. The general idea of brain-area takeover was introduced in the discussion of Einstein's brain in the first lecture.

    C. Some amazing cases show the degree to which brain function can be made up by parts of the brain not intended for those functions at all.

1. Experiments with ferrets have shown that it is possible to rewire visual perception to the auditory cortex: Ferrets can learn to see with those parts of their brains wired for sound.

2. Surgeons removed the half of three-year-old Jody Miller's brain that controlled the left side of her body. Within days, the brain compensated so that she could walk out of the hospital.

IV. One of the most fascinating manifestations of brain plasticity and body image is the phenomenon of *phantom limbs*.

A. Lord Nelson, hero of Trafalgar, lost his right arm in battle. He took the persistent sensation that the arm was still there as "direct evidence for the existence of the soul."

B. The American physician Silas Weir Mitchell coined the term *phantom limb* on the basis of repeated experiences of the phenomenon in amputees from the Civil War.

C. The explanation for phantom limbs was long thought to be stimulation of the nerves in the stump. Ramachandran has proposed an alternative theory, backed up with a range of case histories.

1. Ramachandran proposes that phantom limbs occur when areas of the brain previously assigned to the missing limb are taken over.

2. In one patient, Ramachandran has been able to show that sensations from parts of the face and shoulder are read as sensations from a missing hand.

D. How do you relieve pain in a limb that no longer exists?

1. If phantom limbs are an aspect of body image, it should be possible in some cases to treat the pain that often accompanies phantom limbs by treating body image.

2. Ramachandran has successfully used a mirror box in which a limb "seen" as the missing one can aid in relieving discomfort.

E. You can perform an experiment that creates something like the sensation of a phantom limb. You'll need a friend, a cardboard box open at both ends, and a rubber hand of the type available from novelty shops.

1. Sit at a table opposite your friend and put your right hand into one side of the cardboard box. You can no

longer see that hand, but your friend can see it and touch it from the other side.

2. Now put the rubber hand next to the box where you can see it, as if it were your right hand lying there.

3. Have your friend draw simultaneous and identical patterns on the rubber hand (which you can see) and your real right hand (which you cannot).

4. For about half of those who try the experiment, the rubber hand starts to feel like their own.

F. The idea that body image can expand to include inanimate objects—tools, for example—is also familiar from everyday experience.

V. How do we learn our bodies?

A. A distinction can be drawn between your conscious impression of your body and your unconscious *body schema.* In learning a skill, what is first intensely conscious can later submerge into body schema.

B. The overwhelming consensus is that our sense of our bodies is learned in this way.

1. Human babies take months to learn that those things waving in front of them are their arms, under their control.

2. To a great extent, our sense of our own bodies must be learned because our bodies change over time.

C. Some evidence suggests that parts of our body image may be hardwired at birth.

1. Within the first few days, newborn infants are capable of imitating facial gestures at better than a random rate, suggesting that they may have a default body image of their own faces.

2. Cases have been reported in which people who have never had limbs experience the sensation of phantom limbs, suggesting a default image of limbs in the brain.

VI. Professor Josh Bongard and his colleagues have constructed a robot that learns its body.

A. The star robot first constructs and tests theories of its own body form in terms of feedback from its sensors.

B. It then constructs and tests theories of how to move in a particular direction, with startling results.

VII. Our bodies are, in some sense, mental constructs. As Ramachandran said, "Your whole body is a phantom limb." Our bodies are also, in some sense, social constructs.

    A. What should our bodies look like? Historically, images of the "perfect body" have varied greatly.

    B. The "beautiful body" is statistically out of reach for almost everyone.

    C. A dark side of the social construction of body image is evident in the eating disorders anorexia nervosa and bulimia.

Further Resources:

V. S. Ramachandran and Sandra Blakeslee, *Phantoms in the Brain: Probing the Mysteries of the Human Mind*, chapters 1–3.

Scientific American Frontiers, *Changing Your Mind*, 1997 video.

Josh Bongard, Victor Zykov, and Hod Lipson, *Resilient Machines through Continuous Self-Modeling*, http://ccsl.mae.cornell.edu/research/selfmodels/ (the star robot in action).

Questions to Consider:

1. Consider the following thoroughly speculative thought experiment: If it were possible to hook up a human brain to an animal's body—a cat's, say—do you think the brain could "learn" the cat's body? Are brains flexible enough to do that, or can a human brain handle only a human body?

2. Short of actually trying the Frankenstein-like experiment in question 1, what kind of evidence would convince you that the answer was yes—that a human brain could learn a cat's body? What kind of evidence would convince you that the answer was no?

Lecture Eight—Transcript
Body Image

The mind-body problem was introduced in the second lecture and further explored in lectures since. How could the forces and particles of physics produce the mental thing that's the taste of pineapple? How could the physical produce the mental? In this lecture, I'll look at the issue of minds and bodies from the other side. You have an impression of your own body, but that's a mental impression. Your body image is just that, a mental image. How is that body image formed? How does the mind produce a body? In exploring that question, I'll emphasize a perspective different from that in much of the history of philosophy of mind. Descartes thought of the mind as something separate from the body, as made of an entirely different kind of stuff. But even philosophers diametrically opposed to Descartes have often started with the idea of the mind as something separate or separable.

A standard philosophical thought experiment is the brain in the vat. We know that your contact with the world is through impulses along your nerves, to your spinal cord, to your brain. Imagine, then, that we took a brain out of a person's body and kept it alive in a vat, carefully reconnecting all nerves to some artificial source of input. With sufficient computing skill, we could hook up the brain so as to create the impression of running through a field of daffodils, or swimming across an icy mountain stream, or playing the part of Hamlet before a crowd of thousands. With sufficient computing skill, we could invent a complete fictional life for such a brain. The idea is central to the series of the *Matrix* movies, but it was an established theme in philosophical literature long before.

One question posed in terms of that thought experiment is this: How do you know that you are not a brain in a vat, with a complete simulated life? How do you know that what you perceive is genuinely real? That question is a contemporary form of Descartes' "evil demon." How do I know that I'm not deceived in all that I perceive? But what I want to emphasize is that this example represents a specific approach to mind. It portrays minds as things we can think of [as] entirely removed from "normal bodies" in normal interactions with the world; it pictures minds as things that could be disembodied. By contrast, the approach I want to cover in this lecture is very different. It's an approach to minds as essentially embodied. The neuroscientist Antonio Damasio rejects what he sees as "Descartes' error." Damasio claims that we can understand minds only when we understand them as "embodied minds."

The embodied mind is entirely in line with Functionalism as we outlined it in Lecture Six. For the Functionalist, mental states are functional states of an entire organism. The Functionalist mind *is* an "embodied" mind. This lecture will explore precisely how that works. Where in the brain do we look for a body image? How does the mind produce our sense of our own bodies? Let's start with a little neurophysiology. Imagine you have a pair of old-style headphones on, the kind with the band that goes over your head. Tilt that band back ever so slightly toward the back. Right under that band, inside your skull, is one of the anatomical landmarks of your brain. The central sulcus is the official borderline between the frontal and parietal lobes of your brain. The central sulcus is a deep fold or canyon in the wrinkled surface of the brain. It runs symmetrically on both sides of the brain, in both hemispheres, from above your ears to the top of your head.

Along the back edge of that canyon runs the somatosensory cortex, which takes in touch sensations from various parts of your body. Along the front edge of that canyon runs the primary motor cortex, which outputs commands to the muscles of your body. Body input and body output face each other across the canyon of your central sulcus. The touch sensitivity of your body is mapped to that strip of somatosensory cortex, but different parts are mapped differently. Some parts of your body are more sensitive to touch than others. Your lips, for example, are packed with touch sensors; your hands are as well. Your sensitivity to touch is significantly poorer on your back than it is on your face. With a trusting friend, some time, and a few toothpicks, you can actually quantify the degrees of sensitivity in different parts of your body. Here's how.

Close your eyes, then have your friend touch your lower lip with two toothpicks ½ inch apart. Can you feel two distinct touches from the two toothpicks? Then have your friend move them closer, ¼ inch, ⅛ inch, until you can no longer tell whether you were touched with one toothpick or two. Record that measurement for your lip—the distance at which two touch points can no longer be distinguished. Have your friend do the same thing with the palm of your hands, the back of your hands, your shoulders. If you map your entire body, you'll find places where you cannot tell if touches almost an inch apart are one touch or two. There are parts of the body where it's almost impossible to get the toothpicks close enough together not to be perceived as two distinct points.

Now return to the somatosensory cortex—that strip of brain tissue that functions as a touch register along the back side of the central sulcus. Those areas of your body that are more sensitive to touch occupy a greater proportion of that brain area. Those areas of your body that are less sensitive occupy a smaller area. The area of your brain assigned to a given area is directly correlated with the degree of touch sensitivity we've just been mapping. If you took the data from the touch test, you could use modeling clay to make a model of this aspect of your brain's body image. It would be a model of a person in which the most sensitive areas are the biggest; those with the lease sensitivity, the smallest. The result would be a strange-looking little person with enormous hands and lips but with a tiny body in almost all other respects. That little person is sometimes called a *sensory homunculus*, though a homunculus in an entirely different sense from that of the inner theater in Lecture Four. That little homunculus is something like what your brain thinks of your sensational body.

Amazingly, that distorted sensory homunculus is draped across your brain. Not only does proportion of brain tissue in the somatosensory cortex correspond to the sensitivity of its associated body area, but the physical map of brain tissue corresponds roughly to the organization of your body. So, for example, the finger areas of the brain connect to the palm areas, which connect to the wrist areas, and then the arms, in your brain. Eyes, nose, and lips are lined up in your brain just as they are on your face. The homunculus mapping in your brain isn't perfect. Each half of the body is mapped to the opposite side of the brain. The map is discontinuous, and part of it is upside down. The head, mouth, and pharynx occupy a full half of the somatosensory cortex, right-side up in the lower portion. The rest of the body occupies the upper area, mapped upside down, with the feet on top and with a very peculiar discontinuity: The genital sensitivity area is tucked in beyond the feet at the very top.

I talked about a sensitivity map for the human body. It's possible to create similar sensitivity maps for other animals. The sensory homunculus for the rabbit shows fairly large ears but an even larger head and mouth. When it comes to body image, it's clear that what's most important for a rabbit are its eating parts. Here's a theme that we'll return to throughout the lecture: If areas of the brain are next to each other, there may be cases in which messages spill over to neighboring areas. That idea is the core of the work of V. S. Ramachandran, Director of the Center for Brain and Cognition at the University of California in San Diego. Here's one way the idea plays out: The area of genital sensitivity, we said, was right next to that of the feet. If messages got crossed at that point, might there be an association between eroticism and feet? Ramachandran wonders whether cross-wiring at that point might explain foot fetishes.

I have outlined the brain's sensory map of the body—the sensory homunculus laid across your brain—as if it were permanent. But some of the most interesting phenomena regarding body image turn on the fact that it's not necessarily permanent. Although there are identifiable areas of the normal brain that are usually associated with specific mental functions, the brain turns out to be amazingly "plastic" or adaptable. Under the right conditions, an area of the brain standardly associated with one function can be put to very different use. Areas of the brain can be recruited or remapped for different purposes. That kind of remapping has been shown experimentally in the hands of monkeys. When nerves are cut so that there's no sensory input to the brain from the thumb and first finger, the sensitivity areas of the other fingers invade and expand into that area in the brain. The rewiring is amazingly fast; the brain rewires itself within months.

In precisely the same way, the brains of people who use their fingers for very fine coordination will differ from the brains of those who don't. Finger sensitivity areas will be larger, expanding at the expense of neighboring areas of the brain. This has been shown both for violinists and for those who read Braille. So it's not merely your talents that will change if you take up the violin or learn to read Braille; your body sense will change visibly in your brain. Your new body sense will emphasize the parts of your body important for your new skills. Areas in your brain will be allotted accordingly.

One of the primary exhibits in the first lecture was Einstein's brain. Was Einstein's brain different from yours? Einstein's brain was actually a little smaller than average. But it did have anatomical peculiarities in neighboring areas, one of which is associated with aspects of language and the other with spatial visualization. According to one analysis, the anatomy of Einstein's brain indicates an expansion of the spatial visualization area at the expense of a neighboring area of language, precisely the kind of plasticity and takeover we're talking about. Imaginative spatial conceptualization is the core of Einstein's work. And he himself said that he thought visually rather than verbally, but he struggled with language throughout his life. There are some amazing cases which emphasize just how far brain plasticity can go, how much of brain function can be made up by parts of the brain not intended for those functions at all. Experiments with ferrets, for example, have shown that it's possible to rewire visual perception to the auditory cortex. Ferrets can learn to see with those parts of their brains initially wired for sound.

Human cases are even more astounding, especially in children. In order to deal with crippling epileptic seizures, surgeons removed half of three-year-old Jody Miller's brain. They removed the entire right hemisphere, which controls the left side of the body. The immediate effect was full paralysis on the left side, but within days, the remaining brain rewired itself to reestablish control of the left side of her body. In ten days, she was able to walk out of the hospital. Beside the modularized and compartmentalized picture of the brain, then, we must put the fact of adaptive plasticity. It's still true that normal brains use particular parts for vision, particular parts for hearing, and particular parts for speech, but it's also true that the brain often has an amazing ability to recruit other areas to pressing purposes.

One of the most fascinating manifestations of brain plasticity and body image is the phenomenon of *phantom limbs*. In London, high above Trafalgar Square stands the statue of the great British naval hero Lord Horatio Nelson. It has only one arm; the other is an empty sleeve. Nelson took a musket ball in the right arm in an unsuccessful military expedition in 1797. The arm was amputated to the shoulder. Nelson referred to what was left as "my fin." After the amputation, Nelson continued to have a vivid impression of that missing right arm, including the sensation of his missing right fingers digging painfully into the palm of his missing right hand. Nelson took these sensations to be "direct evidence for the existence of the soul." If an arm can sensibly exist long after it's gone, he reasoned, why not the whole person after the whole body is gone?

Nelson's right arm was a *phantom limb*, a phenomenon that became all too familiar with the thousands of amputations during the American Civil War. It was on the basis of experience with Civil War soldiers that the distinguished Philadelphia physician Silas Weir Mitchell coined the term *phantom limb*. But the phenomenon seemed so unworldly that he published his work under an assumed name and in a popular magazine, rather than subject himself to the ridicule of his professional colleagues. Why do people seem to feel limbs that are no longer there? It was long thought that the explanation was stimulation in the nerve endings of the stump, that it was Nelson's fin that was causing his phantom limb. On that theory, there were often secondary amputations performed in order to get rid of the phantom limb. It's unclear how that would have worked even if the theory were true; you'd just end up with nerve endings higher up, which could be expected to create a new phantom limb.

V. S. Ramachandran has proposed an alternative theory, backed up with a range of case histories. The core of the theory is brain plasticity and the takeover phenomenon of one area of the brain by another. When a hand is lost, its associated brain area no longer receives stimuli. But that means the neighboring areas of the brain, like the area of the face, may invade the area and take over. The neural stimulations in what was the hand area are now coming from the face but may still be interpreted as coming from the original limb. It's not stimulation of the stump that's creating the sensation of a phantom limb but stimulation of the face.

In the case of a young man who had lost an arm in an automobile accident, Ramachandran was able to trace precisely what areas of the young man's face were felt as coming from the missing hand. There are, in fact, two areas that border the hand and arm in the somatosensory cortex: the face on one side and the shoulder on the other. Ramachandran was able to map the phantom hand on both the young man's shoulder and his face. The invasion that was creating the phantom limb had occurred within four weeks of the original accident. Ramachandran has also developed some effective therapies for phantom limbs, again based on the concept of body image. When the phantom appears, it often appears complete with previous pain. Soldiers who have lost a hand because a grenade they were holding exploded may have a phantom that perpetuates the pain at that moment of the explosion.

How do you treat pain in a limb that no longer exists? Ramachandran thinks that the pain, like the limb, is an aspect of body image. To treat phantom pain, you somehow have to treat body image. In some cases, for some forms of phantom pain, Ramachandran has been successful at using an astoundingly simple device, a mirror. Here, Ramachandran's theory gets slightly more complex and involves the motor cortex as well as the somatosensory cortex. Body image includes both a static snapshot of your body and an image of how your body moves. So consider an example of motor action. If you clench your fist right now, what happens is that your motor cortex sends a message to the muscles of your hand. But there's also a feedback loop sending signals back to your somatosensory cortex. At some point in the process, your fist is clenched enough, and a message is sent back dampening the original motor impulse. This keeps you from clenching your fist to the point that you actually harm yourself.

Remember Lord Nelson's complaint: that the fingers of his missing hand would dig painfully into his palm. Ramachandran proposes that what's happening is that motor neurons are sending a message as if to the hand, but there is no hand to give the feedback that says "enough already." The phantom fingers continue to dig into the phantom hand without anything to stop them. The result is Nelson's painful spasm in his phantom hand. Ramachandran's solution in cases like this is to offer some body-image feedback, indicating that the phantom fingers should stop. But how can you do that? There's no hand there to give that feedback. What he does is to set up his patients with a mirror box in which they can see an arm and a hand precisely where their missing arm and hand would be and fully under their control. What they really see is the reflection of their other hand. When the phantom fist clenches, about half his patients found they could relieve it simply by opening their other fist in the mirror box. The mirror makes it look like they can open their phantom hand, and that visual feedback is enough to relieve the pain.

If you'd like to experience a phantom limb, there's an experiment that creates a similar sensation that works for about 50 percent of the people who try it. The experiment reveals still more about how minds create our bodies. In order to do this experiment, you'll need a cardboard box that's open at both ends, a friend, and a rubber hand of the type available from novelty shops. Here's how to perform the experiment: You sit at a table opposite your friend, and you put your left hand into one side of the cardboard box. You can no longer see that hand, but your friend can see it and touch it from the other side. Now put the rubber hand next to the box where you can see it, as if it were your left hand lying there. The setup for the experiment is complete.

Now have your friend draw simultaneous and identical patterns on the rubber hand, which you can see, and your real [left] hand, which you can't. Your friend touches each with a light patter of her fingertips, or she draws a spiral on each, or a square. For about half the people who try this, the rubber hand starts to feel like their own. They feel themselves in the rubber hand despite the fact that they know all about the setup, despite the fact they know it's a rubber hand. Their body image has changed; this obviously inanimate thing starts to feel like part of their body. The sensation can appear even without a rubber hand. With identical patterns of simultaneous touching, it's sometimes possible to feel as if a coffee cup or a tabletop is part of your own body. Are you fooling yourself? Absolutely, but the feelings are real.

This phenomenon of feeling yourself in something inanimate can be crucial to the successful adoption of artificial limbs. For those who have lost a limb, it's important to have a phantom. It's in terms of that phantom limb that they can come to feel a prosthetic limb as their own. I've introduced images of extended body issues in terms of phantom limbs and a rubber hand, but the basic idea—the idea that your body image can expand to include inanimate objects—should be familiar from everyday experience. When you've worked repeatedly and consistently with a tool—a hammer or a wrench, for example—it's as if it becomes part of your body. You act unerringly and unthinkingly as if the hammer were as natural as your hand. You may even sense the world through the head of the hammer.

How do we learn our bodies? We can draw a distinction between your conscious impression of your body and your unconscious assumptions regarding it—what some philosophers call your *body schema*. That unconscious body schema is something you don't think about. It's a sense of your body through which you just act. As you know from your own experience, over time, your conscious body image can be incorporated into this unconscious body schema. The first time you hold a tennis racket, or ride a bike, or try to drive a car, you are conscious of everything. The first time you try to play a violin, you are intensely aware of how you are standing, where the violin is resting on your shoulder, how you're holding the bow, where your fingers are on the fingerboard, the height of your elbow, how your fingers are moving. Your body perception—your thinking about your body—your body image is working overtime.

Learning to play an instrument, or to drive a car, or to ride a bicycle, or to swing a tennis racket involves submerging some of those aspects of awareness into something less than conscious. Now that you know how to ride a bicycle, you don't think about all aspects of your body all the time; you don't have to. Your body awareness and your actions have become automatic. The overwhelming consensus is that our sense of our own bodies is learned in precisely this way. This doesn't appear to be true for all mammals. Calves walk within hours of birth. They either come with a fully equipped body image or learn one in an amazingly short space of time. Human babies, on the other hand, take months to learn that those things waving in front of them are their own arms and that they can even control them.

There's also clearly a way in which our sense of our own bodies has to be learned and even re-learned. Our bodies at 20 are very different from our bodies at birth. Were we hardwired with just one body image—whether that of an infant or that of an adult—we'd be at a severe disadvantage at some important period in our lives. At periods of rapid change in our physical bodies, our body image may take a while to catch up. Adolescents are notoriously clumsy, all arms and legs. They knock the ketchup over when they reach for it because their arms are longer than they expect them to be.

Although the overwhelming consensus is that body image is learned, there's some qualifying evidence on the other side, evidence that some of it, or a default basis for it, may be hardwired at birth. Within the first day or two, newborn infants seem capable of imitating facial gestures at better than a random rate. That might suggest that they have a default body image of what their own faces are like. There's also some evidence of innateness from phantom limbs. There are some cases in which people who have never had limbs nonetheless sense phantom limbs. Explanation of that kind of phantom limb seems to require a body image of limbs laid down to begin with. In order to interpret the evidence, it may turn out that we have to suppose at least a default body image from the beginning, a default mapping of certain areas across your somatosensory cortex, for example. Nevertheless, innate does not mean unchangeable, and that default mapping may still be adaptable in all the ways we've talked about.

In the last lecture, I traced the history of robotics; that comes in here, too. Professor Josh Bongard has constructed a robot that learns its own body. They call it the star robot. It has roughly the shape of a starfish but with only four limbs rather than five. Each of its limbs has two knuckles powered by motors. Its sensory equipment includes touch sensors on the tips of its limbs and a positional sensor at its center. To begin with, the robot is given no data regarding the length of its limbs or how they're connected. In order to figure out its own body, it's programmed to generate random pictures of possible body configurations. It tests each picture for goodness of fit by firing its motors randomly and collecting sensory feedback.

In essence, the star robot is asking itself: "How does the sensory feedback correspond with this theory of my body? Does it correspond better to this image or that one?" The robot picks its best-scoring theories and builds further hybrids and variations from those, testing each theory in turn. In a sense, it's generating and testing possible body images against incoming data. In most test runs, the robot is able to figure out what kind of body it has within minutes. It settles on a body image that's very close to the one it actually has. At that point, Bongard assigned it the task of moving a certain distance across a tabletop. "If this is what my body is like, how can I get it to move over there?" Once again, the star robot spins theories; once again, it sorts them for the best, and eventually, it finds a way to move its newly learned body.

How do you think the four-legged starfish is going to move—two legs on one side and two on the other or crawling one leg at a time? There's a video online at a website listed in your references. In the run shown there, the robot learned to propel itself forward by throwing one leg back and over like a scorpion's tail. The robot scoots forward with the inertia generated by flinging that leg back and over. That movement is not what you'd expect. It's certainly not what anyone would have programmed in. The star robot has formed an image of its own body and has figured out a novel and surprising way to move it.

To a great extent, our body images are learned; they are mental constructs. Ramachandran at one point says, "Your whole body is a

©2008 The Teaching Company.

phantom limb." Like many things, there are certain aspects of our body images that are learned socially, that are social constructs. We not only have an image of what our bodies are like, [but] we have an image of what our bodies should be like—what makes a body beautiful or handsome and how our own bodies measure up. Historically, images of the "perfect body" have varied greatly. Renoir was known for painting beautiful women and for painting them beautifully. But to contemporary eyes, Renoir's women look distinctly short and plump. Boticelli's *Venus*, standing nude in a shell, is muscular and small chested, with wide hips and thighs. Albrecht Dürer's women look positively pregnant.

One of the oldest pieces of human art we have is the *Venus of Willendorf*, found in Austria and dated to at least 25,000 B.C. It might have been an image of the ideal female, fertile and well fed. By contemporary standards, the *Venus of Willendorf* is obese. Differences in conceptions of beauty are evident even over the course of the 20th century. Mary Pickford was America's sweetheart in the films of the 1920s and had the tiny cupid-bow lips considered beautiful in the period. Julia Roberts was America's sweetheart starting in the 1990s and has an enormous mouth by comparison. Mary Pickford struggled to perfect her ringlet curls. By the 1960s, women were ironing their hair in order to be beautiful. In order to fulfill concepts of beauty in the 1930s, Jean Harlow plucked out her eyebrows entirely and penciled in thin lines to replace them. Very few women do that now.

Our contemporary images of "beautiful bodies" are statistically out of reach for almost everyone. The average American woman is 5'4" and weighs 140 pounds. The average fashion model is 5'11" and weighs 117 pounds. That simple contrast accounts for an astounding amount of unnecessary negative body image. Eighty percent of American women say they are dissatisfied with their own bodies. And then there's Barbie. Were she enlarged to 6' tall, Barbie would weigh in at 100 pounds. Her back would be too weak to support the weight of her upper body, and her torso would be too narrow to contain more than half a liver and a few inches of bowel.

The dark side of social norms for body image also shows up in eating disorders, like anorexia nervosa and bulimia. Both of these are complex disorders with clusters of psychological symptoms, including low self-image, anxiety, and depression. In each case, there's evidence that serotonin levels in the brain play a part, that there may be genetic links. But it's also clear that social pressures are part of that mix, the socially inculcated and often damaging pressures to have a "beautiful body," a model's body, a "perfect body." The mind-body problem is cast in terms of two entities: body and mind. In order to understand the organisms we are, we have to understand both aspects. In order to understand our bodies, we have to recognize that they are mind-driven. In order to understand the mental, we have to recognize that our minds are embodied. The theme in this lecture has been our sense of our own body. In the next lecture, I'll take a further step, exploring our sense of self.

Lecture Nine
Self-Identity and Other Minds

Scope:

"I think, therefore I am." But what is it to be me? The mirror test for self-identification, first used by Charles Darwin, shows that chimpanzees have a reflective self-concept, but other primates do not. Children acquire a self-concept and pass the mirror test at about the age of two.

What is it to be the "same person" over time? The ship of Theseus is the classic example of problems of identity, but the issue comes in a variety of forms. What makes your body the same body over time? What makes you the same person? Thought experiments in terms of science fiction teletransporters highlight important problems for major theories of personal identity. The problem becomes real in consideration of puzzling experimental results with split-brain patients. Could it be that you have two seats of consciousness?

How do we know what other people feel and think? Here again, an ancient philosophical question—the problem of other minds—meets contemporary work in psychology and neuroscience. A recent philosophical theory emphasizes the role of simulation in our understanding of other minds—our ability to put ourselves in another's place. Results in the study of autism, brain scans, and the *mirror neurons* of macaque monkeys offer supporting evidence.

Outline

I.   This lecture explores both our sense of ourselves and our sense of other people.

   A. Descartes said, "I think, therefore I am." William James noted, "I am never uncertain as to whether this consciousness is mine." Bertrand Russell asked, "[W]ho is this *me*? Who is this *I*?"

   B. This lecture explores our concept of ourselves, how far it extends in the animal kingdom, and some of the puzzling questions about self posed by split-brain cases.

   C. This lecture also explores the other side of the coin: our concept of other people or other minds.

II. Do animals have a sense of self?

    A. Charles Darwin put mirrors in front of young orangutans to see whether they would realize they were looking at themselves.

    B. Since Gordon Gallup's work in the 1970s, recognition in a mirror has become the standard test for sense of self. If an animal sees a mark on the forehead of its reflection, will it reach for its own forehead to further explore the mark?

        1. Chimpanzees immediately reach to touch the marks. Other monkeys do not.

        2. Gorillas generally fail the test, with the exception of Penny Patterson's Koko.

        3. Human children pass the test at about the age of two.

        4. Elephants also seem to recognize themselves in a mirror.

III. What is our sense of self? What is it to be the "same person" over time?

    A. The metaphysical problem of identity over time appears in a number of forms. A classical version is the ship of Theseus.

        1. In Greek legend, Theseus slew the Minotaur and brought the youth of Athens home. Plutarch writes that the ship of Theseus was preserved for generations in honor of the feat.

        2. Plank by plank, each part of the ship is replaced. In his *De Corpore* of 1655, Thomas Hobbes adds a further spin: What if the old pieces are crutched together in the junkyard?

        3. Which is the real ship of Theseus, the pristine ship celebrated in the harbor or the assemblage of rotting timbers in the junkyard?

    B. The problem of identity also appears in other forms.

        1. Given that your cells are constantly replaced, what makes your body the same body over time? You are a walking ship of Theseus.

        2. Hobbes took a pragmatic approach to questions of identity: The answer depends on what you are talking about. Conditions of identity for one kind of thing may be different than for another.

C. When is something the same person?
  1. In his *Essay Concerning Human Understanding* of 1689, John Locke gives a Functionalist account of when someone is the same man. In order for someone to be the same man, the same functional organization must be continuous over time.
  2. Locke gives a different account for when someone is the "same person." In this case, it is continuity of consciousness through memory that Locke thinks is important.
  3. Locke's view faces some problems. If the "same consciousness" were tied so closely to memory, amnesia patients would automatically and invariably be different people than they were before they experienced amnesia.

D. Teletransporter thought experiments pose problems for many accounts of personal identity.
  1. The teletransporter maps all information about the chemical composition of your body and brain. The information is then sent to Alpha Centauri, where a perfect duplicate is assembled. "Ah," you say as you step from the teletransporter, "here I am." Is it really you that stepped out on the other side?
  2. Consider a "branching" case, in which the signal is sent to two different places, two people step from the transporters, and they go on to live two different lives. Both cannot be identical to you because they are not identical to each other.
  3. No one has used teletransporter examples better than the Oxford philosopher Derek Parfit.
  4. In the end, bodily continuity, causal continuity, and continuity of memory do not seem to fare well as accounts of personal identity. Locke's identification of the "same person" with the "same consciousness" seems right but simply shifts the question: What is it that makes a consciousness mine?
  5. Just what is this sense of self?

IV. Split-brain cases offer real instantiations of the philosophical problem.
  A. The corpus callosum is a thick connection of nerves that transfers information from one side of the brain to the other.

When it is severed as a last-ditch effort to control severe epilepsy, lines of communication between the hemispheres of the brain are cut.

B. Roger Sperry's experiments show that under specific test conditions, the behavior of split-brain patients can be very strange.

    1. A woman shown a picture of a cup in her right visual field can answer what it is.

    2. When shown a picture of a spoon in her left visual field, she says she can see nothing, but when asked to find the object with her left hand, she does so successfully.

    3. According to Sperry, "Everything we have seen indicates that the surgery has left these people with two separate minds … that is, two separate spheres of consciousness."

    4. In one case, when asked what he wanted to be, a young split-brain patient answered "draftsman" with his left hemisphere but spelled out "automobile racer" with his right hemisphere.

V. How do we *know* that other people and consciousnesses exist?

A. A standard answer to the *problem of other minds* is the *argument from analogy*: We know that other minds exist by inference or analogy from our own case.

B. Philosophers and psychologists have used the term *mind reading* to label our ability to read one another's mental states. How do we do that?

    1. One hypothesis, known as the *"theory" theory*, is that we have a theory that links behavior and context to mental states.

    2. Another hypothesis, known as the *simulation theory*, is that we know what someone else is feeling by directly simulating his or her situation in our minds.

C. Some examples can be interpreted in terms of either the "theory" theory or the simulation theory.

    1. In the *false belief* test, a child sees Katie put a marble in a drawer. When Katie is gone, the child sees Sally move Katie's marble.

    2. When Katie returns, where will she think the marble is? Before the age of three or so, children say that Katie will think the marble is where Sally moved it. After about the age of four, they say that Katie will think the marble is where she originally placed it.

D. Other examples favor the simulation theory.

    1. The majority of normal children and children with Down syndrome pass the false belief test by the age of four, but only a small minority of children with autism pass.

    2. Autistic children do well on many theory-like cognitive tests, while Down syndrome children do poorly on many. These results suggest that it is not a theory that is being mastered in mind reading.

    3. Results from brain scans show that the same areas of the brain are activated when a strong emotion is seen and when it is felt. This finding, too, fits the simulation theory.

    4. Studies with macaque monkeys have shown that *mirror neurons* are activated both when the monkey sees a particular action performed and when it performs that action—precisely what the simulation theory might predict.

Further Resources:

Marc D. Hauser, *Wild Minds: What Animals Really Think*, chapter 5.

John Locke, *An Essay Concerning Human Understanding*, Book II, chapter XXVII.

Derek Parfit, *Reasons and Persons*, chapters 10–11.

Questions to Consider:

1. Here's another thought experiment: Your family is waiting for you on Alpha Centauri, and the teletransporter crew is ready. In a few seconds, someone will step out of the teletransporter at the other end, and it will be you. Are you ready to step into the transporter, or do you have doubts? If you hesitate, what is it that you are worried about?

2. Review what you have learned in this lecture about mind reading, "theory" theory, and simulation theory. What evidence from your own experience favors one theory over the other?

Lecture Nine—Transcript
Self-Identity and Other Minds

Descartes thought there is one thing of which I can be absolutely certain: "I think, therefore I am." William James added that there's one thing about our conscious experience that we're never uncertain about; we're never uncertain whose conscious experience it is—it's *mine*, of course. But who is this "me"? In his analysis of Descartes' argument, Bertrand Russell thought that Descartes' "I think, therefore I am" said something more than what was absolutely certain because it smuggled in a full notion of an "I," a self, a "me," lasting over time. What was absolutely certain was merely that thinking is happening. Something is doing the thinking at this particular moment, certainly, but I have no right to think that something really had a past and really will have a future, no right to think that thing did. I have no right to assume it really is an "I."

The topic of the previous lecture was our concept of our own bodies. What I explore in this lecture is our concept of self, of an "I." I will consider what that self-concept consists of, how far it extends in the animal kingdom, and some of the puzzling questions about self posed by split-brain cases. In examining our concept of self, the other side of the coin is our concept of other people, the concept of other minds. There, too, I want to look at issues using both the data from the neurosciences and the conceptual resources of philosophy. In a study in 1872, Charles Darwin describes putting a mirror in front of two orangutans.

> At first they looked at their reflections in surprise. They protruded their lips as if to kiss [the mirror] like another orangutan. They put their hands behind the mirror, looked behind it, and finally became cross and refused to look any longer.

Darwin's orangutans seemed to see an orangutan in the mirror. What's not clear is whether they saw the reflections as reflections of themselves. Since the work of comparative psychologist Gordon Gallup in the 1970s—100 years after Darwin—a recognition test using a mirror has become the standard test for a sense of self across the animal kingdom. The test involves introducing an animal to a mirror and then surreptitiously putting a mark on the animal's face at some other time, a red mark above its right eyebrow and its left ear, for example. When it returns to the mirror and can see the red mark, will it investigate the mark on its own body? If so, it must conceive of the reflection as a reflection of itself.

Chimpanzees immediately reach to touch the red marks above their eyebrow and ear. Sometimes they then look at their fingers; did it rub off? Rhesus monkeys, capuchin monkeys, and marmoset monkeys don't. They generally fail the test, as do gorillas. Of 25 gorillas that have been tested, only one seemed to recognize the animal in the mirror as itself. The one gorilla with a sense of self was a very special gorilla, moreover; it was Koko, raised from infancy by Penny Patterson and taught a form of sign language. Human children start to pass the mirror test at about the age of two. Self-recognition isn't limited to the primates. Elephants see themselves in the mirror and explore the mark on their foreheads with their trunks.

What is our sense of self? The 1944 movie *To Have and Have Not* is based on a novel by Ernest Hemingway and stars Humphrey Bogart and Lauren Bacall. At one point, someone says to Bogart, "You have to excuse her; she's not herself." Bogart says, "Who is she, then?" When I think of myself, I think of myself as the same person over time. I was that little boy running to the top of the hill. That's me in the old photograph. Yes, I have to admit it was I who wrote that brash article early in my career. Those are all the same person; those are all me. Indeed, some seem more like me than the old guy that stares out at me from the mirror as I shave in the morning. But what's this notion of the "same person"? What does it mean to be the "same person" over time? This is the philosophical problem of personal identity. What is it for the person in the photograph and me to be the "same person"?

Concepts of identity are often problematic. In Greek legend, Theseus slew the Minotaur deep in the labyrinth on the island of Crete. He sailed back the young people he had freed, back to their homes in Athens. Plutarch writes that the ship of Theseus was preserved for generations in honor of the feat. Like all ships, it's constantly in need of repair. Part of the decking has to be replaced. New boards have to be put in for rotting parts of the hull. Plank by plank, every piece of the honored ship is eventually replaced. In his *De Corpore* of 1655, Thomas Hobbes adds a further spin: What happens to the old pieces? The worn and rotted pieces go off to the junkyard, where the manager amuses himself by putting them back in their original arrangement. So here is the problem: Is the ship of Theseus the pristine ship on display in the harbor or the rotting hulk crutched together in the junkyard? Who has the *real* ship of Theseus? Plutarch writes that even in ancient times, the ship of Theseus was an example disputed among the philosophers.

The same problem can be repeated for almost any historically important object existing over time. Museum curators face it every day. Picasso sometimes reused his canvases. The Guggenheim has announced that the first piece he painted in Paris has been found beneath one of his later works. Which layer of paint is the Picasso that should be on display? The problem can be repeated even for our own bodies. Our cells are constantly replaced. There's no cell in your body that's identical to any cell in your body when you were two. You are a walking ship of Theseus. The major question at issue here is what makes you the same person you were then. But what makes your body even the same body?

Here's another spin on the problem of identity: Wild Bill Hickok was playing poker in the gold rush town of Deadwood, South Dakota, in 1876 when he was shot in the back of the head by Jack McCall. Wild Bill was holding two pair—aces and eights—known ever since as the "dead man's hand." If you go to Deadwood today, you'll see two separate shops with signs billing themselves as "Where Wild Bill Hickok was killed." One's on the north side of the street; the other is on the south. Where exactly was Wild Bill Hickok killed? Is one of the two shops lying? Is there some historical mystery about the shooting? Not really, but there is a philosophical puzzle of identity. Wild Bill Hickok was killed in Saloon #10 on the south side of the street. But Saloon #10 was later moved across the street to the north side. So where do you go if you want to see where Wild Bill Hickok was killed? Do you go to the geographical location on the south side of the street or to the building on the north?

Hobbes took a pragmatic approach to questions of identity: It all depends on what you're talking about. For some kinds of things, it's what it's made out of that's the core of identity. A gob of wax may be like that. A gob of wax is the same gob of wax no matter what shape you make it into. For some things, like the ship of Theseus, it may be the form or the organization of the thing that matters. Which is it that's important when we're talking about people or about ourselves? What does it mean to say that the young upstart in the photograph and I are the same man? In his *Essay Concerning Human*

Understanding of 1689, John Locke gives a surprisingly modern account of when something is the same man. His account is a Functionalist account. According to Locke, something is the same animal at different times when the same functional organization is continuous over time. Man's an animal. What makes me the same man as that young guy in the photograph is the fact that his is an earlier stage—mine's a later stage—in the history of the same functional organization.

Locke then makes an interesting distinction. I'm the same man as the guy in the photograph because of functional continuity. Whether I'm the same person may still be an open question. Whether we're talking about the same man is a matter of functional continuity, but whether we're talking about the "same person" is a matter of whether we're talking about the "same consciousness." Locke says:

> [I]n this alone consists personal Identity ... and as far as this consciousness can be extended backwards to any past Action or Thought so far reaches the Identity of that person; it is the same self now it was then ...

It is, in particular, the continuity of consciousness through memory that gives us personal identity, that gives us our self-identity through time. Locke uses an example of a prince and a cobbler that reads a lot like a science fiction story of switching brains. Suppose the consciousness of the prince, complete with all his memories, were transplanted into the body of a cobbler. The cobbler awakes with the prince's memories and the prince's consciousness. He thinks of himself as the prince. And wouldn't he then really *be* the prince? One of the things that's so disheartening about Alzheimer's is the deterioration of memory. "Mother doesn't recognize me anymore. She asks me who I am. We no longer have a past in common. She just isn't the same person anymore."

Locke's view captures much of what we seem to mean when we speak of someone being the "same person" over time, but let me outline some problems. Locke ties the "same consciousness" so closely to memory that discontinuity of memory would automatically make someone a different person. That would mean that amnesia patients must automatically and invariably be different people than they were before. That doesn't seem right. Surely someone could be the same kind, loving, and thoughtful person, with the same wonderful sense of humor, despite the fact that they can't remember much of their past. Locke used the science fiction thought experiment of the prince and the cobbler. I'll use another one in order to pose a problem for Locke's account, indeed, for many accounts of personal identity.

A device that appears in many science fiction stories is the teletransporter. If you want to be across the galaxy in a short span of time, we put you into the teletransporter. What it does is map all your atoms and molecules; all the information about the chemical composition of every bone, every muscle fiber, every neuron and its state; a total map of you and your brain. Your brain and body here on Earth are then destroyed, but the information is sent to Alpha Centauri in seconds and is used to assemble identical atoms and molecules in an identical structure. Neurons function in all the same ways. Memory traces are of precisely the same form. You've been faxed to Alpha Centauri. "Ah," you say as you step out of the transporter, "here I am."

Is that really you that stepped out of the teletransporter on the other side? If it's not the precise atoms of a body that matter but the form, it looks like it would have to be. We've mapped the form exactly. If causal connection from the past to the future is what matters, it looks like the teletransporter gives us a causal connection from you at the sending end to you at the receiving end. If it's personality that matters, sense of humor, likes and dislikes, goals and hopes, it still looks like it has got to be you. If it's the same memories that matter, as Locke seems to insist, he has got all your memories as well, so it must be you. He must be you, mustn't he?

Well, maybe not. Here's a complication. Suppose we say that it is you that steps out at the other end, complete with all the same memories, goals, expectations, and personality traits. Consider then a second case, in which we send the same message across space, but something goes wrong. It ends up at two receiver stations. Out step two people on two different planets, each of whom says, "Ah, here I am." From then on, of course, they may go on to have very different experiences and to lead very different lives. Which of those two people is you? This is a "branching" teletransporter scenario. If our criteria of personal identity—same memories, personality, atom-by-atom duplication, even causal connection—say that it's you that steps out of a single transporter, it looks like we have to say that both of those people are you in the double-reception case.

But that won't work. Remember Leibniz. If two things are identical to the same thing, they have to be identical to each other. That would mean that those two people—clearly distinct people, leading different lives on different planets—have to literally be the same person. That seems wrong. What philosophers do when a thought experiment reaches an unacceptable conclusion is to try to figure out where the reasoning went wrong. But in this case, it looks like we'd have to give up the idea that either of those people who stepped out of the teletransporter was you. That seems to be grounds for denying that it's really you that steps out of the teletransporter in the single-message case, too. It wasn't really you; it was just a Xerox.

Perhaps no one has used teletransporters to better effect than the Oxford philosopher Derek Parfit. Parfit has you imagine you're about to step into the teletransporter. Yes, you're a little nervous. The technicians tell you that you'll fall asleep for a bit, they'll map your body down to the atom, send the signal, and then you'll wake up at the other end. That's what they say—but is it true? Then you remember your wife laughing at your nervousness over the breakfast table. As she reminded you, she has been teletransported many times. She giggled, "And there's nothing wrong with me, is there?" So you begin the procedure, but they've been having problems with the machine. A duplicate of you appears at the other end all right—"Ah, here I am"—but the machine neglected to destroy your brain and body at this end. You're still here. There's also some bad news, I'm afraid. Your body here wasn't destroyed, but it was negatively affected. I'm afraid we have to tell you that you can expect to have a fatal heart attack in the next few days.

To console you, the teletransporter staff allows you to talk to yourself, to talk to the "you" that walked out of the other end. "Don't worry," he says. "I'll love your wife faithfully and take care of your children. I'm really you, after all, so you'll live in me to see them grow and prosper." Just how consoling is that? If you're like me, the answer is: *not at all*. I'm going to die, and this guy is going to be frolicking with my wife and kids. That's not me; no thanks. The interesting thing about such a case is that it makes it look like none of the standard accounts of personal identity really captures our sense of self. It's not bodily continuity that seems to matter. It's not personality continuity. It's not continuity of memory traces. Locke's account of personal identity in terms of memory seems wrong for two reasons. It's wrong because someone could remain the same person despite losing memories. It's also wrong because identical memory traces in the guy who steps out of the transporter at the other end don't guarantee that he's really me.

Despite that, Locke's idea of the "same person" as tied to the "same consciousness" seems right. Perhaps what I'm not convinced of when I step into the teletransporter is that it'll be my consciousness in that being that appears at the other end. That doesn't really get us out of the problem; it just shifts the question. What exactly is it that makes a consciousness mine? It doesn't appear to be any qualitative characteristic of the consciousness; all of those might be duplicated in the guy at the other end. It's not even continuity of consciousness that I'm worried about because I break that continuity every night without thinking I'm going to cease to exist. Just what is this sense of self? What philosophy has to offer here, I'm afraid, is not an answer but an appreciation of the difficulty of the question. Parfit has an interesting take on the whole thing. He thinks that what we care about is this elusive sense of self, in which it may not be me at the other end of the teletransporter. But perhaps that isn't what we should care about. Perhaps the continuity and continuance of our memories and plans, of our dreams and ideas, of our ideals and goals should be more important to us than merely perpetuating our selves.

I've used science fiction cases to raise questions about our notion of personal identity. There are real cases from the annals of neuroscience that are equally puzzling. Our brains are divided into a left and a right hemisphere, and they're cross-wired. The right hemisphere processes data for the left side of the body and also for the left side of the visual field. The left hemisphere processes data for the right side of the body and also for the right side of the visual field. People are generally right- or left-handed; one hand is generally dominant. In much the same way, one of the hemispheres of the brain is usually dominant. It's usually the left, and it's also usually the left hemisphere that controls language.

Between the two hemispheres runs the corpus callosum, a thick connection of nerves that transfers information from each side of your brain to the other. In some people, as a last-ditch effort to control severe epilepsy, that connection between the hemispheres is surgically severed. The idea is that the electrical storms that cause seizures are at least blocked from transferring from one side of the brain to the other. For some patients, such an operation can be life transforming, reducing the frequency and severity of seizures to the point that they can once again function normally. But under specific test conditions, the behavior of split-brain patients like these can be very strange.

In 1981, Roger Sperry won the Nobel Price for his work with split-brain patients. In one of his experiments, a California housewife who had undergone the procedure was shown a quick picture of a cup on just the right side of her visual field, thereby sending the information to the left hemisphere. "What do you see?" Sperry asked. "A cup," she answered. The left hemisphere had seen it, and it's the left hemisphere that controls language. Sperry then flashed a picture of a spoon to just the left of her visual field, sending the information to just the right hemisphere. "What do you see?" Sperry asked. "Nothing," she replied. It was the left hemisphere that answered— the hemisphere with language—and it had seen nothing. Sperry then asked the patient to reach under the table with her left hand, the hand connected with the right hemisphere. "There are a number of things under there," he said. "Pick out the one you saw." She still claimed, with her left hemisphere, that she'd seen nothing; but her left hand, connected to her right hemisphere, correctly picked out the spoon.

In representing his results, Sperry said, "Everything we have seen indicates that the surgery has left these people with two separate minds … that is, two separate spheres of consciousness." Sperry's interpretation remains controversial. To the extent that it's right, it looks like split-brain patients are essentially two people in the same body, two minds in the same skull. Some split-brain patients experience an "alien hand," usually a left hand, controlled by the right brain, which works at cross purposes to what they say they want to do with the left brain. In one case, the person would see his left hand try to unbutton his shirt as he tried to button it. In another, a man reported reaching out to give his wife a hug with his right hand, and the left hand punched her instead.

Language—in particular, speech—is usually under control of the left hemisphere. In some cases, however, it's more distributed than that. In one particularly striking case, a young man whose corpus callosum had been surgically cut was asked what he wanted to do when he graduated. "I want to be a draftsman," he said, speaking with his dominant left hemisphere, "I'm already training for it." But when the question was addressed to his right hemisphere alone, it was able to spell out its answers by arranging scrabble letters. The answer wasn't draftsman; it was automobile racer. Something in there wanted to be an automobile racer, but it didn't have access to the microphone. The only difference between split-brain patients and us is that our hemispheres still have the corpus callosum as an information highway between them. What that raises is the unsettling image of a second "you" inside—a second consciousness trapped inside the subdominant hemisphere of your brain.

So far, in exploring our sense of self, I've raised more questions than I've answered. There's another side of the issue that raises just as many. In Lecture Five, I outlined an extreme form of Idealism called *Solipsism*. Solipsism holds that the only thing that's real in the entire universe is my mind. That is, after all, the only thing I have direct evidence for. Unless we are Solipsists, we think we are not alone, that there are other people out there with minds like ours, forms of consciousness like ours, and subjective experiences like ours. We don't treat this as a mere guess; we *know* that other people and other consciousnesses exist. How do we know? This is the *problem of other minds*. A standard answer is the *argument from analogy*. We know that there are other minds like ours by inference or analogy from our own case. How do I know there are other minds? I experience my mind as a link between my environment and my behavior. I see other people's bodies respond in similar environments with similar behavior. I infer other minds—I infer their minds—on the analogy of my own as the missing link between sensation and behavior in their case, too.

The question becomes more specific when we ask not merely how do we know there are other minds, but how do we know about other people's mental states. How do we know, when we do know, what other people believe, or what they want, or how they feel? One approach is to say that we have a theory about beliefs, wants, and feelings, a theory of how these hook up with particular behaviors in particular contexts. The idea is that we operate in ordinary life with a fairly well developed psychology—a folk psychology—that links behavior and the postulation of certain mental states. When someone grimaces on putting a lemon in their mouth, we figure it didn't taste good. When someone says, "I'm sure it's all right; I'm sure there won't be a problem," but is constantly fidgeting, we figure they might not really believe what they've said.

Philosophers and psychologists have used the term *mind reading* to label our ability—our quite normal but very extensive ability—to read each other's mental states. The folk psychology approach that I've just talked about has been called the *"theory" theory* of mind reading. How do we figure out what people believe, what they want, how they feel? We use a theory that links behavior and context to mental states. The "theory" theory is highly cognitive. How do I know there really are other minds? I infer it like a scientific hypothesis from data on behavior. How do I know what someone else is feeling? I use inferences from the data based on my theory of folk psychology.

There's another and more recent approach to the issue, however. It's called the *simulation theory*. Here, the idea is that I know what someone else is feeling not by an elaborate process of inference but by directly simulating their situation in my own mind. I don't figure out what you're thinking by making inferences from a theory but, rather, by running mental simulations in my head. I see you bite the lemon. I rehearse doing that same thing in my mind, and I grasp what that taste must be like for you. I see you fidget, rehearse it in my own mind, and link it with a feeling of uncertainty. The simulation theory makes the whole operation of mind reading less cognitive and more direct. I figure out your mental states by putting myself in your shoes and figuring out what my mental states would be.

There are a number of results regarding mind reading that could be interpreted in terms of either the "theory" theory or the simulation theory. I'll give you just a few examples. The ability to figure out what other people are thinking appears at a very particular point in human development and seems to be following a standard trajectory. By the age of one, people can tell when they and someone else are looking at the same object. They can understand other people's actions as operating in terms of wants and goals. As toddlers, at 18 months or so, they can engage in pretend play that includes pretend mental states. By age four, they're pretty good at figuring out what other people think. They've become mind readers like the rest of us. The developmental story doesn't decide the issue between the two approaches I've mentioned. It might be that children are mastering a theory, as the "theory" theory would have it. It might be that they're acquiring skills of simulation, as the simulation theory would suggest.

One of the standard tests for development of mind reading is the *false belief* test. In the test, a child sees Katie put a marble in a drawer. Katie leaves the room, and while she's away, the child sees Sally come in and move Katie's marble from the drawer to the cupboard. Then the child is asked the following question: When Katie comes back, where will she look for the marble? Before the age of three or so, children will say that Katie will look for the marble in the cupboard. They know that's where the marble is, and they haven't yet mastered the idea that other minds have other beliefs. By the age of four, children know better. Where will Katie look for the marble? In the drawer, of course; that's where she put it, so she will still think it's there. She doesn't know what we know. She doesn't know that Sally came in and moved it.

The false belief test also casts an interesting light on childhood autism. Autism is one of the most severe of psychological conditions to appear in childhood. Alarmingly, rates appear to be on the rise. It's a complex syndrome, but one of the clear central strands in autism is abnormal social and communication development in the first few years of life. Some have referred to autism as a form of *mindblindedness*. One proposal is that it's the normal development of mind reading that has been interrupted. The child with autism hasn't developed full conceptions of other minds and how they function. Comparisons using the false belief test have been done between normal children, children with autism, and children with Down syndrome. The majority of both normal children and Down syndrome children pass the false belief test by the age of four; only a small minority of children with autism does.

The simulation theory seems to fit this last result better. Autistic children do well on many cognitive theory–like tests. Down syndrome children do poorly on many. Yet many Down syndrome children show an understanding of other people that autistic children do not. That suggests it's something other than mastery of a theory that's at issue. There are also other results that clearly favor the simulation theory. Brain scans have shown that the areas of the brain that are activated when you see someone else showing a strong emotion are precisely the same areas that are activated when you feel that emotion yourself. The same phenomenon shows up at the level of individual neurons called *mirror neurons*. Studies with macaque monkeys have shown that there are neurons that are activated both when the monkey performs a certain action and when it sees another monkey performing the same action. The activity of another monkey is mirrored in the same neurons when another monkey acts and when the monkey itself acts—precisely what the simulation theory would predict.

This lecture began with a study involving mirrors—Darwin's early experiments with orangutans. It ends with mirror neurons, neurons that react with immediate simulation or sympathy to the actions of another. Between those reflections, however, a basic philosophical question remains unanswered: the question of personal identity and of our concept of ourselves. What is it to be the "same person"? What is it to be me? The next time you see yourself in a mirror, try to figure out just what that self is. In the next few lectures, I'll move from seeing reflections to seeing in general. Our concepts of our bodies and our concepts of ourselves inevitably involve our concepts of the world beyond us. We are creatures in the world, and it's the world that we perceive and react to. How exactly does that work? In the next lecture, we'll begin to explore the question of perception using data from the neurosciences, theories from both psychology and philosophy of mind, and a range of psychological experiments. In some of those, you'll be participating as a subject. What do you really see?

Lecture Ten
Perception—What Do You Really See?

Scope:

What do we really see? What do we really hear? The focus of this lecture is on the Empiricist theory of perception, which argues that what we really perceive are not things in the world but subjective sense-data—colored patches in our visual fields, for example. It is from these private sensations that we infer the existence of real things in an objective world.

The lecture centers on several auditory illusions and experiments. It also describes visual experiments that seem to support the Empiricist picture.

Despite the theory's appeal, the lecture argues that Empiricism proves inadequate as a picture of perception. Core problems appear in the central concept of inference, in the reintroduction of the "little man" in the inner theater, and in the question of whether the theory really does justice to the data of experience.

Outline

I.   Sensory perception—hearing, seeing, feeling, smelling, and tasting—is the topic of both this lecture and the next.

    A. Both lectures put facts from psychological experiments and neuroscience to philosophical work.

    B. Three very different theories have been put forth to explain perception: an Empiricist theory, an Intentionalist theory, and an Evolutionary theory. The focus of this lecture is on Empiricism. Intentionality and Evolution will be the focus of the next lecture.

II. What do we perceive? The Naïve Realist view says that we see things … things in the world.

    A. Naïve Realism takes perception to be a two-place relation. We have immediate perceptual contact with the things themselves.

    B. But contact seems to vary with different senses.

        1. Do you hear the locomotive or just the rumble of its engine?

      2. Do you smell the cookies or just the aroma of the cookies?

  C. For seeing, touching, and perhaps tasting, perception seems to be a *two*-place relation. For the other senses, it is tempting to think of perception as a *three*-place relation.

      1. In smell, perception seems to be a relation among you, the aroma of the cookies, and the cookies themselves.

      2. In hearing, perception seems to be a relation among you, the sounds of the locomotive, and the locomotive itself.

  D. A little scientific knowledge pushes one to a three-place relation for all the senses. Sight is a three-place relation among you, the light reflected from an object, and the object itself.

III. In an Empiricist theory, perception is even less immediate.

  A. The theory can be introduced in terms of illusions.

      1. Artists are familiar with the fact that things at a distance look bluer.

      2. If an orange is put under a green light, it looks distinctly gray.

      3. The Shepherd tones offer an auditory example. The bells seem to descend endlessly in pitch, but they couldn't possibly do so.

  B. If you cannot tell the difference between something gray and something orange under a green light, what is it that you really see?

      1. According to the Empiricist theory, what you really see are sense-data, the colored patches in your field of vision, for example.

      2. Everything else—your knowledge of the external objects you are looking at, for example—is the result of an elaborate inference from immediate sense-data.

      3. Empiricist theory claims that all perception is a three-place relation among you, your sense-data, and the objects from which the data stem.

  C. The theory appears with variations in the work of the Empiricists: John Locke, Bishop Berkeley, and David Hume, writing in the first half of the 1700s.

      1. Is Empiricism a psychological theory or a philosophical theory? It is both.

2. Empiricism was a dominant theory well into the 20th century.

IV. Empiricist theory has two important parts.

A. The first part relates to the theory's fundamental entities: sense-data.

1. The theory explains how things appear in terms of how other things are. When the orange looks gray, something really is gray: your sense-data.

2. The classic hallucination in Shakespeare's *Macbeth* fits the Empiricist theory exactly:

> Is this a dagger which I see before me,
> The handle toward my hand? Come, let me clutch thee.
> I have thee not, and yet I see thee still.

B. The second part of the theory is inference. What you directly perceive are sense-data. From those, you infer the existence of external objects.

C. Some psychological evidence seems to support the Empiricist picture.

1. The *glissando illusion* was discovered by Diana Deutsch of the University of California at San Diego, one of the primary researchers in the psychology of sound and music. Although it's actually composed of little bits that are cut up, the glissando sounds continuous.

2. The two horizontal lines in this picture are exactly the same length. Why does the top line seem longer than the bottom line?

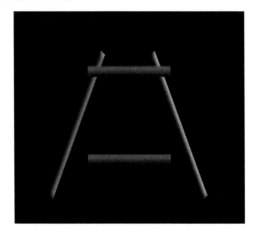

The Empiricist answer is that you read the vertical lines as if they were railroad tracks going away from you into the distance. If they were, something that appeared the way the top line does would have to be longer; thus, you see it that way.

3. In Diana Deutsch's *phantom words*, different people hear different words repeated: *respond, Congress, conscious, Christmas, miss me, mistress.* The sounds are actually syllables of *Boris* alternating in the two speakers.

D. The process of filling in also seems to go along with the Empiricist picture of perception. This experiment shows you your blind spot:

1. Close your right eye and hold the page about a foot in front of you. Focus with your left eye on the x. Although you will not be looking at it, you will be able to see the dot to the side.

2. Continuing to focus exclusively on the x, move the page slowly closer to your eye.

3. When the page is about six inches from your eye, the dot will disappear. All you will see is white paper to the left of the x.

4. If you keep focusing on the x and move the paper closer, the dot will reappear when it is about three inches from your eye.

E. An experiment created by psychology professor Arthur Samuel shows that the same kind of filling in happens with what we hear.

V. How good is the Empiricist picture of perception? Despite its appeal, it has a number of problems.

    A. One problem is in the use of the term *inference*.

        1. Did you infer the continuity of the glissando, or did you just hear it that way?

        2. What is going on seems too simple and immediate to be inference. The term *inference* makes the process sound more cognitive and deliberative than anything we have evidence for.

        3. Doubting the use of the term *inference* does not challenge the data, but it does challenge the interpretation of the data.

    B. The Empiricist picture seems to reintroduce the homunculus. Who is seeing the sense-data, and who is doing the inferring?

    C. An Empiricist might say that the inference involved is unconscious inference or implicit inference, but this explanation creates another problem.

        1. If the inference is unconscious, the inference step in the theory is invisible. But the Empiricist insists that first we see sense-data, then we make an inference. If the inference is invisible, why not think it comes first?

        2. In many of our examples, that seems to be how it works. By the time you have sense-data, the processing has already been done.

VI. The specific problems also introduce a more general reflection.

    A. The story that Empiricism tells about perception is a cognitive or rational story. Perception is portrayed as a rational inference from data.

    B. The history of philosophy is a history of people intensely devoted to rationality. It is perhaps not surprising that philosophers have tended to portray perception, too, as a rational process.

Further Resources:

Donald D. Hoffman, *Visual Intelligence: How We Create What We See*, chapter 1.

Diego Uribe, *Truly Baffling Optical Illusions*.

Michael Bach, *77 Optical Illusions and Visual Phenomena* http://www.michaelbach.de/ot/.

Diana Deutsch, http://psy.ucsd.edu/~ddeutsch (additional links with auditory illusions).

Exploratorium: The Museum of Science, Art and Human Perception, http://www.exploratorium.edu/seeing/exhibits/index.html (a number of visual illusions).

Questions to Consider:

1. When Grandma baked cookies for you, did you smell
   a. the cookies?
   b. the aroma of the cookies?

2. When the ambulance is approaching, do you hear
   a. its siren?
   b. the sound of its siren?

3. When the locomotive is coming down the tracks, do you see
   a. the locomotive?
   b. the sight of the locomotive?

4. If your answers to questions 1 through 3 were not all a's or all b's, what explains the difference?

Lecture Ten—Transcript
Perception—What Do You Really See?

What do we really see? This lecture and the next are structured around experiments from psychology and the neurosciences regarding perception. I want to put those experiments to work in guiding us through the philosophical debates regarding the nature of perception. There are three very different theories of what perception is all about: an Empiricist theory, an Intentional theory, and an Evolutionary theory. In this lecture, I'll focus on Empiricism. We'll pick up the other two theories next time. Let's start with our own immediate take on our own perception. What do you see? You see things, things in the world. You see a cat sleeping in the corner, a cup of coffee steaming on the kitchen counter, a book lying on a table. That's what you see—the cat, the cup, the book—things. The impression in seeing something is that we are in immediate perceptual contact with the thing itself. Seeing is a relation between us and it.

This is a starting point for the main theories I want to talk about. When this idea is formulated as a theory and given a name, the name is *Naïve Realism*. The theory is that perception is a two-place relation, a relationship between you and the world. You see things. What do you see? Things in the world. How good is that intuitive theory? We're interested in perception in general. It may help to think about the issue in terms of our different perceptual modalities: seeing, hearing, feeling, tasting. With regard to hearing, the initial intuition of direct contact may not be as strong. What do we hear? My inclination is to say "sounds." Do I hear the ambulance or the sound of its siren? Do I hear the locomotive approaching or the rumble of its engine and the clatter of its wheels on the rails? Do I hear the oboe or the sounds it's producing?

How interesting. It seems easy to say that we hear sounds of things rather than the things themselves. The parallel would be sights of things, but we don't say that what we see are the sights of things. We say we see the things themselves. Seeing seems somehow more immediate, or at least we talk about it that way. Touch also seems immediate. You feel things—duck feathers and upholstery and people's hands. You don't feel just the *feel* of those things. You feel the things themselves. What do you smell? Do you smell the cookies or just the aroma of the cookies? Do you smell the dirty tennis shoes or just their odor? What do you taste? Do you taste the taste of the cilantro, or do you taste the cilantro?

For seeing and for touch, the *two*-place relation seems intuitive. For those, the Naïve Realism view seems somehow right. When you see something or touch something, you're in immediate contact with it. Maybe the same is true for tasting; people seem to disagree there. For the other senses, it's tempting to go for a *three*-place relation. In smell, there are really three things in play: you, the aroma of the cookies, and the cookies themselves. In hearing, there are three things in play: you, the sounds of the locomotive, and the locomotive itself. Beyond these immediate intuitive impressions, however, there doesn't seem any reason to think that the senses are inherently different. Moreover, it takes just a little scientific knowledge to put immediacy in doubt in the case of *all* of the senses. Do you really see things? We know that light is reflected and refracted from objects and enters our eyes. So do we really see things or just light? Isn't that a three-place relation, too—you, the light reflected from an object, and the object itself?

When described like that, seeing no longer seems so immediate. When described like that, our Naïve Realism concerning perception seems less convincing. Maybe seeing is even less immediate than that. Light impinges on your retinas, stimulating a pattern of firing in the retinal cells. What you really see, then, is not the light but the pattern it creates on your retinas. That seems even less immediate. We are already on the road that leads to the Empiricist theory of perception. A good way to introduce the theory is in terms of illusions. Here's one example: Things at a distance look bluer. If you're looking at mountains at the far edge of the desert, you might think they have a distinctly blue tinge. The rocks and trees of those mountains are actually no different in color from the brown rocks and the green trees of the mountains you see closer up.

Artists have long been aware of that. One of the things Renaissance artists did to make part of the landscape look farther away was to make it look bluer. Leonardo da Vinci wrote about the trick in his notebooks, later published as his discourse on painting. If you look at the *Mona Lisa* and focus not on her but on her background, you'll see that da Vinci made the distant landscape distinctly bluer. Here's another example. Put an orange under a green light, and it doesn't look orange anymore; it'll look distinctly gray. People who put together restaurant buffets know all about this one. They don't put food under fluorescent lights because it looks unappetizing under fluorescent lights. That roast chicken looks so much better and warmer when there's a red light on it.

Let me give you an auditory example. What you're going to hear is a falling glissando, each instant lower than the moment before. [Audio demonstration, Shepherd tones.] The pitch slides down, and down, and down, but it couldn't possibly keep going down—you can't hear that far. And besides, the tone somehow seems to be back in the middle again. Philosophers have long been obsessed with illusions. Part of the obsession is epistemological—an obsession relevant to theory of knowledge. How can we know whether what we perceive is not just an illusion? You'll remember that was part of Descartes' methodology of doubting, outlined in the second lecture. But questions of philosophy of perception and philosophy of mind are just one step away from questions of knowledge. There'll be cases in which I can't tell whether I'm looking at something that's really gray or something that's orange under a green light. If I can't tell the difference between visual illusion and reality in some cases—if there is no perceptual difference in the two cases—what is it that I really see?

The same issue arises in case of hallucination. If I can't tell the difference between visual hallucination and reality—if there is no perceptual difference between the two—what is it that I really see? The Empiricist theory has a clear answer to that question. What is it that you really see? What you really see are sense-data. Consider what's now in your visual field. Consider those patches of color, those shadings moving across your visual field. Those are your sense-data. Those are what you really see. Everything else is an inference from those. Your knowledge that it's objects you are looking at, real and external to you, is an elaborate inference on the basis of your immediate sense-data. For the Empiricist theory, all perception is a three-place relation. It's a three-place relation between you, the sense-data that you immediately perceive, and the objects behind those sense-data. You don't have immediate contact with those objects even if they originally caused your sense-data.

The theory is set out with variations by philosophers known appropriately as the Empiricists—John Locke, Bishop Berkeley, and David Hume, writing in the first half of the 1700s—but it has ancient precursors and contemporary representatives as well. Is it a psychological theory or a philosophical theory? It's both. In Lecture One, I pointed out that different scientific fields have only gradually peeled off from philosophy, and Empiricism first flourished as a theory at a point before psychology had peeled off as a distinct field. It remained a dominant theory well into the first half of the 20th century. Here's Bertrand Russell taking an Empiricist line:

> To say that you see a star when you see the light that has come from it is no more correct than to say that you see New Zealand when you see a New Zealander in London … The physical space in which you believe the "real" star to be is an elaborate inference; what is given is the private space in which the speck of light you see is situated.

That speck in a private space is a sensation, a [point of] sense-data. Russell says, "You see certain patches of color differently situated in visual space and say you are seeing things outside your body." What you really see are just the patches of color; the rest is an elaborate inference.

There are two important parts to the Empiricist story of perception. First, its fundamental entities, sense-data: The theory is based on an explanation of how things appear in terms of how the sense-data are. The theory offers an immediate explanation for illusion, for example. Why is it that the orange looks gray under green light? The orange looks gray to you because you see something that really is gray, that gray patch in your visual field, the gray sense-data. What happens in hallucination? Here's a classic hallucination. Shakespeare's Macbeth is a character who's tormented by hallucinations. He has horrible dreams. He sees ghosts. He's spoken to by witches. He has decided to murder the king in order to usurp his crown. But Macbeth is wracked by anticipatory guilt, and he hallucinates a murder weapon. His is a visual hallucination. He grasps for it in the air.

> Is this a dagger which I see before me,
> The handle toward my hand? Come, let me clutch thee.
> I have thee not, and yet I see thee still.
> Art thou not, fatal vision, sensible
> To feeling as to sight? or art thou but
> A dagger of the mind, a false creation,
> Proceeding from the heat-oppress'd brain?

> . . . .

> Mine eyes are made the fools o' the other senses,
> Or else worth all the rest; I see thee still,
> And on thy blade and dudgeon gouts of blood …

Macbeth is the victim of his own sense-data. He has the visual sense datum of a dagger before him: "A dagger of the mind, a false creation, proceeding from [his] heat-oppress'd brain."

The second major part of the Empiricist theory is inference. What you see are sense-data, the patterns in your visual field. From those, you infer the existence of external objects and what they're like. There [are] a great deal of psychological data that support the Empiricist picture. Here's an auditory illusion discovered by Diana Deutsch at the University of California at San Diego, one of the primary researchers in the psychology of sound and music. This is called the *glissando illusion*. In order to hear this to best advantage, you want to listen to it through loudspeakers rather than headphones. Ideally, the speakers should be in front of you, perfectly balanced in loudness and equidistant to your left and right. What you will hear is an oboe note that bounces back and forth between speakers, but you will also hear a glissando, a sine wave that glides up and down in pitch. Pay attention to where you hear that as it moves in space. [Audio demonstration.]

Here's the amazing thing about what you just heard: The oboe tone that sounds like it bounces back and forth between speakers does exactly that, but the glissando is actually cut into little bits that do precisely the same thing. The glissando sounds continuous, one smooth sound moving through space in accord with its change in pitch, but it's actually composed of little bits that are cut up just like the oboe tone. They alternate with the oboe tone in each speaker, so that the oboe tone is coming from one speaker when a fragment of the glissando is coming from the other. Here's a sample of what was actually coming out of one speaker. Here is a sample of what was coming out of the other. [Audio demonstrations.] And yet when we put them together, you hear a bouncing oboe tone discretely in the two speakers but a glissando that's smooth and continuous. Here it is one more time.

Why does that happen? The Empiricist has an explanation. We have to make sense of a complicated mixture of sounds all the time, and we do so by identifying them with particular sources. That ringing is the sound of the crossing signal—I better stop. That rumble is the engine of the car behind me. He needs a muffler. That's the whistle of the approaching train. We associate sounds with sources in order to make sense of them. Because the pieces of the glissando are clearly related to each other—one piece continues where the last piece left off—we infer that the sound is coming from a single source. That's why we hear it that way.

The same thing happens with vision. There's an optical illusion reproduced in your outline that consists of two more-or-less vertical lines far apart at the bottom of the page [and] closer together at the top, something like the sides of a capital *A*. Across these are drawn two bold horizontal lines of the same length, one across the two vertical lines toward the bottom of the page, the other across them toward the top. Even if those two bold horizontal lines are exactly the same size, the one toward the top where the vertical lines approach each other will look longer. Why? The Empiricist answer is that you read the vertical lines as if they were railroad tracks going away from you into the distance. You read the vertical lines not as slanted toward each other but, rather, as parallel receding lines. If they were, then something that appeared the way the top horizontal bar does would have to be longer. You infer that it's longer and, therefore, see it as longer. How strong is this pattern of inference? Very strong.

Here's another illustration from Diana Deutsch called *phantom words*. This again is heard to best effect with loudspeakers rather than headphones. The speakers should be in front of you, balanced in loudness and equidistant to the left and right. I want you to listen through the sounds you hear for the words that are being repeated. The words may change as you listen; I want you to pay attention to that, too. They may even change as you change the position of your head. [Audio demonstration.] What words did you hear? Some people have heard the words *respond, Congress, conscious, Christmas, miss me, mistress*. Different people hear different words and hear different words at different times. What was actually coming out of the speakers were syllables of the repeated name *Boris*, alternating in the manner of the glissando illusion. All that's coming from the speakers are bits of *Boris*. Where did all those phantom words come from? From the power of inference. You put them there. But you really did hear them, didn't you?

There's a process of filling in that also goes along with an Empiricist picture of perception. When you look at the scene in front of you, it's all there. You can see everything in front of you without any gaps. If you close one eye, you can still see it all. But in fact, there's something surprising going on in that process. In your outlines, there's an illustration with which you can perform an experiment that reveals the existence of a blind spot in each eye. The illustration consists of a black dot on the left side of the page and a little x on the right, about 2½ inches apart. The experiment runs like this: You close your right eye and hold the page at about a foot in front of you. Focus with your left eye on the x, and you'll be able to see both the dot and the x with no problem. You then move the page slowly closer to you, focusing on the x the entire time.

If you do this right, as the paper gets to be about 6 inches from your eye, the dot will disappear. All you will see is the x, [with] nothing but white paper to the left of it. If you keep moving the paper toward your eye—still concentrating on the x—the dot will reappear at about 3 inches from your eye. Why? Our eyes aren't designed very well. The nerves that run from your retinal cells actually run across the front of the retina rather than behind it. They form a bundle, the cable that's the optic nerve. It then plunges through your retina and back toward your brain. It has to go through at some point, and you won't have photoreceptor cells at that point. That's your blind spot. The dot disappears when its image falls across that blind spot. There's another blind spot in the other eye, of course. You can repeat the experiment for the right eye by closing the left and turning the page over.

When the dot disappears, you don't see a gray area. You see white paper. Your perceptual system has filled in an appropriate background. In variations of the experiment in which the x is in a yellow area and the spot is in a green area, your perceptual system fills it in green—the right color. If you do it with a wallpaper of bricks or little pictures of Marilyn Monroe, it fills in the missing area with bricks or pictures of Marilyn. We have a blind spot because our eyes are wired from the front of the retina, and the optic nerve has to pass through to the brain. Octopus eyes are better designed. They're conveniently wired from the back, and octopi have no blind spot.

Here's an auditory form of filling in from my colleague Arthur Samuel in psychology at Stony Brook. I want you to listen to a recording of music, but unfortunately, it gets interrupted. It'll sound like scratches on an old 78 record, but you can hear the music through the scratches. [Audio demonstration.] You were able to filter out the scratches in order to hear the basic melody, right? Now I'll let you hear what was actually behind the scratches. Why did it sound like there was continuous music there when there wasn't? You filled it in. You inferred it. All of that is perfectly in accord with the Empiricist theory.

We've surveyed some important psychological data in support of the Empiricist theory, the theory that what we perceive are sense-data, from which we infer a world out there. But Empiricism also faces some important problems. One problem has to do with the description of the data. In thinking about perception, we want to take in all the scientific data available. But in order to really understand what the data [are] telling us, we have to be wary of conceptual errors that can slip in with description and interpretation of the data. According to the Empiricist reading of the data, what you have immediate access to are sense-data. From those, you infer other things, the size of objects and the continuity of sound and music, for example. The notion of inference is crucial to the theory, but that concept may be misapplied here. Did you infer the continuity of the glissando?

In its ordinary sense, at least, inference is a conscious and cognitive process, a rational process of moving from one thing to another in thought. Were you aware of any cognitive process, or did you just hear the glissando without doing any explicit thinking at all? We could put the point this way: In the Conan Doyle stories, Sherlock Holmes makes some brilliant and masterful inferences; Conan Doyle calls them "deductions," but never mind that. From footprints, Holmes infers the height and weight of the man who made them. From the mud on Watson's boots, he infers what route Watson took. But does Holmes ever infer that he lives at 221B Baker Street? Does he infer that he is Sherlock Holmes? No, he just knows those things. *Infer* is the wrong word there. Those are too simple and too immediate to be inference. The same thing seems to be true of our perceptual data. *Inference* makes the process sound more cognitive and deliberate than anything we have evidence for here. It's important to note what we're doing here. In asking whether the term *inference* is right, we're not doubting the data. What we're questioning is the Empiricist interpretation of the data. What is it that the psychological data [are] really trying to tell us?

Here's another objection to Empiricism: In Lecture Four, we talked about the inner theater and the conceptual problems it presented. One of those was the problem of the homunculus—the little guy inside your head. If seeing things really were like seeing something on an inner screen, who would be looking at that inner screen? A major problem for Empiricism is that it suggests a homunculus theory all over again. What you see are not things themselves but sense-data, those colored patches in your visual field, for example. On the basis of those, you infer the existence of external objects, of other people, of the entire world around you. But who would be seeing the sense-data, and who would be doing the inferring? The whole Empiricist theory suggests that we should understand perception by understanding what some little inner man would have to do—what he'd have as data and what he'd have to do with it: *infer* things from it.

A third problem is actually a continuation of the first one. That problem was that the term *inference* in the Empiricist theory didn't seem true to our experience. What might an Empiricist say in reply? One thing he could say is that what's going on isn't conscious inference but unconscious inference or implicit inference. That certainly makes the theory more plausible. But note what happens when he does that. The inference step in his theory becomes invisible. You can't see it anymore. You're not supposed to see it. It's unconscious or implicit. That's where the third problem comes in. The Empiricist theory, at its best, says that what you really see are sense-data. Those should be perceptually obvious to you, like Russell's colored patches, in your field of vision. You see those first, and you then infer the existence of real things on the basis of them.

The Empiricist theory is that the sense-data comes first; the inference comes second. But why think things happen in that order? If the inference step is now invisible, why not think it works the other way around: inference first and sense-data second? In many of our examples, in fact, that does seem to be how it works. There isn't a first stage of unprocessed sense-data that's immediate and in your face. When you do get something immediate and in your face, it's already the result of unconscious processing. In many of our examples, sense-data appear to be not the raw materials that go in for unconscious processing but the final product that comes out packaged at the other end. That's true of the glissando illusion, for example. You don't have a first stage of little cut-up bits of glissando. You can't even hear those when you *want* to. What you hear, your sense-data in any sense you can access them, is the already processed smooth glissando. That's true in many of the other cases as well. You don't first have sense-data and then proceed to inferential processing. By the time you have sense-data, the processing has already been done.

Let me step back from those specific problems to a more general reflection. The story that Empiricism tells about perception is essentially a cognitive or rational process—a process of inference from data, whether conscious or unconscious. In Locke, in Kant, in Russell, in much of Western philosophy, the story is told as if our development in the world were the development of isolated individuals caught behind a veil of perception. Something like this: Your task, should you accept it, would be to figure out the nature and character of the external world. We want to see if you can reason your way out of this paper bag of immediate sensations. Maybe that's to be expected. The history of philosophy is a history of people intensely devoted to rationality. It may be an inevitable professional liability that they tend to portray things, even perception, in terms of some kind of rational inference.

The result is that the history of philosophy has tended to portray perception on the model of fairly high-level processing, some kind of rational inference from limited data. But is that the right way to understand perception? There are two other theories that say maybe not. Maybe perception isn't much like inference from sense-data after all. I'll talk about two of these alternatives next time: the Intentionalist and Evolutionary theories of perception.

Lecture Eleven
Perception—Intentionality and Evolution

Scope:

What really happens when we see? Intentionalist and Evolutionary approaches offer alternatives to the Empiricist picture.

In the Intentionalist picture, which can be traced back to the work of Franz Brentano in the 1800s, the "aboutness" of perception is essential to it. Brentano's slogan was: "All perception is perception of." The strange story of Oliver Sacks's patient who mistook his wife's head for his hat fits the theory nicely. So does a wide range of other work in the brain sciences on agnosia and prosopagnosia—the inability to recognize faces. But is it true that *all* perception is "perception of"?

The Evolutionary approach represents a different and more recent theory. What we should expect to find in perception, the Evolutionary theorist says, is not a single tidy picture but an assorted bag of adaptive tricks. Because we are evolved creatures, we will arrive with all the bits and pieces of perceptual equipment that proved evolutionarily successful in the past. Both the results of easy experiments and data from the neuroscience of perception are examined as evidence supporting the Evolutionary approach.

Outline

I. What really happens when we see? The core of the Intentionalist approach is the claim that perception comes with content.

   A. One objection to Empiricism was that the notion of inference seems too conscious, deliberate, and rational. That is precisely where the Intentionalist steps in.

   B. When we feel feathers, we do not feel sense-data from which we infer feathers. We feel the feathers directly. Content is not added; perception comes with content.

   C. The theory traces to Franz Brentano, writing in the late 1800s. Bretano's slogan was: "All perception is perception of." The term *Intentionalist* comes from a term used by the Scholastic philosophers of the Middle Ages to mean "conceptual content."

II. Intentionalism accords with a range of results from the brain sciences.

    A. *Agnosia* means "not knowing" and is used to classify a range of cases in which perceptual content seems to drop out.

    B. Oliver Sacks talks of a patient, Dr. P., who suffers from agnosia.

        1. Dr. P. can describe things before him in detail. "*What is this?*" "About six inches in length … a convoluted red form with a linear green attachment."

        2. But Dr. P. cannot identify the thing as a rose.

    C. Prosopagnosia is an inability to recognize faces.

        1. To a person with prosopagnosia, faces are no more individuating than elbows. Some with prosopagnosia cannot even recognize their own faces.

        2. Often a person with prosopagnosia will not recognize family members or close friends until they speak—it is visual recognition in particular that is affected.

        3. Measures of emotional response may indicate that emotional recognition is in place even when visual recognition is not.

III. Is *all* perception "perception of"? All things considered, how good is the theory?

    A. The theory seems to be incomplete in an important respect.

        1. Smelling the soup is qualitatively different from tasting the soup. Seeing the train approach is qualitative different from hearing the train approach. These perceptions are "about" the same thing but are qualitatively different.

        2. An account in terms of "aboutness" seems to leave out that qualitative difference. But that qualitative character is what the account of the sense-data theorist is built on.

        3. Perhaps neither theory is adequate alone. Empiricism leaves out "aboutness," and Intentionalism leaves out qualitative character.

    B. Further, we can identify apparent counterexamples to the theory. Suppose I just hear a bass rumble or see a pure blue field. Would not those be perceptions that were not perceptions "about" anything?

1. The Intentionalist might say that these cases do have an object: These perceptions are "about" themselves. But that attempt to save the theory weakens it. Even the Empiricist's pure sense-data would count, and the Intentionalist's claim was that we do not perceive sense-data.

2. The Intentionalist might say instead that the bass rumble and the blue field do not qualify as cases of perception. This response, too, weakens the theory: It becomes not a theory of perception in general but merely of perceptual recognition.

C. Our ordinary talk of perception is complex. Some of the ways we think and talk about perception demand a concept of recognition and may, therefore, fit an Intentionalist theory. Other ways we think and talk about perception do not necessarily involve recognition. There, Intentionalism will fail.

IV. The Evolutionary approach is a more recent alternative to Empiricism. It offers a view of perception that is radically nonindividualistic and nonrationalistic.

A. According to the Evolutionary approach, we are evolved organisms and can expect to carry a legacy of bits and pieces of perceptual equipment that proved evolutionarily successful in the past.

B. Saccades offer one piece of evidence in support of an Evolutionary approach.
1. If you track a tennis ball moving in front of you, your eyes move in a smooth pattern.
2. If you try to trace the same route without a moving ball, your eyes move in little jumps called *saccades*.
3. You seem to have two systems of eye-tracking. Why? An Evolutionary explanation is that you have two different systems for two very different tasks: (a) tracking moving prey or predators and (b) scanning a space in front of you.

C. The neurological details of perception offer further support.
1. Ganglion cells respond to *on-center* and *off-center* features in their receptive fields in the retina.

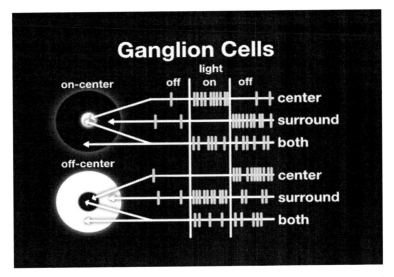

Ganglion Cells

2. On-center cells fire when you shine a light just in the center of the receptive field or if light around the edges goes off. Off-center cells fire when a central light goes off or when light around the edges comes on.

3. The neurons in the primary visual cortex V1 appear to be *line detectors* and *edge detectors*. From there, processing goes to at least 20 higher layers.

4. Visual processing is not deferred to some inner theater in the brain. This, too, fits an Evolutionary picture.

D. The phenomenon of *blindsight* offers further support.

1. People who have suffered damage to the V1 area are cognitively blind. If you ask them to guess simple shapes in front of them, however, their answers are fairly accurate.

2. Nicholas Humphrey, who first studied blindsight in monkeys, thinks that we see in two ways. One is conscious, through V1. When that is knocked out, an evolutionarily older form of vision can remain in place.

V. Which theory of perception wins?

A. Paul Bach-y-Rita has developed an aid for the blind that uses a thin plastic film placed on the tongue.

1. Electrodes on the tongue encode signals from a video camera.

2. Within a short period, blind subjects can recognize shapes and motions well enough to catch a ball thrown to them.
3. The part of the brain recruited for the task is the visual cortex, the same part you use to see.

B. In this lecture we have considered a variety of extraordinary cases: Dr. P's agnosia, blindsight, and blind subjects equipped with a device that stimulates their tongues.
   1. Which of these is really perception? Can these people see or not? The major conceptual mistake may be to think that such questions have a single answer.
   2. Important conceptual work needs to be done in distinguishing and articulating subtleties of the concepts of seeing, recognizing, reacting to, discerning, observing, watching, looking at, attending to, seeing that, glancing, and the like.

Further Resources:

Francis Crick, *The Astonishing Hypothesis: The Scientific Search for the Soul*, chapter 10.

Oliver Sacks, *The Man Who Mistook His Wife for a Hat*. chapter 1.

Michael Bach, *77 Optical Illusions and Visual Phenomena*, http://www.michaelbach.de/ot/.

Exploratorium: The Museum of Science, Art and Human Perception, http://www.exploratorium.edu/seeing/exhibits/index.html (a number of visual illusions).

Questions to Consider:

In this lecture series, we have often tried to decide not whether a theory was absolutely right or absolutely wrong but what might be right about it and what might not be.

The Empiricist says that perception is a two-step process: (1) Sense-data are received and (2) inference is then made on the basis of the sense-data. When you see a house, a hammer, or a friend's face, what you see is really the result of an elaborate process of inference from sense-data.

The Intentionalist says that perception is more immediate than that. "All perception is perception of." Content is not something that needs to be added by inference. Perception *comes* with content: What you see is a friend's face.

To what extent do you think each theorist is right? To what extent is each wrong? To what extent might they be talking past each other?

Lecture Eleven—Transcript
Perception—Intentionality and Evolution

The focus of the last lecture was the Empiricist theory of perception. In this lecture, I want to look at two very different approaches to perception, the Intentional and the Evolutionary approaches. You'll remember that according to the Empiricist theory, what we immediately see [are] not objects but sense-data. Our contact with the objects themselves is indirect. We infer the existence of outside objects on the basis of our sense-data. One of the conceptual problems that I pressed last time was that the notion of *inference* seems inappropriate here, a normal term hijacked for a theoretical purpose. The term *inference* seems too deliberate, cognitive, too rationalistic to fit the facts of perception.

That's precisely where the Intentionalist steps in. The Empiricist picture, says the Intentionalist, doesn't reflect the reality of perception as we know it. When I feel the duck's feathers, I don't feel something else from which I infer the feathers; I feel the feathers. When I see the car in front of me swerve, I don't see patches of color from which I infer the existence of a car and its movement; I see the car swerve. Isn't this just Naïve Realism again? Not quite. The Naïve Realist says that we really are in contact—directly and without mediation—with the world. That's a claim about the real machinery of perception. The Intentionalist starts with something more subtle, a claim about what perception is like in terms of how it feels. What he is saying is, look at how it feels to feel duck feathers. Look at your experience of seeing the car swerve in front of you. Whatever the facts are about light and neurons, that's an experience that comes to you as, or at least as if it were, an experience of direct contact.

Another way of putting the Intentionalist perspective is this: According to the sense-data theory, experience doesn't come with content. Content is something we add; content is something we infer. But our perceptual experience isn't like that. What the Intentionalist points out is that experience, as experienced, comes fully loaded with content. The core idea is that perceptions, as perceived, already have a content, or a direction, or something they're "about." They come that way. The sound I hear already has the content of an ambulance siren and may even arrive loaded with alarm. My visual perception comes fully loaded with content: It's a book I see, the car keys I see, my wallet that I see. This essential perceptual "aboutness," or direction, or content holds even for what happens in illusion and hallucination. Macbeth's hallucination was a hallucination of a dagger. That's what it was "about," and its "aboutness" was built into his perception itself, even if it was a mistaken perception.

Why is the theory called *Intentionalism*? It actually has very little to do with intentions. A major figure in the history of the theory was Franz Brentano, writing in the late 1800s. Brentano's slogan was: "All perception is perception of." He borrowed the term *intentionality* from the word that Scholastic philosophers in the Middle Ages used for "conceptual content." The core of the Intentional theory, then, is that directedness or "aboutness" is essential to perception. Does that accord with results in the neurosciences? Yes. Essential to much of our perception is its direction, what it's "about." Cases in which there is brain damage and perception goes wrong in strange ways make it immediately evident how much of what we think of as normal perception is content-driven. Let's look at some examples.

A range of conditions are categorized under the term *agnosia*. *Agnosia* just means "not knowing" or "lack of knowledge," as in the term *agnostic*. What I want to emphasize is that these might equally be thought of as conditions in which perceptual content drops out, conditions in which patients' perception loses precisely the "aboutness" that the Intentionalist emphasizes. What's intriguing is the specific kind of content that can be knocked out while everything else remains. Oliver Sacks talks of a patient, Dr. P., an intelligent and well-adjusted adult, a very successful music teacher. But Dr. P. has a perceptual problem; he's blind in a certain way. He's object-blind. There's no problem with his eyes; those work just fine. He can describe in minute detail the things that are in front of him. Indeed, if you ask him to describe them in terms of sense-data—the colored patches and movements in his visual field—he'd pass the test without a problem.

Dr. P.'s problem is one of perceptual content. Although he can describe the things in front of him, he can't recognize what they are. His visual agnosia—I'd like to say his "content blindness"—is an inability to see what objects are. If you offer Dr. P. a rose and ask him what it is, he'll say, "About six inches in length, a convoluted red form with a linear green attachment." "*And what is it, Dr. P.?*"

"Not easy to say. It lacks simple symmetry, though it may have a higher symmetry of its own." Interestingly, if you have Dr. P. smell it, he instantly knows what it is; it's a rose. For Dr. P., smell still comes with rose content even though vision doesn't.

If you hand Dr. P. a glove and ask him what it is, he'll say, "A continuous surface infolded on itself. It appears to have five outpouchings, if that's the word." *"A perfectly detailed description, Dr. P., but what is it?"* "A container of some sort?" *"And what would it contain?"* "There are many possibilities. It could be a change purse, for example, for coins of five sizes." *"Could it contain a part of your body?"* Dr. P. shows no light of recognition. And then, of course, there's the fact that as he's leaving the office, he reaches for his hat, grabs his wife's head, and tries to put it on his own. The case of Dr. P. gave Oliver Sacks the title for his book *The Man Who Mistook His Wife for a Hat.*

That kind of case reveals the essential "aboutness" in our perception, an "aboutness" that we might not notice otherwise, precisely because we take it for granted. It's cases like that of Dr. P. that reveal the crucial perceptual role of "aboutness" by showing us what can happen when it's compromised. The content that can drop out in agnosia can be very specific. For example, *prosopagnosia* is an inability to recognize faces. There appears to be a localizable area in the brain that's crucial for recognizing faces. Knock it out with a lesion or a stroke, and people lose that particular kind of perceptual content. Here's a quote from a 50-year-old with prosopagnosia:

> When I was about six, I told my brother I thought robbers were really dumb to cover their faces with masks when they held up a bank. Why bother, I said, when the rest of their body still showed?

To someone with prosopagnosia, faces are no more or less individuating than elbows are. You don't recognize your friends by their elbows; you recognize them first and foremost by their faces. But if you knock out that part of your brain, faces will become like elbows to you; they will lose their distinctive content. In an important sense, you'll no longer see them as faces. In some cases of prosopagnosia, people can't even recognize their *own* faces. Present a middle-aged man suffering from this disorder with a photograph of himself and ask, *"Who is this?"* "Oh, he looks nice, sort of middle-aged. Could it be a senator?" *"No, as a matter of fact, it's you*." Dr. P. could recognize a rose by smell even when he couldn't recognize it by sight. The same kind of thing can happen with prosopagnosia. What's knocked out is often person content just in visual recognition. A person won't recognize a parent, a brother, or a sister until they speak. Upon hearing the voice, the patient will know immediately who it is.

Although visual recognition of faces is knocked out, emotional response may not be. Someone with prosopagnosia won't have any idea who they're looking at, but we can measure their body's emotional response. If you show them a stranger's face, they won't know who it is, and we don't get any particular emotional response. If you show them a picture of their son or their lover, they still won't know who it is, but all measures of their emotional responses will be fully positive. The neuroscientific evidence, then, seems to underscore the central point of Intentionalism: that "aboutness" or "of-ness" is essential to perception as we know it. But let's return to the theory on a conceptual level and in its full form.

What Intentionalism claims is not just that perception often seems to come with content. What Intentionalism claims is that *all* cases of perception are inherently "of" something, and they wouldn't be cases of perception if they weren't. There could be no seeing, no hearing, no feeling, no tasting that didn't come with that kind of content. Intentionalism is the core of Brentano's theory. It's central to the work of Edmund Husserl in the early part of the 20th century. From Husserl, through many twists and turns, it continues as a core thesis of the phenomenological tradition today.

All things considered, how good a theory of perception is Intentionalism? Here's a respect in which the theory seems to be incomplete: There are clearly differences between forms of perception that may have the same intentional object, the same "of-ness" or direction. So smelling the soup is qualitatively different from tasting the soup. Seeing the train approach is qualitatively different from hearing the train approach.

An account in terms of "aboutness" doesn't seem to tell us about the qualitative difference between these perceptual states. Even if all perception has an "aboutness," that's not all it has. In these cases, what an account in terms of "aboutness" seems to leave out is the qualitative character of the perception itself: what it's like to hear the train as opposed to seeing the train. That qualitative character of experience is precisely what the sense-data theorist built his entire account on—visual sense-data of the train as opposed to auditory sense-data of the train. So maybe neither approach is adequate alone. Maybe Empiricism leaves out intentionality and Intentionalism leaves out the qualitative sense-data.

Let's also take a hard look at Intentionalism's core claim, the claim that all cases of perception have an "of-ness" or an "aboutness." Is that true? Certainly, many cases of perception have an "aboutness," but is it really true that they all do? This looks like a counterexample: Suppose I hear a bass rumble. It's not an electric guitar string; it's not an approaching locomotive. It's just a sensation of a bass rumble. It's just that sound, and it's just there. Or here's another case: I open my eyes in the hospital, and I see a blue field before me. That's all I see. I distinguish no ceiling; I recognize no building parts. I'm not even sure that I'm looking at something external to me. Can those things happen? Certainly. Aren't they direct counterexamples for the claim that all cases of perception are about something? There are two directions the Intentionalist can take in the face of these examples. Let's follow his argument through both of them.

First, the Intentionalist might say that these are not counterexamples because these cases *do* have an object. In the case of the bass note and the blue field, Intentionalists have often said those, too, are about something. If nothing else, they're about themselves. Although that's an attempt to save the theory, I think it just weakens it. Part of the impetus for the theory was a criticism of Empiricism. We don't perceive sense-data because perception essentially has content; it's perception of things, about things. If the theory has to say that the experience of the bass note and the blue field are still of things, about things, then even the Empiricist's pure sense-data would qualify as of things, about things. On that line, the Intentionalist critique of Empiricism would fail.

Here's a second tack the Intentionalist could take: Instead of saying that there's something these experiences are about, he can admit that there isn't. How can he save the claim that all perception involves content? By denying that those cases really count as perception. So the Intentionalist might say the case of the bass note and the blue field do happen; it's just that they're not perception. Something is happening in the case of the bass note—even something experiential—but it's not hearing, not even the illusion of hearing, precisely because it doesn't come with an of. Something's happening in the case of the blue field—even something experiential—but you don't see anything because that requires content. That again would save the theory by weakening it.

On that interpretation, the theory is no longer a theory of the full range of perceptual experience. It has protected itself by limiting itself just to perceptual recognition. Indeed, all the support from studies of agnosia can be interpreted this way. What the object-blind Dr. P. has lost, we might say, isn't his vision but his ability to recognize the things he sees as gloves, or hats, or as his wife's head. If Intentionalism shrinks to just a theory about the recognition aspects of perception, it's a much thinner theory than it might have at first appeared. It would amount to this simple claim: that perceptual recognition is always of something. Since recognition is always of something, that's hardly surprising. We'd like our theories to be more informative than that.

So what's the verdict on Intentionalism? The truth is that the ways in which we ordinarily think and talk about perception are complex. We can say yes, you saw the signal, but did you *really* see it? What we mean in context may be, did you see that the signal had changed to yellow? Someone might say, yes, you saw her dress, but did you really see her dress? In one context, that might be meant as, did you see the incredible handwork in the embroidery? In another context, what might be meant is, did you notice that her dress was identical to her sister's? In the way we think and talk about perception—this is complex—some concepts may fit an Intentionalist account and some may not. Sometimes we use perceptual concepts in a way that requires certain kinds of recognition; sometimes we don't. "I saw the signal swinging in the wind, but I didn't realize it had changed to yellow."

Let me turn to a third theory, and a more recent contender, the Evolutionary approach. In the last lecture, I ended with a reflection on the fact that Empiricism—indeed, the whole history of philosophy of perception—emphasizes rationality and the perspective of the individual. The history of philosophy has tried to tell the story of perception as if it were the single individual attempting to rationally construct a world from the limited input of sense-data. The Evolutionary approach is entirely the opposite. It's radically nonindividualistic and radically nonrationalistic. I'm not sure this approach has yet crystallized as a full philosophical theory of perception, but here's the general line of thought: We are evolved organisms. We had to develop certain skills to survive in a certain environment. Successfully dealing with important aspects of that environment has been absolutely necessary for our survival.

But evolution is a "catch-as-catch-can" process. If there's something in the way an organism interacts with the world that increases the chances of survival and reproduction, that something will be passed onto future generations, whatever that something is. There will be thousands of characteristics of an animal—anatomical characteristics, behavioral characteristics, information-processing characteristics—that arise by chance but turn out to be advantageous and, so, are passed on. The Evolutionary approach predicts that when we look at perception, we'll find that it, too, is a hodgepodge of inherited tricks. What we should expect to find is a bunch of different perceptual traits that could have developed any which way, adopted just as long as they work: overlapping forms of sensory processing, redundant perceptual systems, built-in tools for gaining food and avoiding prey, hardwired shortcuts for fast and effective decision-making.

If the Evolutionary story is right, we'll also find that those perceptual abilities may be severely limited. They arose as tricks to increase the success of particular kinds of organisms in particular kinds of environments. They may, therefore, be limited to the environments from which our kind of organism came. Let me outline some of the data that fit this Evolutionary approach and [those that don't] seem to fit either of the other theories we've considered. First, some simple facts about how your eyes move. This is an experiment you can do with a friend or two. Suppose we put you in a chair [and] tell you not to move your head, but you're perfectly free to move your eyes from side to side, not your head, just your eyes. There you sit. All that'll be moving is your eyes. We throw a tennis ball across the room in front of you, and we have you track the ball with your eyes. Maybe one friend throws the ball while the other watches your eyes. Here's how your eyes will move: smoothly and evenly, tracking the tennis ball as it moves from one side of the room to the other.

Now we ask you to do the same thing without the tennis ball: Move your eyes across the room just *as if* a tennis ball were sailing across in front of you. Imagine it's passing in front of you, and make your eyes track the imaginary tennis ball. Here's what happens: The second time, your eyes will not move smoothly. They'll traverse the route of the tennis ball in little jumps, little fits and starts—jerk, jerk, jerk, jerk, jerk. The fact is that when you scan any stationary scene, your eyes always move in those little jumps; they're called *saccades*. When you scan a room, your eyes are jumping from the car keys, to the counter, to the refrigerator, to the windowsill—jerk, jerk, jerk, jerk, jerk. They always move that way whether you know it or not. In fact, you can't consciously make your eyes move any other way. When you're tracking a moving object, on the other hand, they can lock on the object and follow it smoothly, no jerks at all.

Your perceptual system, then, uses two radically different kinds of eye motion. Why? There's no explanation for the two kinds of eye motion on the Empiricist account. There's no explanation on the Intentionalist account. But it fits an Evolutionary account very nicely. You have two different eye-motion systems because your evolutionary forebears needed to move their eyes in two different ways for two different purposes. For tracking moving food or watching moving predators, eye tracking that locked on the moving target was a good idea. That's why you have it. For looking around for something important in a static scene, on the other hand, it's a matter of little bits of information that matter. "Food here, food there?" Why waste time moving your eyes slowly from one spot to another when you can just jump from place to place in order to scan for important information? It has been hypothesized that frogs have only the moving-target perception system. They can, therefore, see things only when they're moving. It's said that's why a frog will starve to death in a box filled with nutritious but stationary flies.

Here's some more data on the brain: When you look at the neuroscience of visual processing, it doesn't suggest either Empiricism or Intentionalism. It's certainly not as if recognition—for example, face recognition—is something that happens immediately in your eyes or optic nerves, like Intentionalism suggests. But on the other hand, the results from neuroscience don't suggest Empiricism either. It's not as if we have to collect all the sense-data and then perform some inference at a distinct stage down the line. In order to sort this out, I'm going to give you some more detailed information about how our visual processing works.

The retina is composed of rods and cones, light-sensitive receiving cells. From there, impulses are sent along the optic nerve by ganglion cells. But the system doesn't work the way you might expect. There's not a single ganglion cell assigned to each rod or cone, and they don't just send a message that this rod is on or this rod is off. What each ganglion cell responds to is not a single rod or cone but several, a certain area of rods and cones. The part of the visual field associated with a particular ganglion is called its *receptive field*. What the ganglion responds to in particular is a small spot of light turned on or off in its receptive field.

There are several kinds of ganglion cells, which respond to specific conditions in their receptive fields. Two of them are *on-center* and *off-center cells*. Here's how an on-center cell works: If it's in darkness, it won't fire. If you shine a light on its entire receptive field, it still won't fire. It fires when a light goes on just in the center of its field. Just to make things complicated, it also fires if light around the edges of its receptive field goes off. Roughly speaking, the off-center cells do the same thing in reverse. They fire when a central light goes off or when light just around the edges comes on. To speak anthropomorphically, what the cells are paying attention to is a very specific pattern of contrast and change between the center and the edges of their receptive fields. An illustration in your outline shows some of the complexities in what ganglion cells respond to. The on-center and off-center are just two types of ganglion cells. There's also a distinction between M cells, which have a larger response area, and P cells, geared to fine detail and especially color. But what even P cells respond to is not color per se but color contrast.

The important point about all of this is that it looks like the information processing of sensory data starts immediately. If what you're trying to do is evolve a successful animal, there's no need for some pure sense-data–level process later down the line. The more processing that can be done up front, the better. The fact is that a lot is done up front. If you follow the optic nerve as it leads back into the brain, it'll take you first to the lateral geniculate nucleus, part of the thalamus, centrally located toward the bottom of your brain. From there, impulses go to what has been classified as V1, or the first visual processing area in the cortex. What kind of computation goes on in the primary visual cortex? What makes the neurons in V1 fire?

The neurons in V1 appear to be *line detectors* and *edge detectors*. It looks like computation has gone from the on-center and off-center detection in the ganglion cells of the optic nerve to higher-order line detection in V1. For any particular neuron there, there's a line orientation at which it fires best. Some neurons fire best for vertical lines, and they stop firing if the line is as little as 15 degrees off. Others fire when there's a line at 45 degrees, for example. The things that your sensory system pays attention to in its early stages, then—the forms of detection critical to the first steps in the brain's processing—don't sound much like the Empiricist's sense-data. What your visual system is paying attention to are contrasts and lines and edges, not the tidy colored patches that the sense-data theorists described. Not the kind of information you might want for a rational reconstruction of perception but exactly what an evolving animal might need to survive.

We've tracked only the early stages of sensory processing, which continues through deeper and deeper layers of processing. First on-center and off-center detection, then lines and edges; how many layers? Researchers have identified at least 20. Somewhere in there, color recognition has to happen. Somewhere in there, face recognition has to appear. But those aspects of processing will be very far down the line. There's an intriguing phenomenon called *blindsight*. There are people who have suffered brain damage to the V1 area I just described. The transfer of neural impulses is fatally interrupted. They can no longer see, not because of eye damage, but rather, because of brain damage.

If you ask them to identify where a light source is in front of them, they'll tell you the task is hopeless; they can't see a thing. They've been blind since the accident. But if you ask them to guess where the light is, their answers are fairly accurate, usually within 5 to 10 degrees. Some blindsight patients can accurately distinguish simple shapes. Two patients denied being able to see an object, but when asked to guess and reach for it, they not only reached for it in the right direction, but they adjusted their hands appropriately to the size and shape of the object. What's going on here? The psychologist and philosopher Nicholas Humphrey, who first demonstrated blindsight in monkeys, thinks there are two ways in which we see. One is conscious; that's the seeing that is no longer available to the blindsighted. What they still have in place, he proposes, is an older evolutionary system that works by different routes.

So which theory wins? Is it Empiricism, Intentionalism, or an Evolutionary approach that's giving us the best story about perception? I think there's a major part of the puzzle that has been insufficiently attended to in theories of perception: the conceptual complexity of our *notions* of perception. Let me add one further example to some of those reviewed in this lecture. Paul Bach-y-Rita was an engineer at the University of Wisconsin who has worked for decades on developing aids for the blind. The latest of his devices is a thin, flexible plastic film that's placed on the tongue. It's embedded with electrodes that carry signals from a video camera, translating visual signals to sensations that can be felt on the tongue. With a short period of training, blind subjects can recognize shapes and track motions. They can see well enough to catch a ball thrown to them. What's even more amazing is the part of the brain that's activated when they do that. It's the visual cortex at the back of the head. It's V1, precisely that part of the brain that's activated when *you* see things.

Now let's review some of the cases we've looked at. There are cases of brain damage in which people's eyes work fine, but they'll tell you they're blind. In blindsight cases, patients can nonetheless distinguish shapes and even navigate through a room by guessing. There are cases in which people's eyes don't work at all, and yet with the aid of impulses on the tongue, they, too, can navigate in the world and catch a ball thrown to them. Dr. P.'s eyes and his visual cortex both work fine, but he can look directly at his wife's head and have no clue as to whether it's a hat. Which of these is really perception? Which of these is really seeing? We can ask in each case, "Well, can he see or can't he?"

The major conceptual mistake may be to think that there's going to be any single answer to those questions. A great deal of conceptual work still needs to be done in distinguishing and articulating the shades and subtleties of the ways we talk and think about perception, in both extraordinary cases and in ordinary, everyday contexts. There's work to be done in clarifying our concepts of seeing, recognizing, reacting to, discerning, observing, watching, looking at, attending to, seeing that, glancing, glimpsing, examining, and the like. There's also a great deal of conceptual work that needs to be done on context because it can depend on context what you're really asking when you ask whether someone saw her dress or not.

©2008 The Teaching Company.

My guess is that the forms of perception that the Empiricists focus on have a small but limited place in that conceptual tangle. My guess is that the Intentionalist's emphasis on recognition also plays an important, but also a limited, role in that conceptual tangle. My guess is that the Evolutionary approach is onto something and onto something important. A number of the results we've reviewed indicate that we don't have a single process of perception. I'm also confident that we don't have a single concept of perception. The conceptual work demanded is to further clarify the meaning of the range of perceptual concepts that we use, how they interrelate, and how they function in context.

In this lecture and the last, we've concentrated on philosophical theories of perception. In the next lecture, I'll take the issue further but with an additional twist that brings in some of the thinking in earlier lectures. I'll look at perception in terms of how our minds function in the world.

Lecture Twelve
A Mind in the World

Scope:

Our understanding of minds demands that we understand both the organisms of which they form a part and the environments crucial to those organisms. In order to understand the mind, we have to understand the mind in the world.

This lecture explores the "mind-in-the-world" approach as it has been developed in psychology, philosophy, and robotics. J. J. Gibson's psychological theory of "affordances" is outlined against the background of its development in training World War II pilots. The classic psychological experiment of inverting lenses directly addresses questions of the mind in the world and is considered in terms of Alva Noë's three-stage analysis of the experiment. Philosophers Andy Clark and David Chalmers offer a thought experiment intended to show that memories, beliefs, and thinking itself can consist of parts of the external world outside our skins. This lecture examines each of these views, highlighting both core truths and misleading overstatements.

Rodney Brooks has arrived at a similar theory in robotics by intentionally negating the assumptions of others in the field. Brooks's robots are built with an eye to embodied intelligence: a mind in the world rather than separate from it.

Outline

I.   This lecture follows the theme of a "mind in the world" through three disciplines: psychology, philosophy, and robotics.

II. The central idea accords with both Functionalist and Evolutionary approaches.

   A. The Functionalist claims that mental states are functional states of an organism, and organisms function in environments. For the Functionalist, the link from mind to world is direct.

   B. The young Charles Darwin was fascinated by differences in the Galápagos finches. Why are there so many different kinds of finches?

1. Darwin concluded that so many different kinds of finches exist because so many different environments exist.
2. Environmental pressure is a crucial element in the evolutionary process. It is environments that do the selecting in natural selection.

III. J. J. Gibson argued that the mind can be understood only in terms of the world of which it's a part.

A. Gibson first developed the theory in training World War II pilots.

B. The core of Gibson's theory is that what we perceive are not sense-data. We do not see base-level sensations of any kind from which we have to infer objects and their motions. According to Gibson, "Eyes evolved so as to see the world, not a picture."

C. What we perceive, Gibson says, are "affordances."
  1. Affordances are possibilities for action.
  2. Perception is direct, rather than inferential. It is tied directly to meaningful action in the world.
  3. Gibson's theory is tied both to the Evolutionary approach and the Intentionalist theory.

IV. Gibson's theory has led to important research, but it is not adequate if taken as a complete theory of perception.

A. Does it tell us the full story of what is happening in perception?
  1. We are sometimes fooled: We think we see an open door, but it turns out to be a clever painting.
  2. Why? Affordances are defined as real features of the environment—for example, real open doors. For that reason, Gibson's theory is unable to explain perceptual error.

B. Is it true that affordances are all we ever perceive?
  1. In order to explain illusions, we could vary the theory to say that what we perceive are apparent affordances: apparently open doors, for example.
  2. What do the real and apparent affordances have in common? The answer seems to demand some lower-level perceptual elements. But that explanation violates the anti–sense-data spirit of the entire theory.

C. We might still agree that we cannot understand the mind unless we understand how the mind works in the world. But we need a critical qualification to Gibson's theory: that "perceiving affordances" is not the whole story of perception.

V. The classic psychological experiment of the inverted lenses underscores the theme.

   A. What happens if you put on glasses that reverse things right to left? The philosopher Alva Noë has analyzed the result in terms of three stages:
      1. The first stage is one of disorientation.
      2. In the second stage, things become clear but are distinctly reversed.
      3. In the third stage, the world "rights itself" again.

   B. The third stage offers clear support for the "mind-in-the-world" approach but remains philosophically perplexing.
      1. In a high school dramatization, the experience of inversion was illustrated by turning the camera over. The subjective experience of things coming "right again" was illustrated by turning the camera upright again.
      2. An alternative view is that one simply gets used to the inversion and is once again able to navigate in the world.
      3. The deepest philosophical question is whether these two accounts are really different. Perhaps they amount to the same thing.

VI. Philosophers Andy Clark and David Chalmers have pressed the idea further in terms of what they call "extended mind."

   A. Where does the mind stop and the rest of the world begin? Clark and Chalmers argue that a range of our mental activities can extend beyond our skin, composed in part of things in the world.

   B. They offer the thought experiment of Inga and Otto.
      1. Inga has a background belief that the museum is on 53rd Street.
      2. Otto suffers from Alzheimer's disease but carries a notebook in which he writes down information. He checks his notebook and finds that the museum is on 53rd Street.

3. Inga's beliefs and memories are in her head in this example. Otto's beliefs and memories are in his notebook.

C. If that account were right, I could announce a complete and total cure for *anterograde amnesia*, a condition in which one is unable to lay down new long-term memories.
   1. The cure: a pencil and notebook.
   2. Clark and Chalmers concede that Otto's beliefs or memories would not normally be classified as such, but the two philosophers think they should be.

D. Many of the things we do involve parts of the external world in crucial ways.
   1. The video game Tetris allows you to think by rotating shapes physically.
   2. The calculations involved in balancing a checkbook would be much more difficult without pencil and paper.
   3. A key to logic puzzles in standardized tests is to make a sketch or diagram.
   4. The mathematician and philosopher Alfred North Whitehead made a similar point in terms of looking for the right symbolism to use in approaching a problem.
   5. Clark and Chalmers mention language and linguistic interaction with other people as a form of "extended mind."

VII. Innovative work in robotics has shown a parallel emphasis on the mind in the world.

A. Rodney Brooks is head of the Robotics Lab at MIT and founder of the iRobot Company. In autobiographical notes, he has said that he tries to find an assumption that everyone is making, then negates that assumption.

B. One goal for robotics has long been the creation of humanoid robots—robots that walk, talk, and think like people.
   1. Brooks points out that evolution did not start with people, and he thinks that robotics should not either.
   2. Brooks attempts to build systems bit by bit, moving slowly toward higher intelligence, just as evolution did.

C. NASA uses robots for space exploration and approached Brooks for ideas in designing a 100-pound robot appropriate for planetary exploration.

    1. Why one 100-pound robot, rather than 100 one-pound robots?

    2. Brooks's proposal was for a crowd of small robots, "fast, cheap, and out of control."

D. In developing robots, Brooks rejects the idea that they must form representations in a central processor. Why not use distributed intelligence?

E. Throughout Brooks's work runs the idea of embodied intelligence: a mind in the world rather than separate from it.

Further Resources:

Rodney Brooks, "Intelligence without Representation," *Artificial Intelligence* 47.

Andy Clark and David Chalmers, "The Extended Mind," *Analysis* 58.

J. J. Gibson, "Autobiography," in *Reasons for Realism: Selected Essays of James. J. Gibson*, Edward Reed and Rebecca Jones, eds.

Errol Morris, *Fast, Cheap, and Out of Control*, 1997, video.

Questions to Consider:

1. If Clark's and Chalmers's extended-mind theory is right, part of your memory is not in your brain but, rather, in a file drawer or a photo album. To what extent does that fit with your experience? To what extent does it not?

2. Consider this thought experiment: NASA has asked you to plan a robot exploration of the planet Jupiter. The agency can afford a payload of only 100 pounds of robotics and must decide among (a) a single large robot, (b) several medium-sized robots with somewhat reduced capabilities, or (c) Rodney Brooks's recommendation of 100 very small robots, each with more reduced capabilities. What strategy do you recommend? Why?

Lecture Twelve—Transcript
A Mind in the World

Lecture Eight emphasized an approach to minds as embodied. The core idea of such an approach is that we won't be able to understand the mind if we insist on thinking of it in isolation, as a brain in a vat or as a mind separate from a body. To really understand minds, we have to understand the organisms whose minds they are. This lecture continues that kind of emphasis but extends it further. Just as we go wrong if we think of the mind in isolation from the organism, we can also go wrong if we think of the organism in isolation. Organisms are what they are, they do what they do, they function as they function largely because of the environment of which they're a part. Our understanding of minds demands that we understand both the organisms of which they form a part and the environments crucial to those organisms. In order to understand the mind, we have to understand the mind in the world.

In this lecture, I want to explore that idea in several different forms: as it shows up in psychology, as it shows up in philosophy, and as it shows up in the development of robotics. The central idea is very much in line with the Functionalist approach. What are mental states? The Functionalist claims that mental states are functional states of an organism. But organisms function in an environment. For Functionalists, the link from mental states to environment—from mind to world—will be quite direct. The central idea is also very much in line with the Evolutionary approach to perception outlined in the previous lecture.

In 1831, the British ship *Beagle* left on an expedition to chart the coastline of South America. The young Charles Darwin signed on as an unpaid naturalist. The Galápagos are a cluster of 19 volcanic islands off the west coast of Ecuador. [Among] the things that impressed Darwin during the voyage of the *Beagle* were the Galápagos finches. The finches of the different islands are clearly related—variations on a theme—and yet they differ from one another in habit, coloration, and in the size and shape of their beaks. There are woodpecker finches, large cactus finches, sharp-beaked ground finches, mangrove finches, vegetarian finches. Why so many different finches with such varied characteristics? The answer that struck Darwin was because of so many different environments.

Environmental pressure is a crucial element in the evolutionary process. It is in particular environments that certain variations succeed or fail. In that sense, it's environments that do the selecting in natural selection. If perception has been molded by evolutionary pressures, we can expect it, too, to be molded by environment. If mind has been molded by evolutionary pressures, we can expect it to be shaped to fit the world. In psychology, it was James J. Gibson who argued most vehemently that you can only understand the mind in terms of the world of which it's a part. Gibson concentrated on perception—in particular, on visual perception—and that's where we'll start.

In World War II, Gibson was assigned to research the training of pilots for the Army Air Corps. Much of his later work stemmed from that experience. In trying to train pilots, it quickly became clear that studying written descriptions of flying maneuvers was of little use. Lectures weren't any better. Static diagrams of landings and takeoffs didn't help much either, particularly when they were drawn from a perspective outside the plane. Motion pictures could be useful, but only when they were motion pictures from the perspective of the pilot. Here are Gibson's words:

> What had to be learned was a system of how to aim at a moving target (a fighter plane) from a moving platform (a bomber). As the situation changed, the action changed. The film showed how one thing varied with another. The book and the talk could graph it, represent stages of it, and describe it in several ways, but it couldn't display the continuous covariation in time. Moreover, the film could make use of the subjective camera, taking the point of view of the learner and displaying how the situation would look to him.

Best of all was a form of training that made learners an active part of that environment, training that put them into something like real situations in something like real time and that demanded interaction with the environment. That's why we now train pilots using flight simulators.

Here's a clear core of Gibson's theory: What is perceived is not sense-data nor anything like it. We do not see base-level sensations of any kind from which we have to infer objects and their motions. Gibson notes that "Eyes evolved so as to see the world, not a picture." What any organism is going to see is what is important for it in the environment. According to Gibson, what it perceives are "affordances." What are affordances? Possibilities for action. The features of your environment afford you certain possibilities. That door is something you can walk through; it affords a certain prospect for motion. That window is something you can look through. That hammer is something you can use to hit nails. Those possibilities for action are affordances, and what you perceive is less the things around you than the things they can let you do.

You can see how this would work in training pilots. You have to train them for fast and accurate action. What they have to be sensitive to in their environments are precisely those aspects that afford effective action. In later work, Gibson generalized that story as a story about all perception. Perception is direct rather than inferential. It's tied directly to meaningful action in the world. He says:

> ... the infant does not begin by first discriminating the qualities of objects and then learning the combinations of qualities [that go together to make objects ... Perceived] objects are not built up from qualities; it is the other way around. The affordance of an object is what the infant begins by noticing. The meaning is observed before ... the color and the form ...

Although perception was his first target, Gibson eventually extended the picture to include all cognition. All aspects of mind are aspects of a mind in the world. I've emphasized the ties between this kind of approach and evolution, but Gibson's approach also ties in with an Intentionalist theory of perception. The Intentionalist theory, like Gibson's, is anti–sense-data. The Intentionalist theory, like Gibson's, claims that perception comes with content up front. The Intentionalist claim is that perception is always perception *of* something, and Gibson agrees. He says that perception is always perception of affordances.

Gibson's theory has important things to say about what perception is really like. It has led to important research on what a perceptual system like ours really picks up on. But a theory can have those virtues and still turn out to be wrong if taken as a complete theory of perception. That was the charge leveled against Intentionalism in the previous lecture. Gibson's approach is open to a similar criticism.

Let's admit that we do often perceive affordances, that what we notice and respond to are, first and foremost, prospects for action in an environment. Two questions still remain: Does that tell us the full story of what's happening in perception? And, secondly, is it true that affordances are all we ever perceive?

In answer to the first question, there's a simple reason to think that Gibson's theory can't be giving us the full story. The simple fact is that we're sometimes fooled. Sometimes we think we see the other train moving forward, but it's actually our train moving backward. Sometimes we think we see an open door, and it turns out to be a clever painting. It's possible to set things up so that someone thinks they're looking through a window open to the outside when what they really see through the window is just a back-projection on a screen. Affordances are defined in such a way that they have to be real features of the environment—real open doors, real scenes through windows. A theory that says you perceive affordances will, therefore, leave something out. It's not going to be able to explain why we're fooled in these cases because the painted door, and the apparent motion of the train, and the scene outside the window *aren't* real.

In answer to the second question, then, it looks like it can't be true that all we ever perceive are affordances. We could vary the theory so that what we perceive are apparent affordances—apparently open doors, apparent scenes through windows. But then we'll want to know what the real and the merely apparent affordances have in common. What is it about the painting that explains the fact that we mistook it for a door? It looks like any theory is going to have to say something like this: "Well, in both cases, what you saw was a door-like shape and what looked like a handle, and the light was right ..." As you can see, that explanation is not written in terms of affordances. That explanation is written in terms of some lower-level perceptual elements that indicate real affordances in one case and [those] that fool us in the other cases. Uh-oh, those are precisely the lower-level perceptual elements that Gibson said we never perceive.

We might still agree that we can't understand the mind unless we understand how the mind works in the world, but it looks like we have to add a critical qualification to Gibson's theory. Just saying that the mind reacts to the world around it or perceives affordances won't be the whole story of perception—there are particular ways that the mind does that—and we'll still want to know how. There's a classic psychological experiment that underscores the theme of the "mind in the world," here again, in terms of perception. This is the experiment of the inverted lenses. If you remove the eyepiece from a microscope or a telescope and you look through just that lens, you'll see everything inverted, exactly like looking at a photograph upside down. What if you wore a pair of glasses with lenses like that for an extended period of time, a pair of glasses that turned everything upside down?

The classic experiments have been done with something similar, with reversing lenses that switch things left to right, like a photograph that has been printed through the wrong side of the negative. What should be on the left is on the right; what should be on the right is on the left. What if you wore a pair of glasses with left-right reversing lenses for an extended period of time? Alva Noë is a philosopher who has continued the Gibsonian tradition by arguing for an "enactment" theory of perception and who uses this classic experiment as a prime piece of evidence for the theory. Noë analyzes what happens when you put on reversing lenses into three stages.

The first stage is one of disorientation. You might think that everything simply looks reversed, but the initial impression is significantly more bewildering than that, particularly when you try to move. One subject described the experience like this:

> ... every movement of my head gives rise to the most unexpected and peculiar transformations of objects in the visual field. The most familiar forms seem to dissolve and reintegrate ... parts of figures run together ... at other times, they run apart ... Countless times I was fooled by these extreme distortions and taken by surprise ...

In the second stage, things become clearer, but they are distinctly reversed. What should be on the right looks like it's on the left. If you try to pour a glass of water from a pitcher, you'll miss the glass. There are also clashes between the senses. You see your left hand on the right, although you still feel it on the left. You see the teakettle steaming on the left, but the sound it's making is clearly coming from the right. The third stage is the one that most effectively shows the "mind-in-the-world" approach, though it's also philosophically perplexing in certain ways. In the third stage, subjects say that the world has righted itself. Things again look the way they should. After a few days of wearing reversing lenses, things on the left look like they're on the left. Things on the right look like they're on the right. Cross-sensory conflicts disappear. Despite the fact that you still have these reversing lenses on, you can ride a bicycle as well as you ever could.

All of this supports the basic story: that perception is keyed to the world and so necessarily adapts to it. The mind is a mind geared to action in the world, and the brain's plasticity adapts perception to fit action in the world. The new environment of reversing lenses is a mirror-image environment, like Alice *Through the Looking Glass*. In order to fit that environment, the mind has to change, so it does. Interestingly enough, different aspects of your mind may accommodate to reversing lenses at different rates. You may be able to ride a bicycle down a normal street, for example, though the writing in the shop windows *still* looks backwards to you.

When you take off the reversing lenses, the mind has to change again. What the classic experiments show is that subjects have to go through the same three stages in order to restore normal vision. Initially, the world will look confused, then reversed right to left, and then it will right itself again. I said that the third stage of the process—in which the world "rights itself"—offers clear support for the "mind-in-the-world" approach, though that stage is still philosophically perplexing in certain ways. The perplexity can be put like this: What happens in that third stage?

I remember a dramatization of the inverted-lenses experiment in a high school science film. It used full inverting lenses so that everything flipped over, up to down. The film followed a script that ran like this: "Here's what the world looks like in the second stage." For that section, the camera itself was turned upside down, filming, as I remember, from a moving car. "But eventually, even though you're wearing inverted lenses, things again look like this." The camera was again rotated on its axis, and everything was right-side up again. That's one account of what happens in the third stage. There is some level of perceptual experience—some sense-data or internal movie—that comes to match precisely the sense-data that you had before putting on the inverted lenses. Things are back to normal in that the sensations you experience are just what they were before.

190

Here's a different account of what happens: You just get used to it. Your visual experience hasn't flipped like the movie camera in the film. It's just that you've become accustomed to the new format of perceptual information. You can move in the world successfully. You do what you need to do. You no longer notice the reversal. Things are back to normal, not in the sense that the sensations are the same as they were, but that they're usable in all the ways that they need to be. Which account is right? This is a philosophical perplexity that I'll return to in Lecture Twenty when I talk about color. What subjects say is that things are "right again," and they can demonstrate it by moving successfully in the world. But that claim could be true on either account. It all depends on what "things are right again" means. Does it mean that the visual sensations have literally flipped and righted [themselves] in that way? Or is it merely that we have cognitively righted ourselves in terms of a different perceptual input?

One aspect of the problem is trying to figure out which of these two different accounts is right. Another aspect is deeper—trying to figure out whether there really are two different accounts here at all. Perhaps it's not so clear that there really is a difference between a flip of sensations and a cognitive accommodation to input. Perhaps they amount to the same thing. If you wear inverted lenses long enough, things will seem "right again." Perhaps that "right again" is all there is to it. After you've worn the inverted lenses for a while and you can once again ride a bike, we could ask you, "Is this a change of sensation and not of cognition or of cognition and not of sensation?" Because sensation and cognition inevitably work together, you may not be able to answer that question. If sensation and cognition *inevitably* work together as part of a mind in the world, the question might not even make sense.

Perception is a primary case in which we can see the mind at work in the world, but it's not the only case. The philosophers Andy Clark and David Chalmers have pressed the idea much further in terms of what they call "extended mind." "Where does the mind stop and the rest of the world begin?" they ask. They don't think your mind ends at you skull, nor does it end at your skin. What they argue is that a broad range of our mental activities—memory, belief, and thinking itself—can extend beyond our skins. They propose that our mental activities are often composed in part of things in the external world. If two scholars write an article, whose name appears first? Usually it's either the senior researcher or the one who has done the most work. A footnote in Clark and Chalmers's work indicates that they did something unusual. They ordered the authors in terms of how committed they were to this central claim. Clark was more convinced that the external world forms a part of our mental events—Chalmers somewhat less—so it was Clark's name that appeared first.

Clark and Chalmers offered this thought experiment: Inga hears of an exhibit at the Museum of Modern Art and decides to go. She thinks for a moment, seems to remember that it's on 53rd Street, and walks in that direction. Clark and Chalmers say:

> Both memory and belief are at work here. Inga retrieves a location from memory. It's also the case that Inga believed the museum was on 53rd Street, even at the beginning of the story and before she thought about it. She had a "non-occurrent" belief, much like your belief that there were people in North America before Columbus arrived—a "non-occurrent" belief on your part that was brought to mind only because I mentioned it.

Now consider the case of Otto. Otto suffers from Alzheimer's disease but has learned to carry a notebook in which he writes down new information. Otto hears of an exhibit at the Museum of Modern Art, and he decides to go. He consults his notebook, which says it's on 53rd Street, and he walks in that direction. Otto's notebook isn't inside his skull, but it does for him just what Inga's memory does for her. Otto's memory, Clark and Chalmers say, is in his notebook. The entries in his notebook, moreover, function just like Inga's non-occurrent beliefs. They say that Otto has beliefs just as Inga does; it's just that Otto's beliefs are entries in his notebook.

It seems to me that there's something right about this batch of claims—and something wrong. If Clark and Chalmers are trying to express their view using normal concepts of belief, memory, and the like, they've gone off the rails. Otto does indeed use things written in his notebook much as Inga uses background beliefs, but that doesn't mean they are background beliefs. A clear indication that they've gone off the rails is this: Suppose I announced a new and revolutionary cure for certain memory problems. The ability to lay down new memories, it turns out, is tied to the hippocampus—curving structures that wrap around the thalamus deep in your head. We know that because people who have had both sides of the hippocampus removed are unable to form new memories. But luckily, I've discovered a complete and total cure. The cure for memory problems? A notebook and a pencil. Ridiculous, you say, and I agree.

There's a movie that uses something like this theme, an interesting but disturbing movie called *Memento*. Leonard Shelby is the protagonist of *Memento*. His wife has been killed, and he's out to get the killer. But Leonard was attacked in the incident as well and suffers from a condition called *anterograde amnesia* as a result. He's unable to lay down new events as long-term memories, and he can't recall anything happening now beyond roughly a 15-minute span. So Leonard will go to sleep; he'll awake and think the attack has just happened, with no memory of anything that has happened since. He writes notes to himself, even notes on his body, to tell him where he is and what progress he has made in locating his wife's killer. But he never really knows when he wrote those notes. He starts to worry that someone has tampered with his notes while he was asleep.

Memories in the normal sense are more than what Leonard writes on his arm, though it may be difficult to say exactly what more they are. Beliefs are also more than what Otto has written in his notebook, though it may be difficult to say exactly what. In the end, Clark and Chalmers are willing to concede that much, but they insist that "the notion of belief ought to be used so that Otto qualifies as having the belief in question. In all important respects, Otto's case is similar."

I'm not sure that Otto's case is similar in *all* important respects. It's enough for the central point at issue that it's similar in some. Once you start to think about it, it is clear that many of the things we do with our minds involve parts of the external world in crucial ways. The video game Tetris involves figuring out how two-dimensional shapes will fit together. You can play Tetris by mentally revolving those shapes in your mind, but you can also rotate the image on the screen. It takes about half the time to rotate it on the screen. Isn't that a form of calculation that involves something in the external world?

There are much simpler examples as well. Balancing a checkbook is a familiar form of calculation but for most of us would be next to impossible if we couldn't do it with paper and pencil. When people used slide rules, part of their calculation was in their hands rather than in their heads. A kind of question that appears on many standardized tests—the Law School Admission Test, for example—is the logic puzzle. An example goes like this: If four men and four women are seated around a table, and no woman is seated next to a woman, and if Adam must be across from Juliet, and George from Henrietta, then who's sitting next to Joe? There's a key to solving all puzzles of this sort. The key is not to try to do it in your head. Organize the information in a visible sketch instead, or a matrix, or a diagram. That way, your hand and eyes can take care of memory and bookkeeping, leaving your cognitive processing for those aspects it's really needed for. That approach to logic puzzles is a kind of calculation that uses a part of the world.

The mathematician and philosopher Alfred North Whitehead made precisely the same point in terms of looking for the right symbolism to use in approaching a problem. He said:

> By relieving the brain of all unnecessary work, a good notation sets it free to concentrate on more advanced problems, and in effect increases ... mental power. ... By the aid of symbolism we can make transitions in reasoning ... almost mechanically by the eye.

What Otto has written in his notebook may not literally be beliefs. It may not even be true that we ought to think of them as beliefs. But the general point is surely right: that we often work best mentally by using parts of the external world. Clark and Chalmers mention one particularly interesting aspect of the external world used as part of an "extended mind" in this sense—language and linguistic interaction with other people. Clark and Chalmers say:

> Language appears to be a central means by which cognitive processes are extended into the world. Think of a group of people brainstorming around a table, or a philosopher who thinks best by writing, developing her ideas as she goes. It may be that language evolved, in part, to enable such extensions of our cognitive resources within actively coupled systems.

When birds soar, they're not moving purely under their own power. They aren't flapping their wings. Birds soar by exploiting the rising air currents of thermals. Thinking as we know it may inevitably exploit the currents of language and an environment of other thinkers.

We've emphasized the notion of a mind in the world in terms of our minds, but if the basic idea is right—if mental functioning is essentially tied to the environment—the idea ought to work in developing artificial minds as well. That's precisely how it has been used in robotics. One of the foremost developers in robotics is also one of its most interesting thinkers. Rodney Brooks is head of the Robotics Lab at MIT. He's also an entrepreneur, founder of the iRobot Company, and developer of the Roomba robotic vacuum cleaner. Brooks has offered some autobiographical notes on how he thinks. What he says is that he attempts to listen to both sides in an intellectual controversy, tries to find an assumption that everyone is making, and then deliberately negates that assumption. Here are some examples of the assumptions he has negated with impressive success.

A standard assumption in robotics has long been that we should build humanoid robots, robots that walked, talked, and thought like a human being. Rodney Brooks negated that assumption. Evolution didn't start with people; it started with bacteria and single-celled animals working toward higher primates only through billions of years. Brooks proposed that we should start with something radically simpler—a machine with the intelligence and functionality of a cockroach, perhaps—then add further systems bit by bit, proceeding step by step toward higher intelligence, just as evolution did.

Here's a second example: NASA is developing robots to explore other planets and approached Brooks for ideas in designing a 100-pound robot appropriate for planetary exploration. The assumption that Brooks tried to negate was the assumption that we should be sending a single large robot. Why not 100 one-pound robots instead? They could explore out in all directions. They could explore, and it might not matter if a few were damaged or lost. He calls it "fast, cheap, and out of control." Within a few years, Brooks predicts, "It'll be possible at modest cost to invade a planet with millions of tiny robots."

What's important here is that the minds of Brooks's robots are essentially minds in the world. Robot development, he insists, should avoid traps of abstraction. It should always be development, stage by stage, of an organism interacting with a dynamic environment. He says:

> Problem-solving behavior, language, expert knowledge and application, and reason, are all pretty simple once the essence of being and reacting are available. The essence is

the ability to move around in a dynamic environment, sensing the surroundings to a degree sufficient to achieve the necessary maintenance of life and reproduction.

In developing robot minds in the world, Brooks rejects the idea that they have to form representations of their worlds in a central brain or central processor. Why even think there has to be a central processor? What if the intelligence is distributed into separate computation centers? Many of Brooks's robots work in terms of distributed, rather than centralized, intelligence. Each leg of one of his insect robots may have a tiny computer. Each of those tiny computers dictates the movement of its leg just in terms of input regarding the position and movement of the legs next to it. It's as if each leg is thinking on its own with local information. No central computer sees the movement of all the legs. With each of its legs moving independently, the robot ambles forward steadily over the terrain. It turns out that many real insects operate that way as well. And why, Brooks asks, do you have to conceive of a robot mind programmed in terms of internal maps, or diagrams, or representations of the world? He says, "The world is its own best representation." Develop robot minds in the world, interactive with the world, and they'll have all the representations they need.

What I've tried to trace in this lecture—in psychology, in philosophy, and in robotics—is a central emphasis on the mind in the world. Occasionally claims are overstated, and I've tried to offer a corrective. But the core claim is solid. Both as individuals and as members of a species—both evolutionarily and individually—our minds have been shaped by our kind of embodiment, action in our kind of environment, in our kind of world. That may not be the whole story, but it's certainly a necessary part of trying to understand the nature of mind. In the lectures that follow, I want to continue exploring minds by exploring how one might try to build them. We'll be looking at intelligence, both natural and artificial. I'll start next time with a history of attempts at building smart machines.

Timeline

B.C.

c. 800 ....Homer, *Iliad* and *Odyssey*.

c. 347–322 ....Aristotle, *Prior Analytics*, *Posterior Analytics*, *De Interpretatione*.

c. 100 ....The Antikythera mechanism, a Greek device used to calculate solar, lunar, and astrological positions. Found in 1902 from an ancient shipwreck.

A.D.

8 ....Ovid, *Metamorphoses*.

1600–1800 ....The golden age of automata.

1614 ....John Napier invents logarithms.

1617 ....Napier's bones.

1623 ....William Schickard mechanizes Napier's bones.

1632–1633 ....Galileo publishes *Dialogue Concerning Two World Systems* and is then tried for suspicion of heresy by the Catholic Church.

1629–1649 ....René Descartes, *Meditations on First Philosophy*, *Passions of the Soul*, *De Mundo*.

1642–1662 ....Blaise Pascal invents the Pascaline calculator and writes *Pensées*.

1651–1655 ....Thomas Hobbes, *Leviathan* and *De Corpore*.

1666 ....Isaac Newton, prism experiments on color.

1672–1715 ....Gottfried Wilhelm Leibniz builds a multiplying machine.

1687	Isaac Newton, *Philosophiae Naturalis Principia Mathematica*.
1689	John Locke, *An Essay Concerning Human Understanding*.
c. 1737	Jacques de Vaucanson builds his famous automatons.
1748	David Hume, *An Enquiry Concerning Human Understanding*.
1748	Julien Offray de La Mettrie, *Man a Machine*.
1769	Wolfgang von Kempelen creates a fake chess-playing automaton.
1781	Immanuel Kant, *The Critique of Pure Reason*.
1800–1821	Francis Gall develops phrenology.
1801	Jacquard's loom, an important step in the history of computing devices.
1810	Johann Wolfgang von Goethe, *Theory of Colors*.
1820–1840	Charles Babbage, Difference Engines #1 and #2 and the Analytical Engine.
1848	An explosion drives a steel bar through Phineas Gage's head.
1854	George Boole, "An Investigation of the Laws of Thought, on Which Are Founded the Mathematical Theories of Logic and Probabilities."
1859	Charles Darwin, *On the Origin of Species*.
1861	James Clerk Maxwell lays the foundations for color photography.

1864	James Clerk Maxwell, "A Dynamic Theory of the Electromagnetic Field."
1872	Charles Darwin, *Expression of the Emotions in Man and Animals.*
1874	Franz Brentano, *Psychology from the Empirical Standpoint*; T. H. Huxley, "On the Hypothesis that Animals are Automata, and its History."
1890	William James, *The Principles of Psychology.*
1891	Sigmund Freud, *On Aphasia.*
1892	Hendrik Lorentz develops the Lorentz field equations.
1904	Alfred Binet develops an intelligence test that lays the foundation for IQ testing.
1910–1913	Bertrand Russell and Alfred North Whitehead, *Principia Mathematica.*
1921	Ludwig Wittgenstein, *Tractatus Logico-Philosophicus.*
1931	Kurt Gödel, *On Formally Undecidable Propositions of Principia Mathematica and Related Systems*, Gödel's incompleteness theorem.
1937	Alan M. Turing creates the Turing machine theory of computation.
1938	B. F. Skinner, *The Behavior of Organisms.*
1943	Jean-Paul Sartre, *Being and Nothingness.*
1946	ENIAC and the von Neumann architecture for computing.

1949	Gilbert Ryle, *The Concept of Mind.*
1950	Alan M. Turing, "Computing Machinery and Intelligence."
1953	James D. Watson and Francis Crick discover the molecular structure of DNA; Ludwig Wittgenstein, *Philosophical Investigations.*
1956	Dartmouth Artificial Intelligence Conference.
1958	Frank Rosenblatt develops the perceptron, a two-layer, feed-forward neural net.
1962	Thomas S. Kuhn, *The Structure of Scientific Revolutions.*
1965	Hubert Dreyfus, "Alchemy and Artificial Intelligence."
1967	Hilary Putnam, "The Nature of Mental States."
1969	Marvin Minsky and Seymour Papert trash Rosenblatt's neural nets in perceptrons.
1974	Thomas Nagel, "What Is It Like to Be a Bat?"
1979	J. J. Gibson, *The Ecological Approach to Visual Perception.*
1980	John Searle, "Minds, Brains, and Computers."
1981	Paul Churchland, "Eliminative Materialism and the Propositional Attitudes."
1982	Frank Jackson introduces black-and-white Mary in "Epiphenomenal Qualia"; Benjamin Libet's experiments on the timing of

readiness potential in the brain and consciousness of willing.

1987 .... The resurrection of neural nets in Rumelhart and McClelland's *Parallel Distributed Processing*.

1988 .... Daniel Dennett, "Quining Qualia"; Hans Moravec, *Mind Children: The Future of Human and Robot Intelligence*.

1989 .... Roger Penrose, *The Emperor's New Mind*; Colin McGinn, "Can We Solve the Mind-Body Problem?"

1990 .... David Rosenthal, "A Theory of Consciousness."

1991 .... Rodney Brooks, "Intelligence without Representation"; Institution of the Loebner Prize.

1994 .... Francis Crick, *The Astonishing Hypothesis*.

1995 .... Patricia Smith Churchland, *Neurophilosophy*; Paul Churchland, *The Engine of Reason, the Seat of the Soul*; David Chalmers, "Facing Up to the Hard Problem of Consciousness."

1996 .... Penrose and Hameroff's quantum theory of consciousness.

1997 .... IBM's Deep Blue wins against chess grandmaster Gary Kasparov.

1998 .... Andy Clark and David Chalmers, "The Extended Mind."

2000 .... The date by which Alan M. Turing predicted in 1950 that a machine would pass the Turing test.

2040 .... The date by which Ray Kurzweil predicts the "coming singularity," in which our machines will surpass us in intelligence.

Glossary

addiction transference: The phenomenon of replacing an addiction to one substance or action with an addiction to another substance or action, usually while attempting to cure the addiction to the first.

affordances: A concept developed in the work of J. J. Gibson, affordances are possibilities for action in an environment.

agnosia: Often the result of brain damage, agnosia is a general term for deficits in a person's ability to interpret information from the senses, despite a lack of damage to the senses themselves. See also **object blindness**, **prospagnosia**, and **visual agnosia**.

Analytical Behaviorism: The view that mental states can be analyzed or defined in terms of behavior or behavioral dispositions. See also **Behaviorism** and **Functionalism**.

Analytical Engine: Charles Babbage drew up plans for this general-purpose computing machine in the mid 1800s; though never built, the device was to be powered by steam and would have used programs on punch cards. See also **Difference Engine**.

Antikythera machine: Discovered just off the coast of the Greek island of Antikythera, the Antikythera machine was a Greek calculating device from about 100 B.C. that could have been used to predict the movement of the Sun, Moon, and major planets.

antinomies: Sets of compelling arguments on both sides of an irresolvable issue. In his *Critique of Pure Reason*, Kant presents the free will and Determinism debate as an antinomy.

artificial intelligence (AI): The science of making machines do things that would require intelligence if done by people. See **Marvin Minsky** in the Biographical Notes.

Asimov's Laws of Robotics: The robots featured in the fiction of writer Isaac Asimov must follow three laws: They cannot intentionally injure human beings; they must obey humans (when this does not conflict with the previous law); and they must protect themselves (again, when this does not conflict with the previous laws).

automata: Machines built to look like and imitate life forms—people or animals—with the appearance of autonomous action.

axiomatic systems: Systems of axioms or first principles from which other claims can be derived as theorems.

axon: Neurons, the cells of nerves, are equipped with a long protuberance called an *axon*. The signal of a neuron travels down the axon and is transmitted to other cells. See also **dendrites**, **neurons**, **neurotransmitters**, and **synapse**.

backpropagation of errors: A training process in which artificial neural nets (computer-instantiated structures loosely based on networks of neurons in the brain) learn from their mistakes.

Behaviorism: In psychology, a research program that seeks to understand the human mind in terms of behavioral inputs and outputs, that is, how humans react to different stimuli and changes in their environment.

binding problem: The binding problem refers to the question of how our brains assemble data from different aspects of perception into the unified consciousness that we experience.

blindsight: Despite their claim to be totally blind, some victims of major damage to the visual cortex are nonetheless able to "guess" about visual information in their environment with amazing accuracy. Paul Humphreys speculates that blindsight functions by means of visual processing through an older and subconscious route.

body schema: Used by some researchers to indicate aspects of body image that are assumed unconsciously and through which one acts.

Boolean function: Any of various functions, familiar from truth tables that take truth values as input and give truth values as output. AND is a Boolean function, for example, which gives "true" as output only when both of its inputs are "true":

P	*Q*	*P* AND *Q*
T	T	T
T	F	F
F	T	F
F	F	F

brain state: A particular configuration of brain activities at a given moment. The term is often used in discussions regarding the philosophy of mind when considering whether mental states, such as belief or love, could reduce to physiological brain states.

Broca's and Wernicke's areas: Two parts of the brain associated with speech functions. Broca's area is involved with the production of speech. Wernicke's area is involved with the comprehension of words uttered by others.

C fibers: A category of slower-conducting nerve fibers responsible for less specific and slower-moving sensations, including pain.

Cartesian doubt: In his effort to determine whether there was anything of which he could be absolutely certain, René Descartes subjected all his knowledge to systematic doubt, rejecting anything about which he might possibly be mistaken or deceived. Descartes concludes that only the fact that he is doubting or thinking is beyond all doubt and, from that conclusion, deduces that he exists. Descartes' *cogito, ergo sum*—"I think, therefore I am"—becomes the foundation of his system.

cognition: A general term for processes of conceptualizing, perceiving, and knowing.

cognitive psychology: In contrast to Behaviorism, a research program that attempts to understand the human mind in terms of the relation of inner mental states.

color circle, wheel, and solid: The color circle portrays colors in terms of similarities and oppositions. The color wheel adds a parameter of saturation, with the colors at the edges fully saturated and progressively mixed as one goes toward the center. The color solid is a three-dimensional portrayal that adds the parameter of intensity or brightness.

Compatibilist strategy: In the context of the Determinism argument, the strategy of challenging the assumption that free will and Determinism are necessarily opposed. The Compatibilist holds that free will, when properly understood, will be seen to be a natural part of a causal universe.

cones: Located on the retina, cones are one of the two types of light-receptive cells: rods and cones. Cone cells function in situations of normal light and register color. Different types of cones, using different pigments, specialize in different ranges of light wavelength. See also **optic nerve**, **retina**, and **rods**.

Connectionism: An interdisciplinary movement that attempts to explain the mind in terms of a large number of simple interconnected units, based on the fact that the brain is composed of an interconnected system of neurons. See also **backpropagation of errors**, **neural nets**, and **parallel distributed processing**.

Copernican theory: Nicolaus Copernicus's heliocentric theory in which the planets revolve around the Sun. See also **Ptolemaic astronomy**.

corpus callosum: The structure connecting the right and left hemispheres of the human brain that allows information to pass between the two. See also **split-brain patients**.

creature consciousness: As outlined by David Rosenthal, creature consciousness is contrasted with state consciousness and transitive consciousness as the state of a creature being awake or aware. Contrast **state consciousness** and **transitive consciousness**.

defeasible reasoning: A form of logic in which default assumptions operate until revised or qualified by new information.

deflationist response: A response that "deflates" a concept—of consciousness or freedom, for example—by showing that an opponent's assumptions regarding the concept are overinflated.

dendrites: Parts of neurons, dendrites serve as the receptors to the signals relayed by other neurons. See also **axon**, **neurons**, **neurotransmitters**, and **synapse**.

Determinism: In one sense, the claim that every event in the universe is the product of earlier events in accord with natural laws. In another sense, the claim that there can be no free will because all events are the product of earlier events. See also **free will**.

Difference Engine: A machine designed by Charles Babbage in the mid-1800s to calculate and print logarithm tables. Although not completed in his lifetime, Babbage's Difference Engine #2 was finally built in the 1990s by the London Science Museum.

dispositional properties: Properties (such as soluble or fragile) that reflect what would happen in certain circumstances. In Analytical or Philosophical Behaviorism, mental concepts are said to be synonymous with behavioral properties, generally understood as dispositional.

Dualism: In classical form, the position that the universe is composed of two radically different substances: the mental and the physical. For Descartes, the mental does not occupy space as the physical does. See also **Epiphenomenalism**, **Monism**, **Occasionalism**, and **Parallelism**.

echolocation: A process of determining distance through the use of sound, used by such animals as bats and dolphins.

Einsteinian physics: Einstein's theory of relativity (general and special) challenged Newtonian tenets, holding, for example, that matter and energy are interchangeable, that time moves at a rate relative to one's rate of speed, and that space itself can be curved by gravity.

empirical: Deriving from experience of the world. *Scientific* is a rough synonym.

Empiricist theory: The theory that perception is a process of inference from sense-data. Classical Empiricists included Locke, Berkeley, and Hume, but the influence of Empiricism extended well into the 20th century in both philosophy and psychology.

Epiphenomenalism: The view that the mind does not have physical effects but merely "floats above" the physical processes of the brain. See also **Dualism**, **Occasionalism**, and **Parallelism**.

epistemology: That field of philosophy devoted to the study of knowledge and how we come to know things.

ethics: The field of philosophy that focuses on moral issues: ethically good actions, ethically right actions, rights, and obligations.

eugenics: The attempt to "advance" humanity by the selective breeding of human beings.

Evolutionary theory: In biology, the theory advanced by Charles Darwin that explains the development and complexity of species through the process of natural selection.

Existentialism: An influential movement in philosophy that took human freedom and one's capacity to create meaning for oneself as starting points.

faculty psychology: An approach to the human mind in terms of a limited number of powers or capacities (that is, faculties).

frame problem: An issue of relevance, the frame problem in artificial intelligence and in understanding human cognition is the problem of deciding what old information should be considered for revision in light of new information.

free will: The question of whether human beings should be considered to have free will, that is, whether they should be understood to have autonomous control over their own actions, is central to the history of philosophy. Answers given also bear on issues of moral and legal responsibility. See also **Determinism**.

frontal lobe: The foremost portion of the brain, understood to be an area important for planning and decision-making.

Functionalism: The position that mental states are functional states of an organism. Mental states, according to the Functionalist, take environmental input and other mental states as input, with behavior and other mental states as outputs.

ganglion cells: In visual perception, the cells that receive information from the retina and transport it to the brain. The long axons of these cells constitute the optic nerve.

Gödel's incompleteness theorem: Kurt Gödel proved that any axiomatic system adequate for simple arithmetic, if consistent, will be incapable of proving some truth expressible in the system.

GOFAI: Short for "good old-fashioned artificial intelligence," an attempt to produce artificial intelligence using rule-governed programs of symbol manipulation. Contrast with **Connectionism**.

halting problem: In the work of Alan M. Turing, the problem of deciding for any given program whether that program will "halt" as opposed to going into an infinite loop.

higher-order thought: Higher-order thought (HOT) theories attempt to analyze consciousness in terms of mental states that are about other mental states.

hippocampus: A seahorse-shaped part of the brain important in the procedures of processing emotions and producing memories.

holistic view (of the mind): The position that the phenomenon of mind is not the result of a specific region of the brain or a single process but emerges from the function of the brain as a unified whole.

homunculus: The "little man inside." In philosophical discussions of the "inner theater," the image of a homunculus is used to denigrate theories that would explain outer perception in terms of some form of inner perception. In brain structure, the term *sensory homunculus* is used to designate a model of the human body in which the proportional sizes of parts of the model correspond to proportional areas of representation in the sensorimotor cortex.

Idealism: Sometimes called *Subjective Idealism*, the response to the mind-body problem that holds that the physical world is illusion and only the mental realm exists. See also **Materialism**.

inference: In logic, the derivation of a conclusion from information contained in the premises.

inhibitory neurons: In contrast to the more common excitatory neurons, these nerve cells inhibit the firing of their target neuron, instructing it not to fire.

inner theater: In the philosophy of mind, the inner theater is used to designate an inner realm in which representations of the world are presented. See also **homunculus**.

intelligence quotient (IQ): The standard way of scoring intelligence tests. In classical form, a person's mental age (the age for which a person's test score is typical) was divided by his or her chronological age in years, with the result multiplied by 100. The average IQ is 100 by definition, with scores for the general population forming a normal or bell curve.

Intentionalist theory of perception: A theory emphasizing that perception is always "perception of" (Brentano), that perception comes with content, rather than content having to be added by inference. Contrast with **Empiricist theory**.

interaction problem: If the mental and the physical are two radically different realms, as Dualism claims, how could they possibly interact? This is the interaction problem posed for Dualism.

inverted lenses experiment: A form of psychological experiment in which a subject's visual stimuli are inverted or reversed by a lens. Results show that subjects accommodate to the reversal over time, though debate remains as to whether this is due to an inner perception that "flips" to accommodate or simply because they learn to work in terms of the new patterns of stimulation.

inverted spectrum: A thought experiment in which one person's color sensations are exactly opposite to another's; one person's qualitative sensations are blue where another's are yellow, for example.

Kurzweil's "coming singularity": Author and inventor Raymond Kurzweil foresees a near future in which our machines will become more intelligent than we are, capable of producing new machines still more intelligent than themselves.

limbic system: A set of structures deep within the brain involved with emotions and emotional memory.

Loebner Prize: A form of the Turing test run each year, offering $100,000 and a gold medal for the first computer program indistinguishable from a human. See http://www.loebner.net/Prizef/loebner-prize.html.

logic: The study of patterns of valid deduction. Formal logic represents the essential structure of claims in symbolic form, codifying logical argument in the form of symbolic derivations. Mathematical logic studies formal properties of systems of logic. Philosophical logic concentrates on philosophical assumptions crucial to different logical systems.

Materialism: A response to the mind-body problem that holds that only the physical is ultimately real. *Reductive Materialism* claims that the realm of the mental somehow reduces to the physical. *Eliminative Materialism* claims that our concepts for the mental will be eliminated in an ultimately satisfactory and entirely physical scientific theory of human functioning. See also **Idealism**.

mental age: A controversial concept found in intelligence testing; used to indicate the age for which a person's score on the test would be typical.

mental set or set expectation: In perception, a background expectation that may influence what is perceived.

metaphysics: The most general conceptual investigation into the nature of reality.

mind-body problem: The mind-body problem refers to our conceptual difficulty in understanding the relation between mental and physical phenomena. For different answers to the problem, see

Dualism, Epiphenomenalism, Functionalism, Idealism, Materialism, Occasionalism, and **Parallelism**.

Monism: In the philosophy of mind, the position that there exists only one basic kind of "stuff" or substance. Both Materialism and Idealism are forms of Monism, as opposed to Dualism, which holds that the universe contains two fundamentally different kinds of things: the realms of the mental and the physical. See also **Dualism**.

multiple instantiation: The notion that mental states might be instantiated in any of various forms of organisms and even, perhaps, in machines.

Naïve Realism: The view that the world as we perceive it is essentially the way the world actually is independent of our perception of it.

NAND: A Boolean connective that means "not both are true." The following is a truth table for NAND:

P	*Q*	*P* NAND *Q*
T	T	F
T	F	T
F	T	T
F	F	T

neural nets: Computational structures instantiated in software but modeled roughly on the operation of neurons in the brain. Trained by backpropagation of errors, neural nets have shown an impressive ability to generalize, that is, to learn patterns applicable to new cases. See also **backpropagation of errors**, **Connectionism**, and **parallel distributed processing**.

neurons: The cells of the nervous system. Stimulated by input at their dendrites, neurons pass a signal down their axons to their terminal nodes, where electrochemicals called *neurotransmitters* are released into a synapse and stimulate other neurons in turn. See also **axon, dendrites, neurotransmitters,** and **synapse**.

neurotransmitters: When one neuron transmits a signal to another, it does so by releasing chemicals called *neurotransmitters* into the small space (or synapse) between the neurons. The neurotransmitters cause a change in the receiving terminal (or dendrite) of the neuron being given the signal. See also **axon**, **dendrites**, **neurons**, and **synapse**.

Newtonian astronomy: Isaac Newton's laws of gravitation codified and explained the movement of celestial bodies in accord with the Copernican (heliocentric) conception of planetary motion. But Newtonian physics also left unsolved a number of problems that paved the way for Einsteinian physics as a replacement.

object blindness: A specific type of visual agnosia characterized by the inability to distinguish the identity of objects.

Occasionalism: A form of Dualism, Occasionalism holds that the mental and physical are, in fact, causally isolated but operate in sync through the action of God at every moment. See also **Dualism**, **Epiphenomenalism**, and **Parallelism**.

optic nerve: The bundle of nerve fibers that brings visual information from the retina (the light-sensitive layer on the rear interior surface of the eye) to the brain.

optical illusion: An image or object that plays upon human processes, leading a person to misperceive what he or she sees. See examples in Lecture Ten.

Panpsychism: A response to the "hard problem of consciousness" defended by David Chalmers and Galen Strawson. The Panpsychist holds that all matter is in some way conscious.

paradigms: In the philosophy of science of Thomas S. Kuhn, a set of background assumptions and explanatory concepts definitive of a science at a particular time.

parallel distributed processing: A term associated with Connectionist neural networks. It involves systematically constructing networked lines of connections between units, which are strengthened and weakened depending on the successes or failures of the processes. See also **backpropagation of errors**, **Connectionism**, and **neural nets**.

Parallelism: A form of Dualism asserting that the mental and physical are, in fact, causally isolated but operate in "pre-established harmony" because both realms were wound up like two clocks by

God at the inception of the universe. See also **Dualism**, **Epiphenomenalism**, and **Occasionalism**.

perception: The process of gaining awareness of something through one's bodily senses.

perceptron: A two-layer neural net developed by Frank Rosenblatt. Perceptrons could be trained using a simple rule to any logical function they could instantiate, but Minsky and Papert showed that perceptrons could not instantiate some simple logical functions, such as *exclusive or*.

phantom limb: The name for the experience of one who has lost an appendage yet has an illusory sensation of its presence.

phenomenology: A tradition in philosophy that takes subjective experience as its starting point. Objectivity and science, in this view, are seen as a second level of abstraction; one must step out of one's experience in attempting to acquire an objective perspective.

philosophy of language: The branch or topic of philosophy concerned with understanding how language is structured and used. Questions arise regarding the relationship between language and reality and how linguistic meaning should be understood.

philosophy of mind: The branch of philosophy concerned with understanding the nature of the mind, the nature of consciousness, and the relationship between minds and brains, or the mental and the physical. Contemporary philosophy of mind is aggressively interdisciplinary, interfacing with psychology, computer science, and the neurosciences.

phrenology: A pseudoscience popular and influential in the 1800s, which studied the bumps of a person's skull to learn about his or her character traits.

plasticity: Also called *neuroplasticity*, *brain plasticity*, and *cortical plasticity*, the ability of brain matter to alter so as to perform different functions. In learning new manual skills, areas of the brain may be recruited to new tasks.

pre-philosophical facts: Commonsense assumptions or understandings in advance of critical reflection.

private language argument: Ludwig Wittgenstein's *Philosophical Investigations* is structured as an assortment of separate comments, seen by many as containing a central argument regarding the essentially public nature of language. In these lectures, the argument is presented in terms of a necessity for public criteria in language learning and, thus, language comprehension, though there is much disagreement as to precisely what the argument is and how or whether it works.

privileged access: The notion that we each have access to the contents of our own minds in ways that others do not.

prosopagnosia: Often the result of damage to the brain, prosopagnosia is a characterized by the inability to recognize faces, despite being able to recognize other objects without difficulty.

Ptolemaic astronomy: Ptolemy's geocentric (that is, Earth-centered) model of the universe was the dominant theory for hundreds of years, rigorously articulated but eventually superseded by Copernicus's heliocentric model. See also **Copernican theory**.

qualia: Plural for *quale*, *qualia* refers to subjective qualitative experiences, for example, the taste of a pineapple or the feel of silk.

quantum mechanics: Developed early in the 20th century, quantum mechanics is a sophisticated theory regarding subatomic events. Although the theory is well confirmed experimentally, its interpretation remains an area of controversy. Its implications or claimed implications extend to whether Determinism is true, whether every event has a cause, whether conscious measurement is constitutive of the universe, and even what the nature of human freedom might be.

quantum randomness: In standard interpretations of quantum mechanics, events occur at the quantum level that have no specific cause and are impossible to predict.

Reductive Materialism: That form of Materialism that holds that the mental can be reduced to the physical. In terms of the relation between the things at issue, Reductive Materialism claims that mental things are ultimately purely physical. In terms of the sciences at issue, Reductive Materialism claims that the science of the mental will follow directly from the science of the physical.

relational properties: A property something has in virtue of its relation or interaction with another thing. "Beside" and "married" are relational properties: One thing cannot be "beside" all by itself, nor can a person be "married" without another person. Relational properties are contrasted with intrinsic properties, which belong to something independent of their relations to others.

retina: The layer of light-sensitive cells that covers the rear interior of the eye. The retina registers incoming light as the beginning of a process of signals sent to the brain. See also **cones**, **optic nerve**, and **rods**.

robotics: The study and design of robots, machines that work somewhat autonomously to perform tasks for humans.

rods: Located on the retina, rods are one of the two types of light-receptive cells: rods and cones. They function in situations of little light and do not register color. See also **cones**, **optic nerve**, and **retina**.

saccades: Our eyes move in swift jumps called *saccades* (or *saccadic motion*) as we scan across something, such as the page of a book or a computer screen.

semantics: The meaning of the symbols of a system of language or the study thereof. Semantics is contrasted with syntax, a matter of the shapes of the symbols and rules in terms of those shapes. Semantics concerns the relation of those shapes to ideas and things in the world. See also **syntax**.

sense-data: In the Empiricist theory, information delivered to the brain via the senses that is then used as the basis for the inferences that form our experience of the world.

sensory cortex: That part of the cortex that registers touch from various parts of the body; the sensory cortex is organized in a way that corresponds roughly to the organization of the body. See also **homunculus**.

Solipsism: The position that the only thing that exists is one's own mind.

spandrels: In Evolutionary theory, properties of organisms that were not directly selected for but nonetheless "came along for the ride."

split-brain patients: People in whom the corpus callosum between the two hemispheres of the brain has been surgically cut, often to relieve extreme epilepsy. Split-brain patients function normally in most contexts but show surprising behavior in carefully constructed experimental conditions because of the lack of communication between the hemispheres.

state consciousness: In the work of David Rosenthal, the sense in which a mental state is conscious—for example, a belief is a conscious belief or anger is conscious anger. Contrast **creature consciousness** and **transitive consciousness**.

Stoics: A school of ancient philosophy known for its work in logic, physics, and ethics. The Stoics held that Determinism was true and that we have no control over the "slings and arrows of outrageous fortune." The rational road to tranquility is to control one's emotional reactions to the inevitable.

strong AI: The position that a machine can have a mental state, such as understanding, in virtue of instantiation of a particular program. Weak AI is a research program in which programs are used to understand mental states. Strong AI is the claim that an appropriate program would be a mental state.

Substance Dualism: Also known as *Cartesian Dualism*, the position that the universe is composed of two radically different kinds of "stuff" or substances: the realm of the mental and the physical. See also **Dualism**, **Epiphenomenalism**, **Occasionalism**, and **Parallelism**.

symbol-processing: The methodical manipulation of symbols. A calculator does math by manipulating symbols according to rules, for example, rather than by dealing with the quantities the numbers may represent.

synapse: In sending a signal to another neuron, the neuron ejects neurotransmitters into the small space between the two neurons. That space is called a *synapse*. See also **axon**, **dendrites**, **neurons**, and **neurotransmitters**.

syntax: The structure of the symbols in a language or the study thereof. Syntax is a matter of the shapes of the symbols and rules in terms of those shapes. Semantics, in contrast, concerns the relation of those shapes to ideas and things in the world. See also **semantics**.

transitive consciousness: In the work of David Rosenthal, transitive consciousness is consciousness of something. Contrast **creature consciousness** and **state consciousness**.

trichromacy: The normal human capacity to see colors. The term refers to the fact that color perception functions in terms of three sets of color-sensitive cones in our retinas. See also **cones** and **retina**.

Turing machine: An abstract machine conceptualized by Alan M. Turing as a formal model for the concept of computation. The Turing machine served as a model for the building of real computers.

Turing test: Alan M. Turing suggested that the question "Can a machine think?" be replaced with a specific test: In communication through a monitor interface, can a computer fool a person into thinking that it, too, is a person?

unity of consciousness: Despite receiving a variety of sensory data, processed in various areas in the brain, we experience consciousness as a seamless unity.

valid: An argument is valid if the conclusion follows from the premises. A deductively valid argument is one in which the connection is logically tight and in which it is logically impossible for the premises to be true and the conclusion to be false.

visual agnosia: A form of agnosia that results in an inability to interpret visual data. Both object blindness and prosopagnosia fall under this subcategory. See also **agnosia**, **object blindness**, and **prosopagnosia**.

visual cortex: Usually used to refer to the primary visual cortex located in the rear of the brain, which processes incoming visual data from the eyes.

volitional (or willing) dysfunction: A disorder that inhibits a person's ability to control his or her own actions.

voluntary action: An act made as the result of one's choice, contrasted with involuntary or reflex actions over which one does not have conscious control.

von Neumann architecture: An overall design for computers presented by John von Neumann in 1945 on the basis of work on the ENIAC. Virtually all contemporary computers have a von Neumann architecture, in which memory functions to contain both data and the program that operates on those data.

weak AI: Weak AI is a research program in which programs are used to understand mental states. Strong AI, in contrast, is the claim that an appropriate program would be a mental state.

zombies: In thought experiments in the philosophy of mind, zombies are supposed to be behaviorally and functionally identical to people but without consciousness or inner experience.

Biographical Notes

Aristotle (c. 384–322 B.C.): A major figure in Western philosophy and science, student of Plato, and teacher of Alexander the Great. His work covers topics in physics, poetics, rhetoric, ethics, epistemology, and metaphysics.

Antoine Arnauld (1612–1694): A French philosopher and theologian, Arnauld is best known for his adaptation and advancement of Descartes' philosophy.

Charles Babbage (1791–1871): A mathematician and mechanical engineer, Babbage is known for pioneering work in the development of computers. Babbage devised plans for Difference Engines #1 and #2, complex, steam-driven calculating machines designed to compute and print logarithm tables. His greatest design was for the Analytical Engine, which would have been a universal programmable computer.

Alfred Binet (1857–1911): In 1904, in an attempt to tailor elementary education to student needs, Binet developed the first modern intelligence test, the foundation for all later IQ testing. Binet's warnings that the test was not intended to measure some single quality called *intelligence*, that it should not be used to rank normal children, and that there was no reason to believe that whatever it measured was innate, were largely ignored.

Ned Block (b. 1942): Block is a professor of philosophy at New York University with research areas in philosophy of mind and cognitive science. He is known for the Chinese nation thought experiment.

Josh Bongard (b. 1974): Bongard, currently teaching at the University of Vermont, is a computer scientist working in robotics. He has built a robot that has the ability to learn its own body.

George Boole (1815–1864): A British mathematician, logician, and philosopher, Boole authored *Laws of Thought* and created what is now called *Boolean algebra*.

Cynthia Breazeal (b. 1967): A professor at MIT, Breazeal is known for the exploration of emotion in robotics. Her most complex robot, Leonardo, can read and respond to emotional cues in interaction with humans.

Franz Brentano (1838–1917): According to Brentano, "All perception is perception of." He is known for groundbreaking work in the philosophy of psychology and for the development of the concept of intentionality.

Rodney Brooks (b. 1954): A professor of robotics at MIT, Brooks has argued against the traditional symbolic manipulation approach to artificial intelligence in favor of an interactive and embodied one. Brooks calls for the progressive development of increasingly complex robots in interaction with the world.

Jerome Bruner (b. 1915): An American psychologist, Bruner's research explored dimensions of cognitive psychology and cognitive learning.

David Chalmers (b. 1966): Chalmers is a prominent figure in contemporary philosophy of mind, currently teaching at the Australian National University. He is best known for pressing the "hard problem of consciousness" and the "explanatory gap": How can subjective experience possibly be explained in terms of any physical substrate or functional organization?

Patricia Smith Churchland (b. 1943): Churchland, currently teaching at the University of California at San Diego, is a philosopher working in close contact with neurophysiology.

Paul Churchland (b. 1942): A philosopher of mind currently teaching at the University of California at San Diego and most well known for his doctrine of Eliminative Materialism. This doctrine proposes that our folk psychological concepts for mental states—belief, love, and consciousness, for example—will simply disappear with the development of an adequate science of humans and their functioning in much the same way that concepts of witches and humors have been abandoned.

Andy Clark (b. 1957): Clark is a professor of philosophy at the University of Edinburgh. Specializing in philosophy of mind, Clark is known for work with David Chalmers on the extended-mind theory. Clark and Chalmers propose that a broad range of our mental activities—memory, belief, and thinking itself—are often partially constituted by things in the world beyond our skins.

Garrison Cottrell (b. 1950): Cottrell, a professor at the University of California at San Diego, is a computer scientist working in cognitive science. One of his achievements is a three-layer neural network successful in learning face recognition.

Francis Crick (1916–2004): Crick, an English molecular biologist, was co-discoverer, with James D. Watson, of the structure of the DNA molecule. In later work, Crick dedicated himself to neuroscience and the study of consciousness.

Antonio Damasio (b. 1944): A behavioral neurobiologist at the University of Southern California who has made important contributions to the interdisciplinary discussion between philosophy and the neurosciences. Damasio's main interest is the neurological systems involved in memory, emotions, and decision-making.

Charles Darwin (1809–1882): The central figure in evolutionary biology and one of the outstanding scientists of all time. Darwin's *On the Origin of Species*, the product of extensive research, provided incontrovertible evidence for the theory that all species evolved through time by a process Darwin called *natural selection.*

René Descartes (1596–1650): Descartes, a major figure in Western philosophy, was also an eminent mathematician and scientist. He is known for both Cartesian coordinates and Cartesian Dualism: the theory that the mental and the physical are two radically distinct aspects of the universe.

Diana Deutsch (b. 1938): Currently teaching at the University of California at San Diego, Deutsch is a perceptual and cognitive psychologist known for pioneering research in auditory illusions and the psychology of music.

Hubert Dreyfus (b. 1929): Dreyfus is a professor of philosophy at the University of California at Berkeley, known for his attacks on the prospects of artificial intelligence.

Euclid (c. 300 B.C.) Euclidean geometry is the historical paradigm of an axiomatically developed system, long thought to be the only possible view of relations in space. Over the last 200 years, alternatives known as *non-Euclidean geometries* have been developed.

Jerry Fodor (b. 1935): Fodor is a philosopher and cognitive scientist currently teaching at Rutgers University and known for his theory of the language of thought. The theory claims that thinking employs a mental language of representations, sometimes called *mentalese.*

Harry Frankfurt (b. 1929): Frankfurt, professor emeritus of philosophy at Princeton University, proposed insightful theories about free will. He argued for a hierarchical understanding of free will, in which free action is not just the ability to act on a desire but also includes a second-order volition that desires what to desire. An act is free if it is in accord with the desire one wants to desire.

Gottlob Frege (1848–1925): A German mathematician, logician, and philosopher, Frege is considered one of the founders of contemporary logic and philosophy of language. His attempt to ground all of mathematics on basic logical axioms inspired Russell and Whitehead's later work in *Principia Mathematica*.

Sigmund Freud (1856–1939): Freud, an Austrian-born psychiatrist and neurologist, founded psychoanalysis.

Phineas Gage (1823–1860): In a railroad construction accident, an iron rod was blasted through Gage's skull. He did not die but underwent a radical change in personality. Although used at the time as an argument for a holistic approach to mind, Gage's story has become a classic example of functional localization in the brain.

Francis Gall (1758–1828): An Austrian anatomist, Gall was the founder of phrenology. Phrenologists thought they could detect the developed areas of the brain by feeling for bumps and valleys on the skull. Although phrenology is now considered a pseudoscience, the idea of functional localization is a basic tenet of contemporary neuroscience.

Gordon Gallup (b. 1941): Currently teaching at the University of Albany, Gallup is a psychologist with a specialty in biopsychology. He is known for the development of the mirror test, used to determine self-awareness in animals.

Howard Gardner (b. 1943): Gardner, currently teaching at Harvard University, is a psychologist well known for his theory of multiple intelligences.

J. J. Gibson (1904–1979): Gibson was an American psychologist with a specialty in the field of visual perception. In *The Perception of the Visual World*, he develops the theory of "affordances." In Gibson's theory, what we perceive are not objects but affordances—possibilities for action in the environment.

Henry H. Goddard (1866–1957): Goddard, an American psychologist and eugenicist, was the first to bring IQ testing to America. In violation of Binet's warnings, Goddard used the test as a ranking, assigning the terms *idiots*, *imbeciles*, and *morons* to those in the lowest three categories.

Kurt Gödel (1906–1978): Gödel was an Austrian American mathematician, logician, and philosopher. His incompleteness theorem had a profound effect on the philosophy of logic and mathematics in the 20th century. Gödel's theorem proves that for any axiomatic system that includes arithmetic, there will be truths about numbers that cannot be proven in the system.

Johann Wolfgang von Goethe (1749–1832): Although also a scientist and theologian, Goethe is best known as a key figure in German literature. His *Theory of Colors* argued, against Newton, that color exists not in wavelengths of light but in the mind.

Stuart Hameroff (b. 1947): Hameroff is an anesthesiologist and professor at the University of Arizona, known for his research collaboration with Roger Penrose. Penrose and Hameroff suggest that the key to consciousness may be found in quantum effects in the microtubules of neurons.

N. R. Hanson (1924–1967): Hanson, an American philosopher of science, spent much of his philosophical energy exploring how observation is influenced by beliefs, making observation theory-laden. In *Patterns of Observation*, he argues that two people with different beliefs will experience the world in radically different ways.

Donald O. Hebb (1904–1985): An American psychologist, Hebb was the first to show how artificial networks of neuron-like devices could learn.

Thomas Hobbes (1588–1679): Although he is best known for his work in political theory in *Leviathan*, Hobbes's views on personal identity in *De Corpore* were also influential.

David Hume (1711–1776): Hume was an influential thinker in the Scottish Enlightenment and is considered one of the giants of British Empiricism. He also outlined an early theory of learning by association.

Nicholas Humphrey (b. 1943): A British psychologist and philosopher, Humphrey has spent of much of his professional life exploring issues of consciousness. In work on monkeys, he was the first to discover a mode of vision called *blindsight*, in which an individual is able to see in a certain sense despite complete damage to the visual cortex.

Edmund Husserl (1859–1938): A German philosopher, Husserl is the father of phenomenology. This philosophical method attempts to engage in a science of consciousness with the purpose of discovering the structure of experience.

Thomas H. Huxley (1825–1895): Huxley was a strong and early advocate of the theory of evolution. He is also associated with Epiphenomenalism, the view that mental states merely "float above" the physical states of the brain.

Frank Jackson (b. 1943): A philosopher at the Australian National University, Jackson has done extensive research in the philosophy of mind, metaphysics, and epistemology. He is best known for his "black-and-white Mary" argument that there are truths of consciousness that will forever escape physical science.

William James (1842–1910): A professor of philosophy at Harvard, James was an original thinker in the fields of both philosophy and psychology. James was a principal proponent of Pragmatism and did much to establish psychology as an empirical science.

Immanuel Kant (1724–1804): Kant is widely considered one of the giants of the European philosophical tradition. At the age of 57, he published his masterpiece, *The Critique of Pure Reason*.

Johannes Kepler (1571–1630): An influential German mathematician and astronomer, Kepler proved in *Astronomia Nova* that the Earth revolves around the Sun in elliptical orbits, which is his principal contribution to science. In communicating Napier's work to William Schickard, Kepler also played a role in the history of calculating machines.

Christof Koch (b. 1956): Koch is a neuroscientist at the California Institute of Technology. In collaboration with Francis Crick, he developed a theory of consciousness in terms of synchronized 40-Hertz firing of neurons in the brain.

Thomas S. Kuhn (1922–1996): A historian and philosopher of science who earned renown with *The Structure of Scientific Revolutions*. Kuhn claimed that the history of science represents not a progressive accumulation of new knowledge but the repeated and revolutionary overthrow of earlier scientific paradigms.

Ray Kurzweil (b. 1948): Kurzweil has made formative contributions in optical character and speech recognition, synthesized music, and speech production. Kurzweil warns of the "coming singularity," a point at which our machines will be more intelligent than we are.

Julien Offray de La Mettrie (1709–1751): A French physician and philosopher who argued in *Man a Machine* that animals were machines and that man is an animal. Man, therefore, is a machine.

Gottfried Wilhelm Leibniz (1646–1716): Leibniz was an influential philosopher, theologian, diplomat, physicist, and mathematician. He developed binary notation and built a complex calculating machine, and his development of calculus paralleled Newton's. He is known for the "indiscernibility of identicals," the principle that if two things are identical, anything true of one will be true of the other. In response to the interaction problems of Dualism, Leibniz proposed Parallelism. According to Parallelism, mind and body are not causally connected but function in parallel, like identical clocks wound up at the same time, because of a "pre-established harmony" initiated by God at the creation of the universe.

Benjamin Libet (b. 1916): Libet, an American physiologist, is an innovator in the science of human consciousness. Libet is known for experiments indicating that the brain's initiation of action often *precedes* conscious decision.

John Locke (1632–1704): A major figure in British Empiricism, Locke also developed a classical position regarding personal identity and memory. His work in political philosophy was highly influential on the American Declaration of Independence.

Elizabeth Loftus (b. 1944): A professor of psychology and law at the University of California at Irvine, Loftus's research has made her one of the world's leading experts on the fallibility of eyewitness testimony.

Hendrik Lorentz (1853–1928): Lorentz won the Nobel Prize in physics in 1902 for his work on electrodynamics and relativity.

Unlike Maxwell, he did not think magnetism could be explained in terms of classical mechanics and, in that way, paved the way for Einstein.

Nicolas de Malebranche (1638–1715): Malebranche tried to address the interaction of mind and body by championing a theory called *Occasionalism*. Mind and body are not causally connected; according to Occasionalism, God is involved at every moment in making them act in parallel.

James Clerk Maxwell (1831–1879): A Scottish mathematician and physicist, Maxwell is best known for the Maxwell equations, which first linked basic laws of electricity and magnetism.

Jay McClelland (b. 1948): McClelland, an American psychologist, is known for his work with artificial neural nets. In 1986, McClelland and David Rumelhart authored *Parallel Distributed Processing*, which introduced backpropagation of errors as a new learning rule for a new kind of net. Their work resurrected Connectionism.

Warren McCulloch (1898–1968): McCulloch was an American neurophysiologist. With Walter Pitts, he demonstrated in the 1940s how simple electrical devices could imitate neural firing.

Colin McGinn (b. 1950): McGinn is a professor at the University of Miami and a *mysterion*: In "Can We Solve the Mind-Body Problem?" McGinn argues that some things are forever beyond the range of human knowledge. One of these is an understanding of consciousness.

John Stuart Mill (1806–1873): A major contributor to the philosophical fields of logic, ethics, and political theory, Mill outlined an early theory of learning by association.

Marvin Minsky (b. 1927): Minsky is a major figure in the theory of computation and a pioneer in artificial intelligence. Shortly after the Dartmouth conference of 1956, he built a program capable of constructing proofs in geometry.

William Molyneux (1656–1698): Molyneux, an Irish-born scientist and politician, posed a question to John Locke that has become known as the *Molyneux problem*. If a man was born blind and learned to distinguish between basic geometric shapes by touch—a cube and sphere, for example—would he be able to distinguish them by sight once his vision was restored?

Hans Moravec (b. 1948): Moravec is professor at the Robotics Institute at Carnegie Mellon University. He lauds robotics as the next step in evolution.

Samuel George Morton (1799–1851): An American physician and natural scientist, Morton collected hundreds of skulls in the attempt to measure the intelligence of different races by comparing brain size.

Thomas Nagel (b. 1937): Nagel teaches at New York University. He has published numerous essays and books, the most important of which may be his essay entitled "What Is It Like to Be a Bat?" Nagel argues that the subjective quality of consciousness cannot be explained through objective science.

John Napier (1550–1617): Napier was a Scottish mathematician and physicist known for the development of logarithms and of Napier's bones, a calculating device for doing multiplication by addition alone.

John von Neumann (1903–1957): Hungarian by birth, von Neumann was a major figure in 20th-century physics, mathematics, and computer science. He is known for the von Neumann architecture that characterizes all contemporary computers, in which memory functions to contain both data and the program that operates on that data.

Allen Newell (1927–1992): Newell was a pioneer in the fields of computer science and artificial intelligence. He and Herbert Simon achieved one of the first major successes in artificial intelligence by creating the Logical Theorist, a program capable of proving theorems in formal logic.

Isaac Newton (1643–1727): Newton, calling himself a natural philosopher, is a paramount figure in the history of science. His 1666 prism experiments laid the foundations for contemporary optics and the theory of color.

Alva Noë (b. 1964): A professor of philosophy at the University of California at Berkeley, Noë specializes in philosophy of mind. In the tradition of J. J. Gibson, Noë argues for an enactment theory of perception: that perceiving is a way of acting.

Stephen Palmer (b. 1948): Palmer is a professor of psychology at the University of California at Berkeley, where he is the director of the university's Visual Perception Lab. Palmer's theoretical work has applied neuroscience to the philosophical issue of the inverted spectrum.

Seymour Papert (b. 1928): Papert, a professor at MIT, is a computer scientist, mathematician, and a pioneer of artificial intelligence. With Marvin Minsky, he launched a devastating attack on Rosenblatt's neural network perceptrons, rendering Connectionism obsolete until the mid-1980s.

Derek Parfit (b. 1942): Parfit, a British philosopher currently teaching at Oxford, specializes in issues of self-identity, rationality, and ethics and the relations among the three.

Blaise Pascal (1623–1662): Pascal was an eminent French mathematician, philosopher, and theologian. The inventor of the Pascaline, a calculating machine, he reacted to Descartes' claim that animals were merely unfeeling machines by saying, "I cannot forgive Descartes."

Roger Penrose (b. 1931): Penrose, professor at the University of Oxford, is a theoretical physicist and mathematician. Penrose has proposed that some aspects of human intelligence are non-algorithmic. Working with Stuart Hameroff, he suggests that the key to consciousness may be found in quantum effects in the microtubules of neurons.

Walter Pitts (1923–1969): A genius in logic and mathematics. Pitts never attended college but frequented lectures at the University of Chicago. With Warren McCulloch, he demonstrated in the 1940s how simple electrical devices could imitate neural firing.

Plato (c. 427–347 B.C.): A student of Socrates as well as the teacher of Aristotle. Plato's work is a formative part in the history of all major philosophical fields of study.

Hilary Putnam (b. 1926): An American philosopher central to 20th-century philosophy of mind, philosophy of science, and philosophy of language. He is known for the development of Functionalism, particularly in terms of the model of Turing machines. Functionalism identifies mental states with functional states of the organism.

Pythagoras (c. 580–c. 500 B.C.): Pythagoras and the Pythagoreans made major advancements in mathematics, including the Pythagorean theorem and the existence of irrational numbers.

V. S. Ramachandran (b. 1951): Born in India, Ramachandran is a neurologist and professor at the University of California at San Diego. He is best known for research that analyzes the phenomenon of phantom limbs in terms of body image in the brain.

Frank Rosenblatt (1928–1969): Rosenblatt developed the perceptron, a two-layer, feed-forward artificial neural net in the early 1960s. Using Rosenblatt's delta learning rule, it was shown that a perceptron could be trained to any pattern of input-output responses it could instantiate. Unfortunately, Marvin Minsky and Seymour Papert showed that some patterns existed that perceptrons could not instantiate, including *exclusive or*.

David Rosenthal (b. 1939): Rosenthal is professor at the City University of New York who focuses on philosophy of mind. He is known for his higher-order thought (HOT) theory of consciousness, according to which a mental state is conscious if it is the target of a higher-order thought.

David Rumelhart (b. 1942): Rumelhart, an American psychologist, is known for his work with artificial neural nets. In 1986, Rumelhart and Jay McClelland authored *Parallel Distributed Processing*, which introduced backpropagation of errors as a new learning rule for a new kind of net. Their work resurrected Connectionism.

Bertrand Russell (1872–1970): Russell was a significant figure in 20th-century logic and philosophy, with major contributions in the philosophy of logic, philosophy of language, philosophy of mind, and epistemology. Russell and Alfred North Whitehead's *Principia Mathematica* showed that all of mathematics could be built from a few simple logical concepts and, thereby, paved the road for contemporary computing.

Gilbert Ryle (1900–1976): Ryle was a follower of Wittgenstein and an influential proponent of Analytical Behaviorism. In *The Concept of Mind*, he attacks Cartesian Dualism, ridiculing the notion that the mind is some separate entity that inhabits a body as the dogma of the "ghost in the machine."

Oliver Sacks (b. 1933): Sacks is neurologist and writer known for a number of popular and influential books. *The Man Who Mistook His Wife for a Hat* and *An Anthropologist on Mars* investigate brain disorders and their relation to consciousness and cognition.

Jean-Paul Sartre (1905–1980): A French playwright, novelist, and philosopher, Sartre built the idea of freedom into the core of his Existentialism.

Roger Schank (b. 1946): With colleagues at Yale, Schank designed a program to address the frame problem in the understanding of narratives. Enthusiasts claimed that programs like Shank's could understand the story, a claim that stimulated John Searle's Chinese room thought experiment as a rebuttal.

William Schickard (1592–1635): On the basis of Napier's work and in communication with Kepler, Schickard developed an early calculating machine.

John Searle (b. 1932): A leading philosopher of mind, Searle is professor of philosophy at the University of California at Berkeley. He is famous for his Chinese room thought experiment, intended as a criticism of strong AI. Searle's example attempts to show that no machine, in virtue of instantiating a program, could be said to understand English or have other cognitive abilities.

Herbert Simon (1916–2001): Simon was a political scientist and a pioneer in the fields of computer science and artificial intelligence. He and Allen Newell achieved one of the first major successes in artificial intelligence by creating the Logical Theorist, a program capable of proving theorems in formal logic.

B. F. Skinner (1904–1990): An American psychologist, Skinner is known as a foremost figure in psychological Behaviorism and, in particular, for the development of schedules of reinforcement.

Roger Sperry (1913–1994): Sperry won the Nobel Prize for his work with split-brain research. In treating epileptics, he severed the corpus callosum, the part of the brain that connects the left and right hemispheres of the brain. According to Sperry, "Everything we have seen indicates that the surgery has left these people with two separate minds … that is, two separate spheres of consciousness."

Thales (c. 624–c. 546 B.C.): Thales is often called the first Greek philosopher and scientist. In contrast to mythological explanations of the world, Thales attempted to devise a natural and rational one.

Louis L. Thurstone (1887–1955): Thurstone, an American psychologist, is known for his work on intelligence testing. He argued against the notion of a general intelligence, suggesting that individuals could possess a number of "primary mental abilities" in varying degrees.

Alan M. Turing (1912–1954): Turing was an inventive logician and mathematician. He conceived of the Turing machine, which is still the major formal model for computation, was crucial to breaking Nazi codes during World War II, and played a major role in the early development of computers. Turing introduced the Turing test as a challenge for artificial intelligence.

Jacques de Vaucanson (1709–1782): A master of automata, Vaucanson created both a flute player and a famous mechanical duck.

Voltaire (1694–1778): Voltaire was a renowned essayist and satirist of the French Enlightenment.

Alfred North Whitehead (1861–1947): Whitehead and Russell's *Principia Mathematica* showed that all of mathematics could be built from a few simple logical concepts and, thereby, paved the road for contemporary computing.

Ludwig Wittgenstein (1889–1951): Wittgenstein was one of the most influential philosophers of the 20th century. Believing that many philosophical problems have their roots in misunderstandings of language, Wittgenstein explored the logic of language with the hope of "dissolving" philosophical problems. His work falls into two distinct periods, marked by the *Tractatus Logico-Philosophicus* and *Philosophical Investigations*. It is the latter work that evokes Analytical Behaviorism, including the private language argument and the parable of the beetles in the boxes.

Bibliography

General Sources and Anthologies:

Beakley, Brian, and Peter Ludlow, eds. *The Philosophy of Mind: Classical Problems/Contemporary Issues*. Cambridge, MA: MIT Press, 1991 (1st ed.), 2006 (2nd ed.). An exhaustive anthology of contemporary work and historical pieces, leaning toward cognitive science.

Block, Ned, Owen Flanagan, and Güven Güzeldere, eds. *The Nature of Consciousness: Philosophical Debates*. Cambridge, MA: MIT Press, 1999. A large but canonical anthology of pieces on consciousness.

Guttenplan, Samuel, ed. *A Companion to the Philosophy of Mind*. Oxford: Blackwell, 1995. Arranged alphabetically by topic, with a helpful introductory mapping of the territory in terms of three levels of analysis.

Heil, John, ed. *Philosophy of Mind: A Guide and Anthology*. Oxford: Oxford University Press, 2004. An anthology of important pieces, historical and contemporary; notable for brief and helpful introductions to each section.

Hofstader, Douglas, and Daniel C. Dennett, eds. *The Mind's I: Fantasies and Reflections on Self and Soul*. New York: Bantam Books, 1981. A rich and enjoyable collection of literature and philosophy, with important pieces mentioned in the lectures by John Searle, Alan M. Turing, Thomas Nagel, and Daniel Dennett.

Velmans, Max, and Susan Schneider, eds. *The Blackwell Companion to Consciousness*. Oxford: Blackwell, 2007. An encyclopedic approach to major theories, authors, and debates.

Interviews:

Baumgartner, Peter, and Sabine Payr, eds. *Speaking Minds: Interviews with Twenty Eminent Cognitive Scientists*. Princeton: Princeton University Press, 1995. Revealing interviews with many of the contemporary figures mentioned in the lectures.

Blackmore, Susan. *Conversations on Consciousness*. New York: Oxford University Press, 2006. A series of informal interviews with many of the contemporary figures mentioned in the lectures.

Works Cited in the Lectures:

Aristotle. *De Interpretatione, Prior Analytics,* and *Posterior Analytics.* In *The Basic Works of Aristotle,* edited by Richard McKeon. New York: Random House, 1971. The birth of logic.

Braitenberg, Valentino. *Vehicles: Experiments in Synthetic Psychology.* Cambridge, MA: MIT Press, 1996. A set of short but thought-provoking chapters on how to design simple machines that seem to show complicated psychological behavior.

Brooks, Rodney. "Intelligence without Representation." *Artificial Intelligence* 47 (1991): 139–159. A manifesto of the Brooks approach to artificial intelligence, robotics, and a mind in the world.

Carter, Rita. *Mapping the Mind.* Christopher Frith, scientific adviser. Berkeley: University of California Press, 1999. An absorbing coffee-table book on the brain.

Chalmers, David. "Facing Up to the Hard Problem of Consciousness." *Journal of Consciousness Studies* 2 (1995): 200–219. Reprinted in Heil, *Philosophy of Mind: A Guide and Anthology,* pp. 617–640. The classic piece on the hard problem.

Churchland, Patricia Smith. "Reduction and Antireductionism in Functionalist Theories of Mind." In *Neurophilosophy.* Cambridge, MA: MIT Press, 1986. Reprinted in Beakley and Ludlow, *Philosophy of Mind,* both editions. In the process of arguing for the philosophical importance of work in neuroscience, Churchland lays out a clear defense of Reductionism.

Churchland, Paul. "Eliminative Materialism and the Propositional Attitudes." *Journal of Philosophy* 78 (1981): 67–90. Reprinted in Heil, *Philosophy of Mind: A Guide and Anthology,* and in Beakley and Ludlow, *Philosophy of Mind,* 2nd ed. A classic statement of the Churchlands' Eliminative Materialism.

Churchland, Patricia Smith, and Paul Churchland. "Could a Machine Think?" *Scientific American* 262 (1990): 32–39. A response piece to Searle's Chinese room thought experiment in the same issue.

Clark, Andy, and David Chalmers, "The Extended Mind." *Analysis* 58 (1998): 10–23. Reprinted in *The Philosopher's Annual,* vol. 21, edited by Patrick Grim, Ken Baynes, and Gary Mar. Atascadero, CA: Ridgeview Press, 1999. Clark and Chalmers's elegant statement of the "extended mind" thesis.

Crevier, Daniel. *AI: The Tumultuous History of the Search for Artificial Intelligence*. New York: Bantam Books, 1993. An entertaining and informative treatment of debates that continue within artificial intelligence.

Crick, Francis. *The Astonishing Hypothesis: The Scientific Search for the Soul*. New York: Touchstone, 1994. An accessible source for a number of topics in neuroscience, including Crick and Koch's theory of consciousness as synchronized 40-Hertz firing across the brain.

Damasio, Antonio. *Descartes' Error: Emotion, Reason, and the Human Brain*. New York: Penguin Books, 1994. Contemporary neuroscience applied to questions in philosophy and psychology; as engaging as it is informative.

Dennett, Daniel. *Brainstorms*. Cambridge, MA: MIT Press, 1981. A collection of Dennett's earlier articles in philosophy of mind, ending with the wonderful "Where Am I?" Accessible and thought-provoking.

——. *Elbow Room: The Varieties of Free Will Worth Wanting*. Cambridge, MA: MIT Press, 1984. Although Dennett has more recent work on free will, this is his classic treatment and, in many ways, still the best.

——. *Freedom Evolves*. New York: Penguin Books, 2003. As always, Dennett is eloquent and entertaining. Here, he outlines Compatibilism in an evolutionary setting.

——. "The Nature of Images and the Introspective Trap." In *Content and Consciousness*. London: Routledge & Kegan Paul; New York: Humanities Press, 1969. Reprinted in Beakley and Ludlow, *Philosophy of Mind*, 1st ed. A classic Dennett attack on the inner theater.

——. "Quining Qualia." In *Consciousness in Modern Science*, edited by A. Marcel and E. Bisiach. Oxford: Oxford University Press, 1988. Reprinted in Block, Flanagan, and Güzeldere, *The Nature of Consciousness: Philosophical Debates*. A difficult but rewarding piece to read repeatedly.

Dennett, Daniel, and Marcel Kinsbourne. "Time and the Observer: The Where and When of Consciousness in the Brain." *Behavioral and Brain Sciences* 15 (1992): 183–247. Reprinted in *The Philosopher's Annual*, vol. 15, edited by Patrick Grim, Gary Mar, and Peter Williams. Atascadero, CA: Ridgeview Press, 1994. Also reprinted in Block, Flanagan, and Güzeldere, *The Nature of Consciousness: Philosophical Debates*. The full development of several objections to the inner theater.

Descartes, René. *Meditations on First Philosophy*. John Cottingham, ed. Cambridge: Cambridge University Press, 1996. Available in many editions, excerpted in many anthologies. A primary source for Cartesian Dualism.

Durrell, Lawrence. *The Alexandria Quartet: Justine, Balthazar, Mountolive*, and *Clea*. London: Faber and Faber, 1962. This set of beautiful novels makes the point that no behavioral description can be interpretationally exhaustive.

Fodor, Jerry. "Observation Reconsidered." *Philosophy of Science* 51 (1984): 23–43. Reprinted in *The Philosopher's Annual*, vol. 7, edited by Patrick Grim, Christopher J. Martin, and Michael A. Simon. Atascadero, CA: Ridgeview Press, 1984. An effective response to overstatements of holism and the influence of belief on perception.

Gardner, Howard. *Frames of Mind: The Theory of Multiple Intelligences*. New York: Basic Books, 1983. A complete but readable outline of his theory, with progressive chapters on different intelligences.

———. *Multiple Intelligences: The Theory in Practice*. New York: Basic Books, 1993. An accessible introduction to his theory and its implications.

Gibson, James J. "Autobiography." In *Reasons for Realism: Selected Essays of James J. Gibson*, edited by Edward Reed and Rebecca Jones, pp. 7–22. London: Lawrence Erlbaum, 1982. A brief but effective introduction to major elements of Gibson's approach.

———. *The Ecological Approach to Visual Perception*. London: Lawrence Erlbaum, 1986. Gibson's major work in applying the concept of perceptual affordances.

Gibson, William, and Bruce Sterling, *The Difference Engine*. New York: Bantam Books, 1991. A novelistic look at what history might have been like if Charles Babbage had succeeded in building steam-driven computers in 1840.

Gould, Stephen Jay. *The Mismeasure of Man*. New York: W.W. Norton, 1981. Gould's outspoken criticism of IQ testing.

Grim, Patrick. "Free Will in Context: A Contemporary Philosophical Perspective." *Behavioral Sciences and the Law* 25 (2007): 183–201.

A survey of current approaches with a concluding outline of contextualism.

Hanson, N. R. "Observation." In *Patterns of Discovery*. Cambridge: Cambridge University Press, 1958. Excerpted in *Introductory Readings in Philosophy of Science*, edited by E. D. Klemke, Robert Hollinger, and A. David Kline. Amherst, NY: Prometheus Books, 1980. A strong classic statement regarding theory-laden perception.

Hauser, Marc D. *Wild Minds: What Animals Really Think*. New York: Henry Holt and Co., 2000. An entertaining discussion of animal cognition that introduces a range of important contemporary research.

Hoffman, Donald D. *Visual Intelligence: How We Create What We See*. New York: W.W. Norton & Company, 1998. A fascinating exploration of optical illusions and what they tell us about perception.

Humphrey, Nicholas. *Seeing Red: A Study in Consciousness*. Cambridge, MA: Harvard University Press, 2006. A short and popular introduction to issues in perception by the man who first studied blindsight in monkeys.

Jackson, Frank. "Epiphenomenal Qualia." *Philosophical Quarterly* 32 (1982): 127–136. The original appearance of black-and-white Mary. A good general discussion of the argument appears in Daniel Stoljar and Yujin Nagasawa's introduction to *There's Something about Mary*.

Kuhn, Thomas S. *The Structure of Scientific Revolutions*. Chicago: University of Chicago Press, 1962; with postscript, 1970. An extremely influential piece of work in philosophy of science.

Kurzweil, Raymond. *The Singularity Is Near: When Humans Transcend Biology*. New York: Penguin, 2005. Kurzweil's predictions regarding the future of artificial intelligence.

Locke, John. *An Essay Concerning Human Understanding*. New York: Dover Publications, 1959. A historical classic of Empiricism, as difficult to read as most things published in 1689.

Loftus, Elizabeth F. *Eyewitness Testimony*. Cambridge, MA: Harvard University Press, 1979. The classic text regarding the fallibility of eyewitness testimony.

McGinn, Colin. "Can We Solve the Mind-Body Problem?" *Mind* 98 (1989): 349–366. Reprinted in Block, Flanagan, and Güzeldere, *The*

Nature of Consciousness: Philosophical Debates. A clearly posed problem with some obscurity in McGinn's answer to it.

Miedaner, Terrell. "The Soul of Martha, a Beast" and "The Soul of the Mark III Beast." In *The Soul of Anna Klane*. New York: Ballantine Books, 1978. Reprinted in Hofstadter and Dennett, *The Mind's I*. Taken together, a wonderful pair of fictional reflections on life and consciousness—human, animal, and mechanical.

Minsky, Marvin, and Seymour Papert. *Perceptrons, Expanded Edition*. Cambridge, MA: MIT Press, 1988. In its original form, this is the book that interrupted fruitful work on neural networks for a generation.

Moravec, Hans. *Mind Children: The Future of Human and Robot Intelligence*. Cambridge, MA: Harvard University Press, 1988. Moravec envisages a beautiful future in which our machines replace us.

Nagel, Thomas. *Mortal Questions*. New York: Cambridge University Press, 1979. A collection of Nagel's essays, with emphasis on ethics. Nagel is always clear, direct, and surprising.

———. *The View from Nowhere*. Oxford: Oxford University Press, 1986. Nagel's defining statement on issues of subjectivity and objectivity across the philosophical spectrum.

———. "What Is It Like to Be a Bat?" *The Philosophical Review* 83 (1974): 435–350. Reprinted in Nagel, *Mortal Questions*, and in Hofstadter and Dennett, *The Mind's I*. Nagel's seminal article on the problem of consciousness.

Noë, Alva. *Action in Perception*. Cambridge, MA: MIT Press, 2004. Noë's enactive approach is a philosophical extension of the Gibsonian tradition.

Parfit, Derek. *Reasons and Persons*. Oxford: Clarendon Press, 1984. Even better than its sterling reputation would lead one to expect. Densely argued, Parfit's work calls for reading in small bits and thinking at large.

Penrose, Roger. *The Emperor's New Mind: Concerning Computers, Minds, and the Laws of Physics*. Oxford: Oxford University Press, 1989. The first of Penrose's two books on undecidability and the limits of algorithms, quantum mechanics, and the brain. Dense but often rewarding.

———. *Shadows of the Mind: A Search for the Missing Science of Consciousness*. Oxford: Oxford University Press, 1994. The second of Penrose's two books on undecidability and the limits of algorithms, quantum mechanics, and the brain. Dense but often rewarding.

Place, U. T. "Is Consciousness a Brain Process?" *British Journal of Psychology* 47 (1856): 44–50. Reprinted in Beakley and Ludlow, *Philosophy of Mind*, both editions. A classic statement of the claim that mental states are brain states.

Putnam, Hilary. "The Nature of Mental States." Originally published as "Psychological Predicates" in *Art, Mind, and Religion*, edited by W. Capitan and D. D. Merrill. Pittsburgh: University of Pittsburgh Press, 1967. Reprinted in Beakley and Ludlow, *Philosophy of Mind*, both editions, and as "Psychological Predicates" in Heil, *Philosophy of Mind: A Guide and Anthology*. A classic statement of Functionalism.

Ramachandran, V. S., and Sandra Blakeslee. *Phantoms in the Brain: Probing the Mysteries of the Human Mind*. New York: William Morrow, 1988. An engaging discussion of neuroscience and its lessons regarding the mind, with a focus on Ramachandran's research regarding phantom limbs.

Rosenthal, David. "A Theory of Consciousness." In Block, Flanagan, and Güzeldere, *The Nature of Consciousness: Philosophical Debates*. A brief and effective presentation of Rosenthal's higher-order thought (HOT) theory of consciousness.

Rumelhart, David E., James L. McClelland, and the PDP Research Group. *Parallel Distributed Processing*, vol. 1: *Foundations*. Cambridge, MA: MIT Press, 1988. The resurrection of neural nets. Only for the initiated.

Russell, Bertrand. *Philosophy*. New York: W.W. Norton, 1927. One of Russell's many works; a bit dated but wonderfully written and always thought-provoking.

———, and Alfred North Whitehead. *Principia Mathematica*. Cambridge: Cambridge University Press, 1927. First published in 1910–1913, this is Russell and Whitehead's demonstration that all of mathematics could be generated from a few logical symbols and rules. Even for the specialist, now of purely historical interest.

Ryle, Gilbert. *The Concept of Mind*. New York: Barnes and Noble, 1950; Chicago: University of Chicago Press, 2002 (a new edition with an introduction by Daniel C. Dennett). Excerpted in Beakley and Ludlow, *Philosophy of Mind*, both editions. The classical statement of Analytical Behaviorism.

Sacks, Oliver. *An Anthropologist on Mars: Seven Paradoxical Tales*. New York: Vintage Books, 1996. Entertaining and enlightening.

———. *The Man Who Mistook His Wife for a Hat*. New York: HarperCollins, 1985; New York: Touchstone 1998. A thoroughly fascinating set of cases, with Sacks's speculations as to what they tell us about the mind.

Searle, John. "Is the Brain's Mind a Computer Program?" *Scientific American* 262 (1990): 26–31. The Chinese room argument in *Scientific American* form, accompanied by a response from the Churchlands.

———. "Minds, Brains, and Programs." *Behavioral and Brain Sciences* 3 (1980): 417–450. Although Searle's text is reprinted in several of the resources listed here (Beakley and Ludlow, *Philosophy of Mind*, both editions; Heil, *Philosophy of Mind: A Guide and Anthology*; and Hofstadter and Dennett, *The Mind's I*), it is best read in its original context, with extensive comments by others and his replies.

Stoljar, Daniel, and Yujin Nagasawa. "Introduction." In *There's Something about Mary*, edited by Peter Ludlow, Yujin Nagasawa, and Daniel Stoljar. Cambridge, MA: MIT Press, 2004. A good overview of Frank Jackson's black-and-white Mary argument.

Vacca, John, ed. *The World's 20 Greatest Unsolved Problems*. Upper Saddle River, NJ: Prentice-Hall, 2005. One of the few books that focuses on what we *don't* know.

Wittgenstein, Ludwig. *The Blue and Brown Books*. New York: Harper and Row; Oxford: Blackwell, 1958. Compiled from students' notes originally distributed in blue and brown covers in mimeograph form, *The Blue Book* offers a good introduction to the private language argument in particular and Wittgenstein's intriguing obscurity in general.

———. *Philosophical Investigations*. New York: Macmillan, 1958. The later Wittgenstein in all his aphoristic obscurity, simultaneously intriguing and infuriating.

Wood, Gaby. *Edison's Eve: A Magical History of the Quest for Mechanical Life*. New York: Anchor Books, 2002. Rich initial chapters on the legend of Descartes' robotic daughter and Vaucanson's automata; somewhat sketchier later on.

Additional Resources:

Baars, Bernard J., William P. Banks, and James B. Newman, eds. *Essential Sources in the Scientific Study of Consciousness.* Cambridge, MA: MIT Press, 2003. Purely for the specialist.

Boden, Margaret A. *Mind as Machine: A History of Cognitive Science*, vols. 1 and 2. Oxford: Clarendon Press, 2006. A vast, detailed, opinionated but valuable research source.

Uribe, Diego. *Truly Baffling Optical Illusions*. New York: Sterling Publishing, 2003. One of the best of many collections of optical illusions, with some discussion of why certain effects occur.

Williams, Michael R. *A History of Computing Technology*. Los Alamitos, CA: IEEE Computer Science Press, 1997. An exhaustive compendium on the history of calculational notations, techniques, and machines. One of the best.

Film and Video Sources:

Lang, Fritz. *Metropolis*. 1927.

Scott, Ridley. *Blade Runner*. 1982.

The following are classic reflections on minds, machines, and society:

- Morris, Erroll. *Fast, Cheap, and Out of Control.* 1997. A cult documentary that mixes footage and interviews regarding lion taming, topiary, naked mole rats, and Rodney Brooks on robots.

- Rose, Reginald, and Sidney Lumet. *Twelve Angry Men.* 1957. A psychological drama that makes memorable points regarding prejudice and misperception. Make sure you see the black-and-white version starring Henry Fonda.

- Scientific American Frontiers. *Robots Alive!*, *Robot Pals*, *Changing Your Mind.* 1997. Alan Alda's entertaining programs on topics covered in the lectures.

Internet Sources:

Bach, Michael. *77 Optical Illusions and Visual Phenomena.* http://www.michaelbach.de/ot/.

Bongard, Josh, Victor Zykov, and Hod Lipson. *Resilient Machines through Continuous Self-Modeling.* http://ccsl.mae.cornell.edu/research/selfmodels/. The star robot in action.

Chalmers, David. This professor and author offers an astounding set of Web pages regarding consciousness and philosophy of mind. When does this man have time to do anything else? Chalmers's sites include the following:

Online Papers on Consciousness. http://consc.net/online.html.

Mindpapers: A Bibliography of the Philosophy of Mind and the Science of Consciousness. http://consc.net/biblio.html. Extensive.

Zombies on the Web. http://consc.net/zombies.html. A compilation of sites on zombies.

Computer History Museum. http://www.computerhistory.org/about_us.html.

Deutsch, Diana. http://psy.ucsd.edu/~ddeutsch/. Auditory illusions.

Duke University, Neurobiology, Laboratory of Dale Purves, M.D. *Color Contrast: Cube.* http://www.neuro.duke.edu/faculty/purves/gallery9.html. Shows the color contrast experiment referred to in Lecture Twenty. Astoundingly, the blue squares on the top surface in the left image are, in fact, identical to the yellow squares on the top surface in the right image. Taken out of context, both are an identical shade of gray. The experiment also appears with some additional discussion at http://discovermagazine.com/2004/feb/neuroquest/.

e-Chalk Optical Illusions. http://www.echalk.co.uk/amusements/OpticalIllusions/illusions.htm. Includes interactive forms of the color contrast experiment and other color illusions.

Exploratorium: The Museum of Science, Art and Human Perception. http://www.exploratorium.edu/seeing/exhibits/index.html. Includes a number of visual illusions.

Home Page of The Loebner Prize in Artificial Intelligence. http://www.loebner.net/Prizef/loebner-prize.html. Includes information on the Loebner Prize and links to recent winning programs that you can review.

Macmillan, Malcolm. *The Phineas Gage Information Page*. http://www.deakin.edu.au/hmnbs/psychology/gagepage/.

Science Museum, http://www.sciencemuseum.org.uk/visit museum/galleries/computing/ondisplay.aspx.

Shore, David I. *Measuring Auditory Saltation*. http://www.mohsho.com/dshore/sound_top.html. A version of the auditory rabbit.

T.I.L. Productions. *Vaucanson and His Remarkable Automatons.* http://www.automates-anciens.com/english_version/automatons-music-boxes/vaucanson-automatons-androids.php. Site shows what may be photos of the remains of Vaucanson's duck.

University of North Carolina at Charlotte. http://www.philosophy. uncc.edu/faculty/phi/Phi_Color2.html. An interactive exploration of the color phenomenon.

Visual Cognition Lab, University of Illinois. http:// viscog.beckman.uiuc.edu/djs_lab/demos.html. Includes the unseen gorilla video mentioned in Lecture Nineteen, together with wonderful exercises regarding change blindness.

Zalta, Edward N., principal ed. *Stanford Encyclopedia of Philosophy.* http://plato.stanford.edu/. An unequaled website source on all philosophical topics.

Permissions Acknowledgments

Notes